# Blender 2.5 Character Animation Cookbook

50 great recipes for giving soul to your characters by building high-quality rigs and understanding the principles of movement

**Virgilio Vasconcelos**

[PACKT] open source *

PUBLISHING     community experience distilled

BIRMINGHAM - MUMBAI

# Blender 2.5 Character Animation Cookbook

First published: June 2011


Production Reference: 1130611


Published by Packt Publishing Ltd.
32 Lincoln Road
Olton
Birmingham, B27 6PA, UK.

ISBN 978-1-849513-20-3

www.packtpub.com

Cover Image by Virgilio Vasconcelos (virgiliovasconcelos@gmail.com)

# Credits

**Author**

Virgilio Vasconcelos

**Reviewers**

Allan Brito

Martin Poirier

**Acquisition Editor**

Sarah Cullington

**Development Editor**

Hyacintha D'Souza

**Technical Editor**

Aaron Rosario

**Project Coordinator**

Joel Goveya

**Proofreader**

Aaron Nash

**Indexer**

Tejal Daruwale

**Production Coordinator**

Aparna Bhagat

**Cover Work**

Aparna Bhagat

# About the Author

**Virgilio Vasconcelos** is an animator based in Brazil, who uses Blender as his 3D tool to produce animations. He is also a university professor, teaching digital 3D and 2D animation at Universidade Federal de Minas Gerais (UFMG). His specialties include character rigging and animation, and his first tryst with Blender was back in 2003. He has worked as lead 3D artist at Nitrocorpz Design Studio, and has several personal and commissioned productions recognized by the Blender community, being awarded and nominated for artistic categories in events such as Blender Conference and BlenderPRO.

You can watch his animations, read his blog and contact him at http://www.virgiliovasconcelos.com.

# Acknowledgements

No book is the product of just the author—he just happens to be under the spotlight with his name on the cover. The contribution of a number of people was crucial to bring this book to fruition, and it would take far more space than I have available to thank each one individually.

A special note goes to Chaitanya Apte, Hyacintha D'Souza, and Joel Goveya from Packt Publishing, without whom this book wouldn't exist. Thank you for believing in me, and for all the wonderful guidance and professionalism throughout these months. You and the entire Packt Publishing team did an outstanding job to help produce a high quality publication.

I must also thank the coding wizards who don't get tired of making Blender such an amazing tool, which crosses the line of being just an open source graphics application to be a respected tool by all CG professionals, regardless of its license. I'm grateful to people such as Ton Roosendaal, the head of the Blender Foundation, who is the main man responsible for what Blender has become; artists such as Bassam Kurdali and Nathan Vegdahl, from whom I've learned a lot by studying their rigging approaches; and the active user community in forums and discussion lists, such as blenderbrasil-dev in Google Groups. Aside from Blender fellows, I'm also very thankful to the guys at Nitrocorpz Design Studio, where I gained more experience and knowledge working on projects to write about in this book.

Along with all these people, a book isn't worth without a reader. If you're reading this now I want to thank you and let you know that I've put a lot of effort into making something very useful for you and your projects.

# About the Reviewers

**Allan Brito** is a Brazilian architect, specialized in information visualization. He lives and works in Recife, Brazil. He works with Blender 3D to produce animations and still images, for visualization and instructional material. Besides his work with Blender as an artist, he also has wide experience in teaching and researching about 3D modeling, animation, and multimedia.

He is an active member in the Blender users community, writing about Blender 3D and its development for websites in Brazilian Portuguese (http://www.allanbrito.com) and English (http://www.blender3darchitect.com and http://www.blendernation.com). Besides his two blogs, he has written three books about Blender, in both English and Brazilian Portuguese, covering topics such as architectural visualization, mechanical modeling, and general Blender guides.

To know more about the author, visit the website http://www.blender3darchitect.com, where he covers the use of Blender and other tools for architectural visualization.

I want to thank my wife Erica for the support during the review of this book.

**Martin Poirier** is a software developer with a Master's Degree in Computer Graphics, specialized in character animation and simulation. He's been involved with the FOSS Blender project since early 2003, soon after its open source debut, working on plenty of things here and there, but mostly on the transformation system. Lately, he has been developing a distributed rendering solution for Blender animations.

Martin has reviewed and contributed to the official *Blender 2.3 Guide*. He is also contributing to the wiki version of the Blender Manual (occasionally).

# www.PacktPub.com

## Support files, eBooks, discount offers and more

You might want to visit www.PacktPub.com for support files and downloads related to your book.

Did you know that Packt offers eBook versions of every book published, with PDF and ePub files available? You can upgrade to the eBook version at www.PacktPub.com and as a print book customer, you are entitled to a discount on the eBook copy. Get in touch with us at service@packtpub.com for more details.

At www.PacktPub.com, you can also read a collection of free technical articles, sign up for a range of free newsletters and receive exclusive discounts and offers on Packt books and eBooks.

PACKTLiB®

http://PacktLib.PacktPub.com

Do you need instant solutions to your IT questions? PacktLib is Packt's online digital book library. Here, you can access, read and search across Packt's entire library of books.

## Why Subscribe?

- Fully searchable across every book published by Packt
- Copy and paste, print and bookmark content
- On demand and accessible via web browser

## Free Access for Packt account holders

If you have an account with Packt at www.PacktPub.com, you can use this to access PacktLib today and view nine entirely free books. Simply use your login credentials for immediate access.

*This book is dedicated to my love, Suryara, who brings so much happiness to my days; and my mom and sister, Leonora and Letícia, who support me unconditionally when I'm trying to draw with a computer.*

*This book would not have been possible without your love and understanding.*

# Table of Contents

# Preface

This book offers clear, illustrative, and easy-to-follow recipes to create character rigs and animations for common situations. Bring your characters to life by understanding the principles, techniques, and approaches involved in creating rigs and animations; you'll be able to adapt them to your own characters and films.

## What this book covers

Chapter 1, *Get Rigging*—It's about the essential concepts and recipes you need to know before creating the controllers for your character. Master them and you'll avoid lots of headaches in the future.

Chapter 2, *Rigging the Torso*—Here we'll begin rigging our character's torso. It's a crucial set of recipes where you'll learn how to control things such as the pelvis, the neck, and how to stretch them in a cartoony way.

Chapter 3, *Eyeing Animation*—Here's a chapter dedicated to controlling our character's eyes. The eyes are what our audience looks at the most, so we have to carefully create good controllers for that part of the body.

Chapter 4, *Poker Face? Facial Rigging*—This chapter is dedicated to teaching you how to enable our characters to talk and express their feelings through facial expressions.

Chapter 5, *Hands Down! The Limbs Controllers*—In this chapter, we'll see how to create all kinds of controllers for arms, legs, feet, fingers, and shoulders.

Chapter 6, *Blending with the Animation Workflow*—It's time for animation, and in this chapter we'll see some important concepts and techniques to get started on the right foot and work efficiently.

Chapter 7, *Easy to Say, Hard to Do: Mastering the Basics*—Here we'll see some very important principles of animation applied to our characters. These principles are crucial for virtually every piece of animation you'll need to create.

*Chapter 8, Shake That Body: The Mechanics of Body Movement*—In this chapter we'll mix everything we've learned until here and apply them to real world situations.

*Chapter 9, Spicing it Up: Animation Refinement*—Now that we have achieved proper movement in our characters, it's time to take them to the next level with refinements.

*Chapter 10, Drama King: Acting in Animation*—Animators don't just move puppets around; they make you believe the characters are alive. Here we'll see some recipes about why our characters move, instead of how.

*Appendix*, Planning Your Animation—The Appendix talks a bit more about some concepts related to animation and how you can prepare yourself to make the perfect shot.

# Who this book is for

This book will be handy for those Blender users who already know the basics of adding, modeling, and rendering objects within the program, but are eager to learn how to turn a character's mesh into a more life like entity.

# Conventions

In this book, you will find a number of styles of text that distinguish between different kinds of information. Here are some examples of these styles, and an explanation of their meaning.

Code words in text are shown as follows: "Select your entire bone, open the **Specials** menu (press the W key), and choose **Subdivide**."

**New terms** and **important words** are shown in bold. Words that you see on the screen, in menus or dialog boxes for example, appear in the text like this: "Open the file 001-Orientation.blend from this book's support files."

> Warnings or important notes appear in a box like this.

> Tips and tricks appear like this.

# Reader feedback

Feedback from our readers is always welcome. Let us know what you think about this book—what you liked or may have disliked. Reader feedback is important for us to develop titles that you really get the most out of.

To send us general feedback, simply send an e-mail to feedback@packtpub.com, and mention the book title via the subject of your message.

If there is a book that you need and would like to see us publish, please send us a note in the **SUGGEST A TITLE** form on www.packtpub.com or e-mail suggest@packtpub.com.

If there is a topic that you have expertise in and you are interested in either writing or contributing to a book, see our author guide on www.packtpub.com/authors.

# Customer support

Now that you are the proud owner of a Packt book, we have a number of things to help you to get the most from your purchase.

## Downloading the example code

You can download the example code files for all Packt books you have purchased from your account at http://www.PacktPub.com. If you purchased this book elsewhere, you can visit http://www.PacktPub.com/support and register to have the files e-mailed directly to you. Alternatively, the author also maintains a copy of the code on his website at http://virgiliovasconcelos.com/blender-animation-cookbook/.

## Downloading the color images of this book

We also provide a PDF file that has color images of the screenshots used in this book. The high resolution color images will help you better understand changes in the output. You can download this file from https://www.packtpub.com/sites/default/files/3203OS_Color_Images.pdf.

The author also maintains a copy of the graphics as well as the other code files from this book at http://virgiliovasconcelos.com/blender-animation-cookbook/.

## Errata

Although we have taken every care to ensure the accuracy of our content, mistakes do happen. If you find a mistake in one of our books—maybe a mistake in the text or the code—we would be grateful if you would report this to us. By doing so, you can save other readers from frustration and help us improve subsequent versions of this book. If you find any errata, please report them by visiting http://www.packtpub.com/support, selecting your book, clicking on the **errata submission form** link, and entering the details of your errata. Once your errata are verified, your submission will be accepted and the errata will be uploaded on our website, or added to any list of existing errata, under the Errata section of that title. Any existing errata can be viewed by selecting your title from http://www.packtpub.com/support.

## Piracy

Piracy of copyright material on the Internet is an ongoing problem across all media. At Packt, we take the protection of our copyright and licenses very seriously. If you come across any illegal copies of our works, in any form, on the Internet, please provide us with the location address or website name immediately so that we can pursue a remedy.

Please contact us at copyright@packtpub.com with a link to the suspected pirated material.

We appreciate your help in protecting our authors, and our ability to bring you valuable content.

## Questions

You can contact us at questions@packtpub.com if you are having a problem with any aspect of the book, and we will do our best to address it.

# 1
# Get Rigging

In this chapter, we will cover the following topics:

- ▶ Defining good orientations for your bones
- ▶ Using separate bone chains for different tasks
- ▶ Customizing shapes and colors for your bones
- ▶ Using corrective shape keys
- ▶ Making an IK-FK switcher
- ▶ Tips on weight painting you characters

## Introduction

So, you've successfully modeled an awesome character in Blender. After hours of careful and detailed work you have built a very appealing protagonist with a good topology for your next animation, but there's an issue: how do we make it look more life like, and also, how do we make it move?

Since a character model can be made of thousands of vertices, moving them individually across the 3D space is virtually impossible. We need an easier way of moving our models, and this way is called rigging.

**Rigging** is the process of creating a series of controls (the "Rig") to deform another object, which is often a character mesh. It involves creating special objects that move selected groups of vertices at once. This is the principle behind Skeletal Animation, where objects called "bones" are used to control parts of our models.

In Blender, there is a special object called **Armature**, which can be described roughly as a set of related bones that are used to control a mesh. To use an analogy, bones are for armatures as vertices are for meshes. Armatures can be added within the 3D View by pressing *Shift + A* and choosing **Armature | Single Bone** on the menu. Similar to meshes, armatures also have an Edit Mode accessible through the *Tab* key, where you can add, change, and remove bones as you wish. Bones can also be linked, creating a chain of hierarchically related bones.

Rigging is often referred to as one of the most difficult subjects in 3D animation. When creating a character rig, there are many aspects that you have to keep in mind, and two of them should be observed as major guidelines:

▶  The rig must be simple enough to be used by the animator

▶  The rig must be complex enough to allow convincing movements for your characters

Finding an ideal balance between complexity of features and ease of use is the Holy Grail of character rigging. On one hand, if a rig is too simple it can be harder for the animator to give the character an "illusion of life". On the other hand, an extremely complex rig can be a nightmare: the animator should not require a tutorial to be able to start posing a character. It has to be straightforward enough to be used instinctively. Of course, a skilled animator should be able to achieve an amazing piece of animation even with a very simple rig, but the job of a character rigger is to make the animator's life easier.

Because every animation project has its own sorts of challenges and demands, there is no absolute right or *wrong* way to build a character rig. What we will see here are best practices that should apply to most situations. These recipes should be dealt with just as in a traditional cookbook: feel free to add spice to suit your personal taste.

# Defining good orientations for your bones

When creating rigs for 3D characters in Blender, there is one mistake that is probably the most common of all, and it is also responsible for lots of headaches in the future: the orientations of the bone chains.

Every time we have to create a bone chain to allow our character to do a specific movement, some people (maybe in a hurry) often overlook this foundation of a good character rig. Since our characters and its bones live in a three-dimensional space, everyone familiar with 3D concepts should know that they are subject of the three world axes: X, Y and Z.

Along these concepts, we should be comfortable with the idea of "local" and "global" coordinates. **Global coordinates** are the ones relative to the scene: every scene has its Up or Down (Z axis), Left or Right (X axis), and Front or Back (Y axis) coordinates. Every object in a scene also has its own, or local, coordinates to allow easier transformations. To make an analogy with our world, "going East" would be the global coordinates while "turning right" refers to your local coordinates.

For instance, we should be allowed to bend a character forward regardless of its rotation and position relative to the scene. This "bending forward" would be too difficult to achieve using only the global coordinates; that's why we can use the local ones.

## Getting ready

Using the concept of local coordinates, we have also to define some conventions such as which axis we are talking about when bending "forward". We have to pay attention to the sane organization of the bones, where a chosen local axis (for instance, local X) would be the same for all "forward" transformations, be it a finger or a knee. The character **Otto**, which is used throughout this book, uses the X local axis for the most common transformations, such as for bending the elbows and knees, closing the fingers, or bending the torso forward. This makes it easier to pose our character without having to worry about which axis you should use: if in doubt, use X!

Here we'll see how to create and correct bone chains in order for them to be more coherent and easier to manipulate.

## How to do it...

Let's suppose you want a chain with three bones for a finger:

1.  Open the file `001-Orientation.blend` from this book's support files. You'll see a hand model with four of its finger bones already set. I've let the ring finger for you to rig, like in the next screenshot:

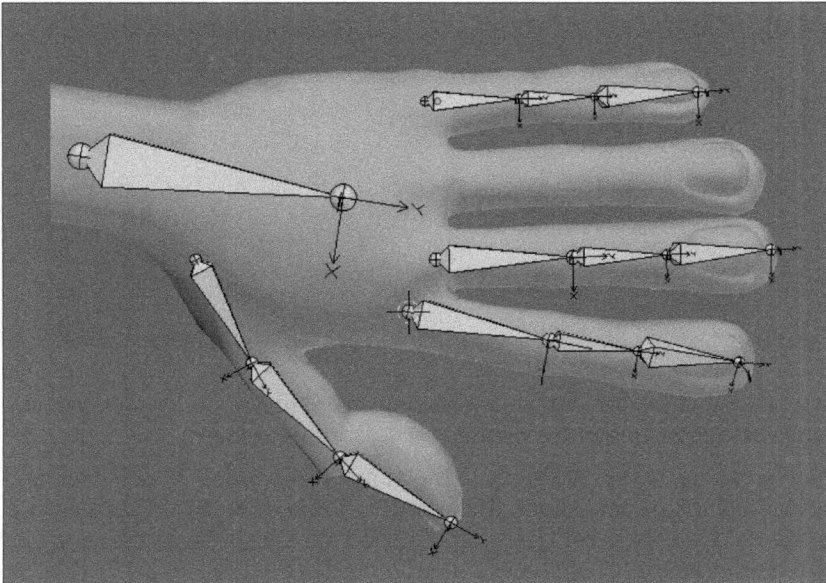

2. Position your 3D cursor where the first finger bone should be created: select your mesh, enter the Edit Mode (*Tab*), select a vertex or group of vertices at the base of the finger and press *Shift + S*. Choose **Cursor to Selected**.

3. Go back to Object Mode (*Tab*), select the armature, enter its Edit Mode (*Tab*) and press *Shift + A* to add a new bone under the cursor location.

> In order to view better what we're doing, I've enabled the X-Ray and Axes display modes, in the **Properties** panel, under the **Object Data** tab.

Now you just move the tip of this bone until the finger's first joint and extrude the bone two times, right? WRONG!

Extruding bones is just what one would normally do in order to create a bone chain, but that brings to our new bones some unwanted rotations.

4. Select the tip of your bone and move (press the *G* key) it until the tip of the finger, as seen in the next screenshot:

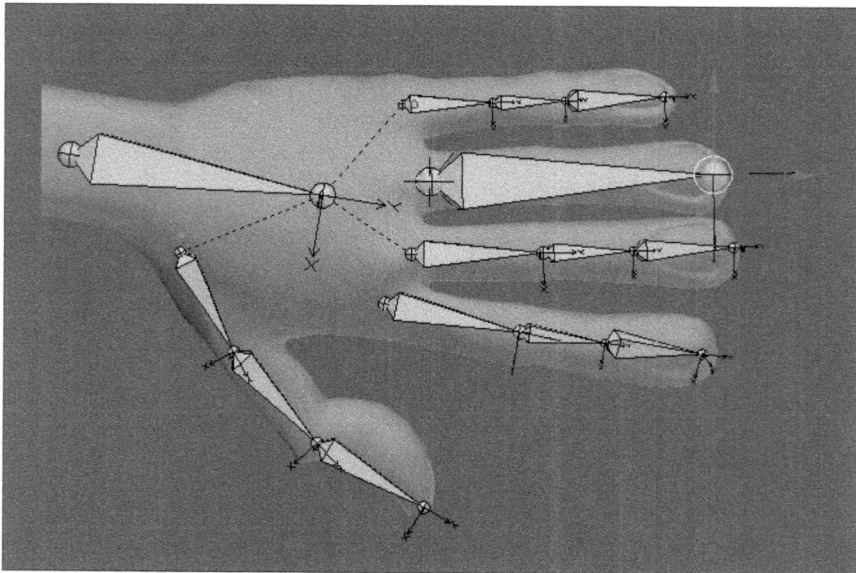

5. Select your entire bone, open the **Specials** menu (press the *W* key), and choose **Subdivide**. Select one of the bones and repeat this process.

6. Move (press the *G* key) the joints to the appropriate places of the finger, and the orientations will be consistent. Note that the X axis of each bone is always pointing toward us, while the other bones on the hand have their Z axes pointing up. We need them all consistent.

7.  Select the bones you have just created, press *Ctrl + R*, and type 90. This will correct their rotations, making their Z axes point toward us (check the *Axis conventions* section at the end of this recipe to know more about this).

8.  Select the hand mesh, hold *Shift*, select a bone, and press *Ctrl+ P*. Choose **With Automatic Weights** to get a basic deformation on the hand.

9.  Now you can rotate the bones under their local X axis (*R + X + X*) to see what happens.

> When you tell Blender to rotate (*R*), move (*G*), or scale (*S*) an object, you can use some key modifiers to tell it in which axis that transformation must happen. If you press *X*, *Y*, or *Z* one time, you're telling it that one of these global coordinates must be used. If you press the modifier key twice (*X + X*, *Y + Y*, or *Z + Z*) you're demanding that the transformation happen regarding that local coordinate.

## How it works...

When using a correct bone orientation upon its creation, you avoid the need to correct the armature later. The orientation of the bones is often overlooked, and problems at this stage will be painfully noticed on later stages, when the animator tries to move the bones in a coherent way.

To demonstrate that, I've created the index finger bones with the usual "extrude" technique. Let's say the animator wants to close the fingers: this should be accomplished by selecting each bone and pressing *R* to rotate and *X* twice to select the local X axis. The next image shows the results of the previous action with the bones hidden, to demonstrate how the extruding technique on the index finger leads to unwanted results. We wanted to close the finger, not twist it like that. An animator would have a hard time trying to figure out which axis should be used for every finger. Talk about being counterproductive!

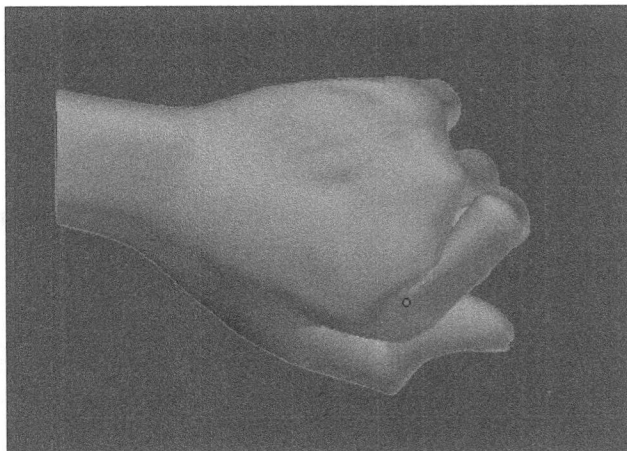

## There's more...

What if you have already created bone chains with this orientation disorder? Do you have to recreate everything from scratch? No, there's hope for us all. This process is just to avoid the need for correcting the bones later, by creating them with the right orientations from the beginning. This means we can adjust the orientation by hand at any moment.

### Correcting the orientation

You can always correct or define the orientation of a bone through its **Roll** value. In the Armature's Edit Mode, select the bone(s) that you want to correct, press *Ctrl + R*, and move your mouse. As with any transformation in Blender, you can use it along with *Ctrl* (to do it in steps of five degrees) or *Shift* (to get softer transformations).

You can manually view and set the **Roll** angle of a bone through the **Properties Panel** (press the *N* key), just below the **Radius** slider, as shown in the following screenshot:

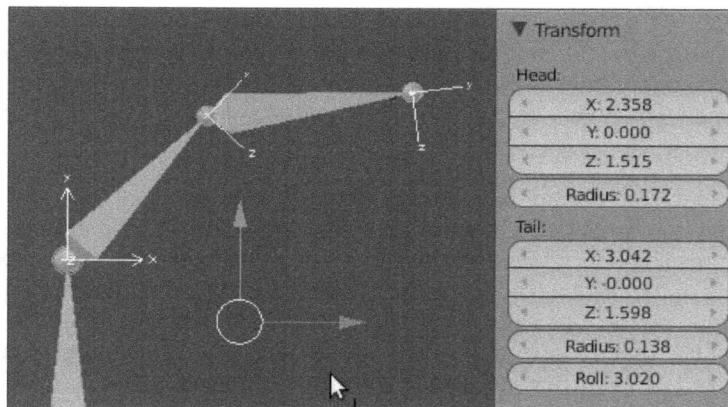

Another shortcut for automatically correcting the **Roll** value is *Ctrl + N*, which tells Blender to guess what the best roll angles are based on their Z axes, which will all point to the same direction ("Up" or the cursor location).

### Axis conventions

Another important thing to keep in mind when creating bones is axis conventions. It means you should always set the "front" of a bone to a given axis. This "front" is the default axis for a transformation, usually a rotation.

For instance, a humanoid character has some default movements, such as bending an elbow, knee, or finger. The bones for all these parts point in different directions, but you can set their roll values in a way that the animator's life becomes a little easier. A common approach is setting the X axis of a bone as the default transformation angle, so when the animator wants to bend and elbow, a knee, or a finger, it's just a matter of using the X local axis for that.

There's no need to wonder "what local axis should I use for this transformation?". In the case of our armature, we can select all the bones, press *Ctrl + R*, and type 90, so the bones' X axes point at us in the Front view.

This way you get consistence throughout your rig, which is a must in professional workflows. I've seen rigs where different fingers in a hand required a different default axes for bending. A nightmare!

### Rigify

A very cool way to add new bones and chains is by using the **Rigify** add-on which comes bundled with Blender 2.5. You can enable it in the User Preferences Window (press *Ctrl + Alt + U*), in the Add-ons tab.

With this add-on enabled you can add predefined bone chains for body parts or even a full human body. The great advantage is that you don't need to worry about names or orientations, since they come configured. You only have to worry about correctly adjusting the preset chains to the proportion of your character mesh.

### See also

*Chapter 5: Controlling fingers*

# Using separate bone chains for different tasks

A useful approach when building rigs is to create more than one bone chain to accomplish different tasks. The idea behind this is to not overwhelm you with so many functions attached to one single bone, making the rig easier to understand and modify.

It is useful to separate the bone chains by their main functions to make things easier to manage: one chain that will only deform your character's mesh, one for creating **Inverse Kinematics** (**IK**) controllers, another for **Forward Kinematics** (**FK**) controllers, interface, helpers, and so on.

By creating them separately, you can make changes without breaking things in your rig. If you stack all the functions and constraints on one single chain, a little change can make a real mess. By separating them you can also make your rig more appealing and usable by defining custom shapes, colors, and hiding bones that shouldn't be touched by the animator.

## Getting ready

You need a mesh to be deformed by the bones you'll create. Open the file `001-Chains.blend` from this book's support files. It contains a tail-like mesh so you can follow this recipe to create separate chains, producing a scorpion-like movement.

## How to do it...

1.  Position the 3D cursor on the base of the tail, with a left mouse click in the 3D View, as seen in the next screenshot:

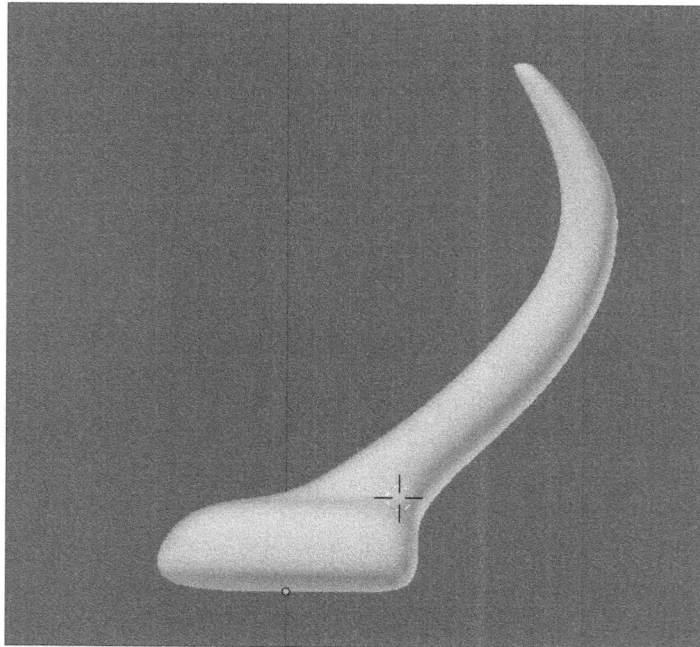

2.  Press *Shift + A* and select **Armature | Single Bone** to create one bone which extends from the base to the tip of the tail. Enter in Edit Mode (press *Tab*), select its tip, and move (press *G*) it to the tip of the tail.

> In order to better see the bones and their axes, go to the **Properties** window, under the **Object Data** panel, and enable the **X-Ray and Axes** properties.

3. Select the bone, press *W*, and select **Subdivide**. Repeat this two more times in order to get eight bones. Select each joint and move (press *G*) it so it fits the tail nicely.

4. Select all the bones (the *A* key), press *Ctrl + R*, and type 90 so their orientation is set with their X axes pointing towards us. The X local axis will be the default to the front or back rotation.

5. Refer to the recipe called *Defining good orientations for your bones* if in doubt. You should end up with something similar to the next screenshot, showing the front and side views:

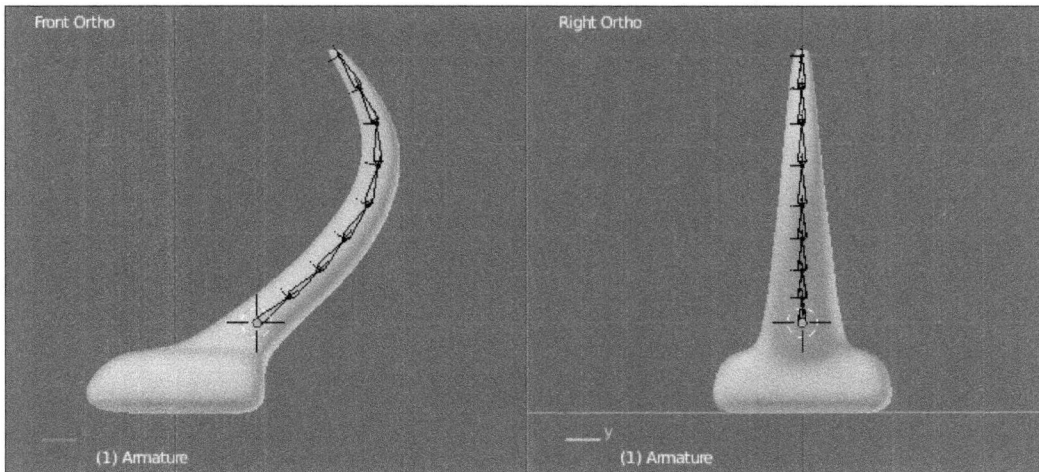

6. Still in Edit Mode, set the bones' names using the **Properties** panel (press the *N* key). For their names, use a prefix such as D_, which stands for "Deformation". That's the role of these bones: they're responsible for deforming our mesh. Good names can be D_tail.1 to D_tail.8.

In Blender versions prior to 2.5, finding the name of a bone in the list displayed by the program could be a tough job, as seen in the next screenshot. Using prefixes are crucial to help you find the desired bone in a list and know its function without having to select it. With the arrival of Blender 2.5, finding a bone (or any object) by its name is much easier: just start typing in the appropriate field to narrow the selection options.

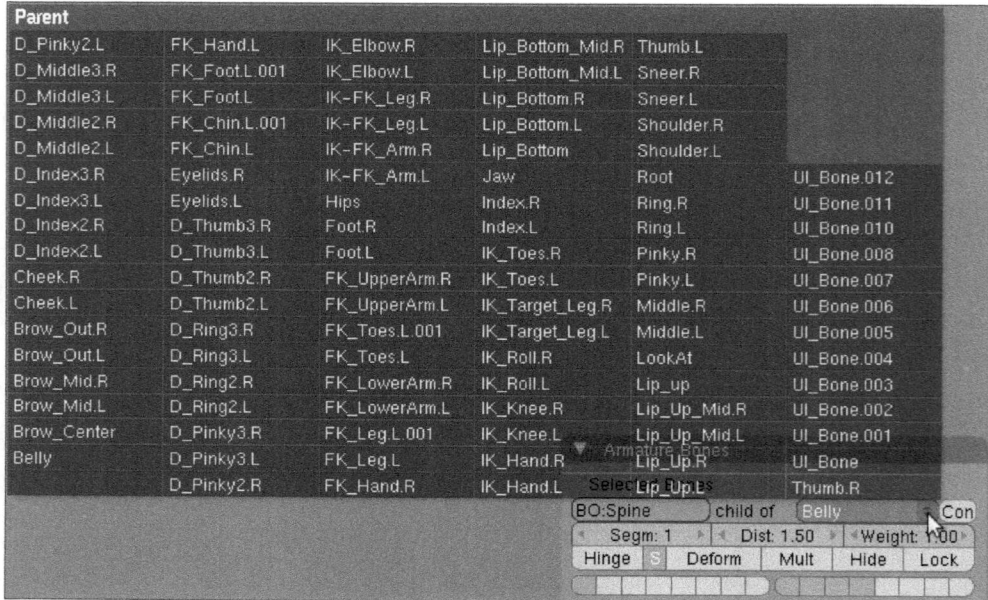

| Parent | | | | | |
|---|---|---|---|---|---|
| D_Pinky2.L | FK_Hand.L | IK_Elbow.R | Lip_Bottom_Mid.R | Thumb.L | |
| D_Middle3.R | FK_Foot.L.001 | IK_Elbow.L | Lip_Bottom_Mid.L | Sneer.R | |
| D_Middle3.L | FK_Foot.L | IK-FK_Leg.R | Lip_Bottom.R | Sneer.L | |
| D_Middle2.R | FK_Chin.L.001 | IK-FK_Leg.L | Lip_Bottom.L | Shoulder.R | |
| D_Middle2.L | FK_Chin.L | IK-FK_Arm.R | Lip_Bottom | Shoulder.L | |
| D_Index3.R | Eyelids.R | IK-FK_Arm.L | Jaw | Root | UI_Bone.012 |
| D_Index3.L | Eyelids.L | Hips | Index.R | Ring.R | UI_Bone.011 |
| D_Index2.R | D_Thumb3.R | Foot.R | Index.L | Ring.L | UI_Bone.010 |
| D_Index2.L | D_Thumb3.L | Foot.L | IK_Toes.R | Pinky.R | UI_Bone.008 |
| Cheek.R | D_Thumb2.R | FK_UpperArm.R | IK_Toes.L | Pinky.L | UI_Bone.007 |
| Cheek.L | D_Thumb2.L | FK_UpperArm.L | IK_Target_Leg.R | Middle.R | UI_Bone.006 |
| Brow_Out.R | D_Ring3.R | FK_Toes.L.001 | IK_Target_Leg.L | Middle.L | UI_Bone.005 |
| Brow_Out.L | D_Ring3.L | FK_Toes.L | IK_Roll.R | LookAt | UI_Bone.004 |
| Brow_Mid.R | D_Ring2.R | FK_LowerArm.R | IK_Roll.L | Lip_up | UI_Bone.003 |
| Brow_Mid.L | D_Ring2.L | FK_LowerArm.L | IK_Knee.R | Lip_Up_Mid.R | UI_Bone.002 |
| Brow_Center | D_Pinky3.R | FK_Leg.L.001 | IK_Knee.L | Lip_Up_Mid.L | UI_Bone.001 |
| Belly | D_Pinky3.L | FK_Leg.L | IK_Hand.R | Lip_Up.R | UI_Bone |
| | D_Pinky2.R | FK_Hand.R | IK_Hand.L | Lip_Up.L | Thumb.R |

Now we're going to create the controller bone. This bone belongs to another "chain" of bones responsible for controlling the deformation ones. The controllers don't perform any mesh deformation by themselves. Although in this example this chain has just one bone for the sake of simplicity, more complex rigs can easily have dozens of them.

7. Still in the armature's Edit Mode, place your cursor just above the tip of the tail and press *Shift + A* to add another bone. Press *Ctrl + R* and type 90 so that its orientation is the same as the deformation chain ones. Define this bone's name as `Tail`. The controller bones are usually named without prefixes in order to be friendlier to the animator, who will look out for `Tail` instead of `C_Tail`.

8. Disable the **Deform** option on the **Bones** tab in the **Properties** window, as seen in the next screenshot, so this bone will not perform any deformations on the mesh:

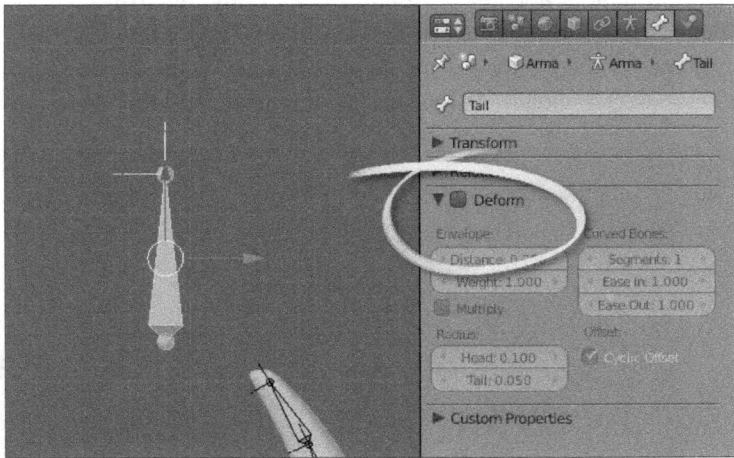

9. Now we're going to add constraints to control our deformation chain. Go to the armature's Pose Mode (press *Ctrl + Tab*). Then, select the bone Tail (which is the controller one), press *Shift* and then select the bone on the tip of the deformation chain, D_tail.8. Press *Ctrl + Shift + C* to bring up the **Constraints** menu and choose **Copy Rotation**.

10. This will make the bone on the deformation chain copy the rotations of the controller one, but you will notice that it will copy the absolute rotation (which is not what we want). To make this bone copy the transformation based on its own rotation, select it and go to the **Bone Constraints** panel, under the **Properties** window. Check the **Offset** option and select **Local Space** on the two drop-down lists, as seen in the next screenshot:

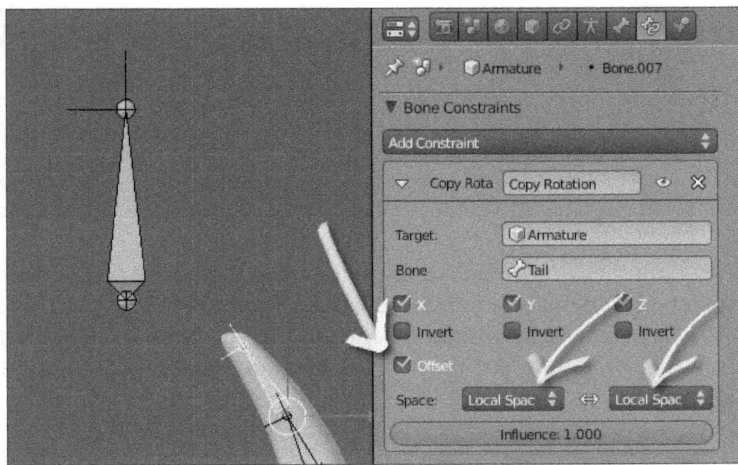

11. Apply the same constraint to all other bones of the deformation chain: select them and, lastly, the bone which has the constraint we want to copy. Go to the **Pose** menu on the window header and select **Constraints | Copy Constraints to Selected**. That will apply the same constraint to all bones of the deformation chain.

12. Still in Pose Mode, select the `Tail` bone and rotate it. You'll see that all the bones on the deformation chain follow its rotation like a real tail, as seen in the next screenshot:

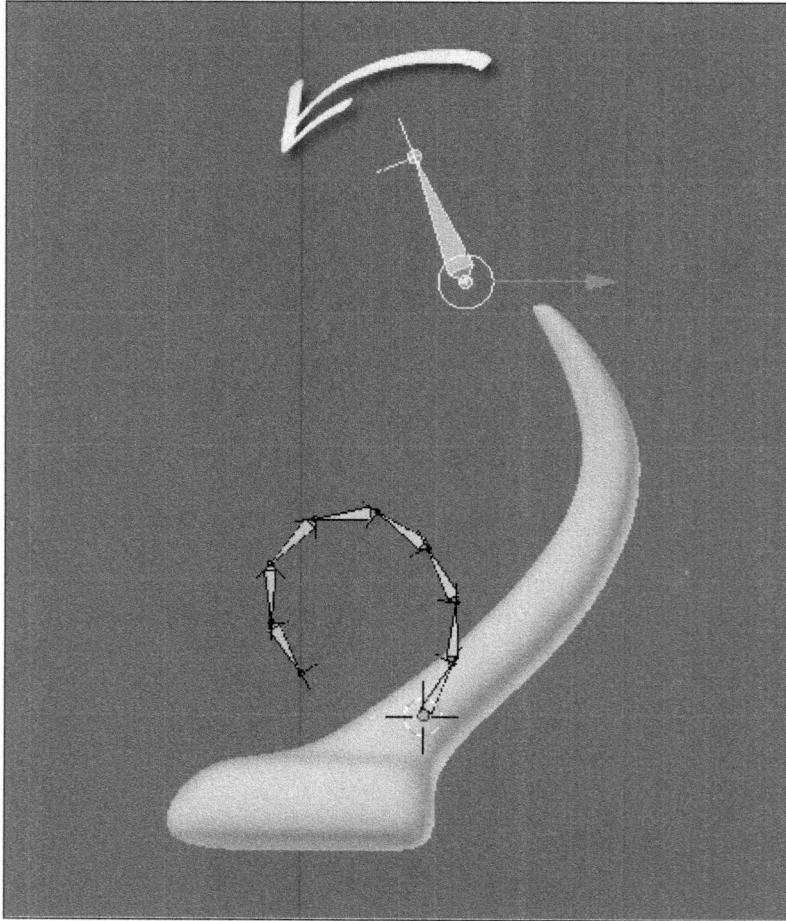

13. Since the animators wouldn't need to see or move the bones on the Deformation chain, you should select and move (the *M* key) them to another (and invisible) bone layer. I usually move my deformation bones to the last layer, so you can do the same for yours. You should now also turn off the X-Ray option for this armature, since it's no longer needed.

14. Lastly, select the Tail mesh, hold *Shift*, click on one bone of the chain, press *Ctrl + P*, and choose **With Automatic Weight** to make our armature object actually deform the mesh, as seen in the next screenshot:

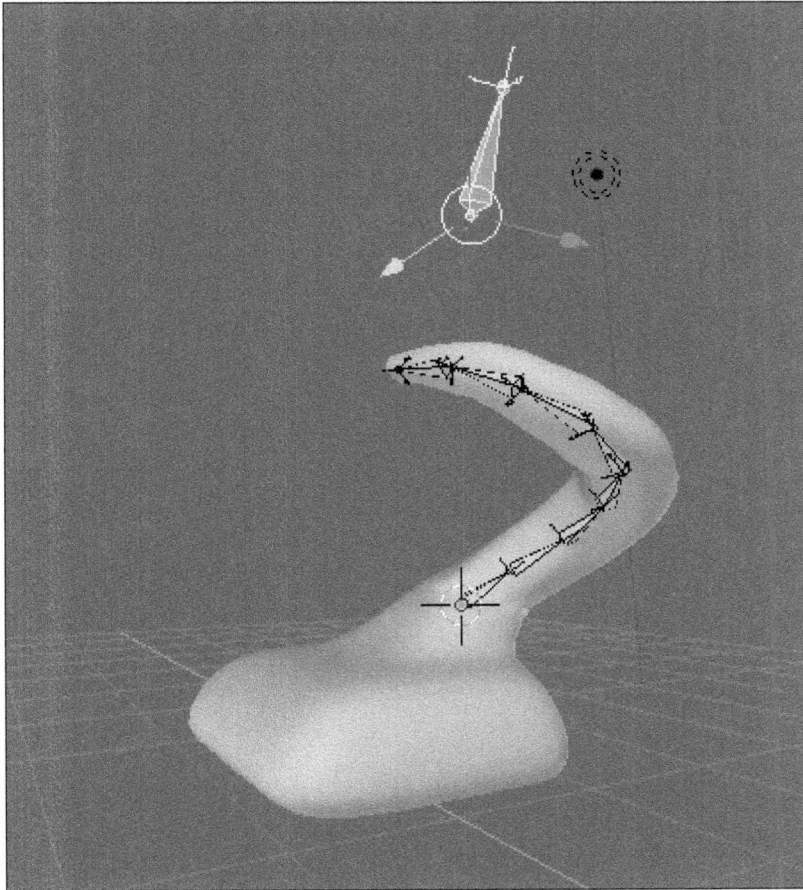

## How it works...

By creating separate bone chains to accomplish different tasks, you end up with a very usable and organized rig, which is easy to animate and to configure, since each bone does only what is meant to do. This approach allows us to have a larger number of deformation bones to achieve softer results while still being simple to animate, having fewer bones to be controlled by the animator. This example showed how a scorpion-like tail can be controlled with only one bone, although eight bones build its structure.

## There's more

The concept of separate bone chains will be discussed further throughout this book, notably when creating different chains to control arms, legs, torso, face, and eyes.

### Don't get tied up on those chains

As your rig grows in complexity, you should use the bone layers that Blender offers you to manage the chains.

In some cases it is interesting to make a bone present on more than one layer. For instance, you may want to keep your main controller bones (limbs, head, torso) only on layer 1 and leave the detail controllers (facial expressions, fingers, eyes) on layer 2. But there are other bones which act only to enable and disable features of your rig, such as the ability to stretch limbs or switch between Inverse and Forward Kinematics (more about this in the recipe *Making an IK-FK switcher*).

These "general rig properties" should be present on both layers 1 and 2. To accomplish that, select the desired bone, press *M* to bring up the layer selection menu, hold *Shift*, and click on all the layers that you want those bones to belong to.

And always remember to use prefixes for your chains in order to find what you want quicker. You can use D_ for deformation bones, IK_ for Inverse Kinematics bones, FK_ for Forward Kinematics chains, T_ for target bones, M_ for mechanism, and so on. There's more on these uses in later recipes.

## See also

*Chapter 3: Controlling the pupils*

*Chapter 4: Creating the jaw controller*

*Chapter 5: Controlling fingers*

# Customizing shapes and colors for your bones

Not only do we need to create rigs that work, but they also need to be usable for the animator. Blender offers us a property for the bones called X-Ray, that allows us to view the bones from any angle, regardless of the mesh it deforms. It can be useful sometimes, notably when editing the bone chains, but using X-Ray in more complex rigs can confuse the animator. Take a look at the clutter in the next screenshot, where all bones of our character Otto are visible and with X-Ray enabled:

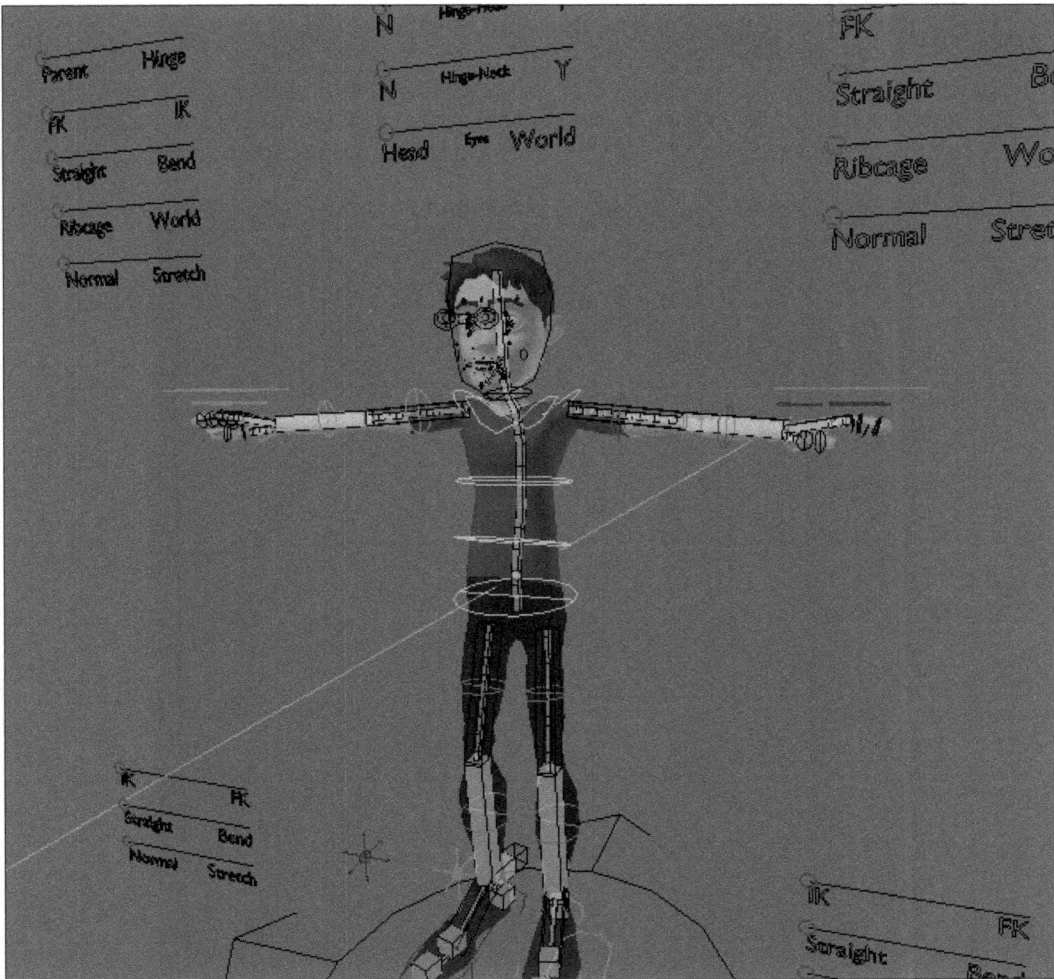

As we mentioned at the beginning of the chapter, a rig must be visually simple and intuitive, so anyone without prior guidance can start moving the character without trouble. It is possible to change the default shape and color of your bones in Blender, making your rig much more usable and intuitive.

## Getting ready

Creating custom shapes and colors for your bones in Blender is easy, and we'll see some good practices for your rigs. You can use any chain of bones in Blender.

## How to do it...

1. Open the file `001-Legs.blend`. It has two chains of three bones indicative of two legs of a human, as you can see in the next screenshot. We're going to make shapes for all the bones, and we'll make the bones of each leg a different color:

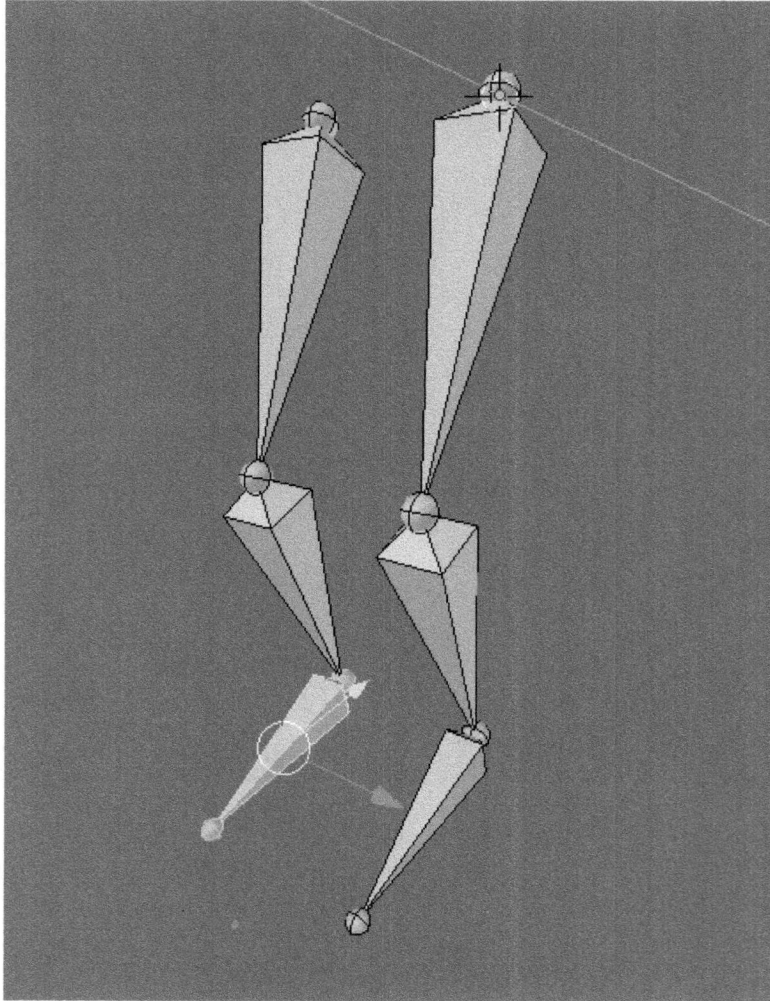

2. In Object Mode, create a single plane through *Shift + A* | **Mesh | Circle**. On the **Operator** tab, in the **Tool Shelf** (press the *T* key to open it), change the values of **Vertices** to 8 and **Radius** to 100.

3.  In the **Properties** panel (press *N*), set the name of this object as SHAPE_Leg. Get in Edit Mode (press *Tab*), select the two vertices positioned over the X axis, and make an edge (*F*) between them. This would make a line to divide the octagon in half, similar to the one in the next screenshot:

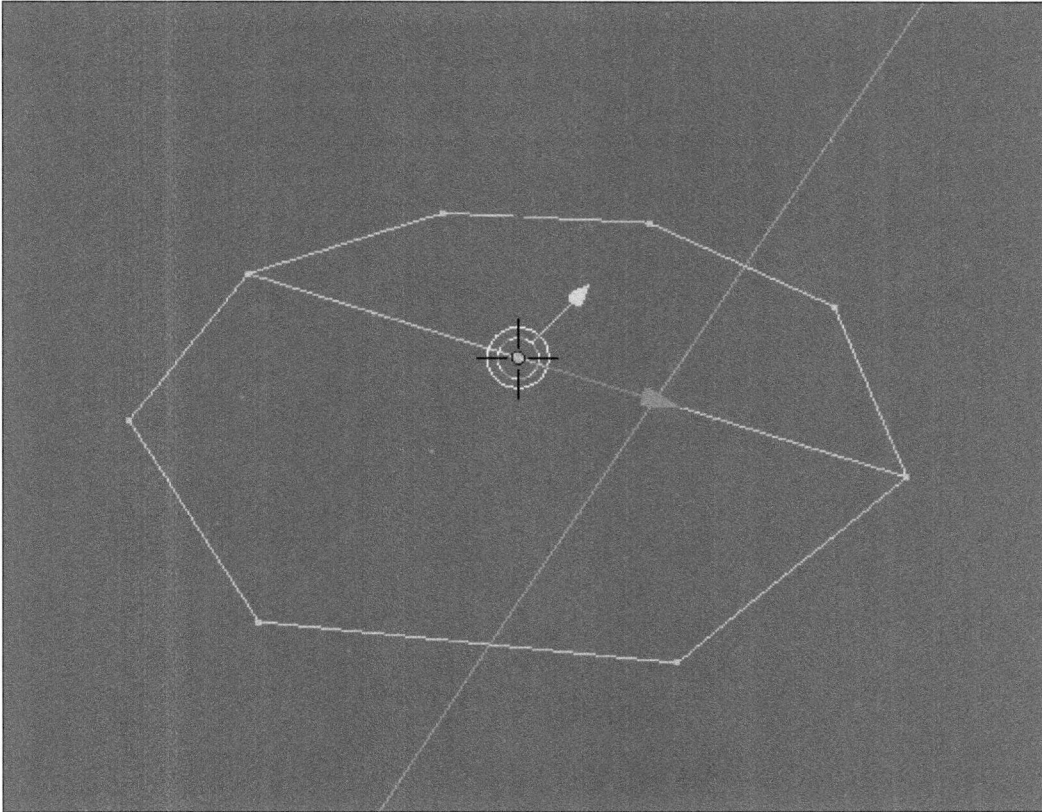

4.  Go back to Object Mode (*Tab*) , select the armature, and enter into Pose Mode (*Ctrl + Tab*).

5. Select **Thigh.L** and go to the **Bone** tab in the **Properties** window. Under the section **Display**, click on the field called **Custom Shape** and select **SHAPE_Leg**. Check the box called **Wireframe**, which will make your custom shape always be drawn in a more pleasing way, regardless of your current viewport shading. The next screenshot shows these fields:

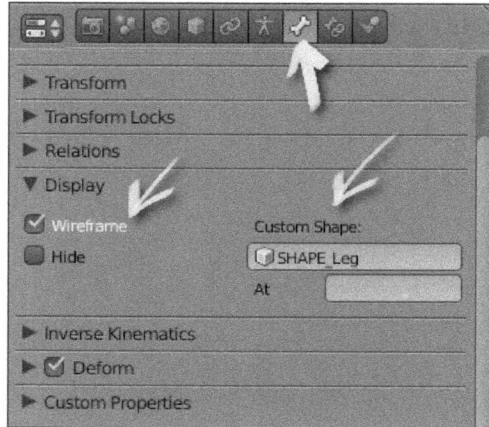

You'll see that your bone will change from the default octahedron to the shape you just created. But you'll also notice that the rotation and position of the shape don't help much, since we need it at the middle of the bone and perpendicular to its direction. The next screenshot shows the problem:

> If you don't see the shapes after this step, go to the **Object Data** tab under the **Properties** window and make sure that the boxes **Shapes** and **Colors** are enabled.

6. Select your shape object again, enter in Edit Mode (*Tab*), select all the vertices (*A*), and rotate (*R*) them 90 degrees in the local X axis. You'll see that the bone shapes update automatically. To fix the position, making the shape stand about half of the bone, move (*G*) the selected vertices in their local Y axes until you are happy with the result. Still in Edit Mode, resize (*S*) the shape to achieve a reasonable size in your rig. The next screenshot shows the result:

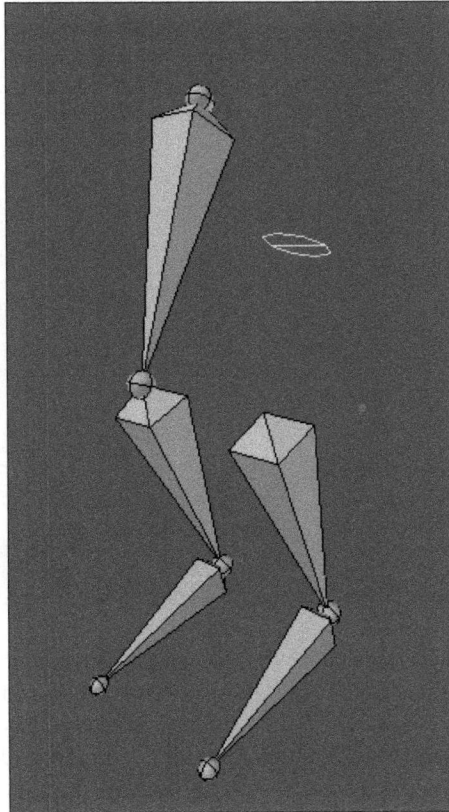

7. Now you can use the same shape for the `Ankle.L` bone, using the **Display** section in the **Bone** tab under the **Properties** window.

8. Repeat the same process and create another shape for the `Foot.L` bone: be creative and make a bi-dimensional shape of a foot. Name it `SHAPE_Foot.L` Repeat everything for the other leg and you should end up with something similar to what's in the next screenshot (I've created a simple character mesh to make it easier to see):

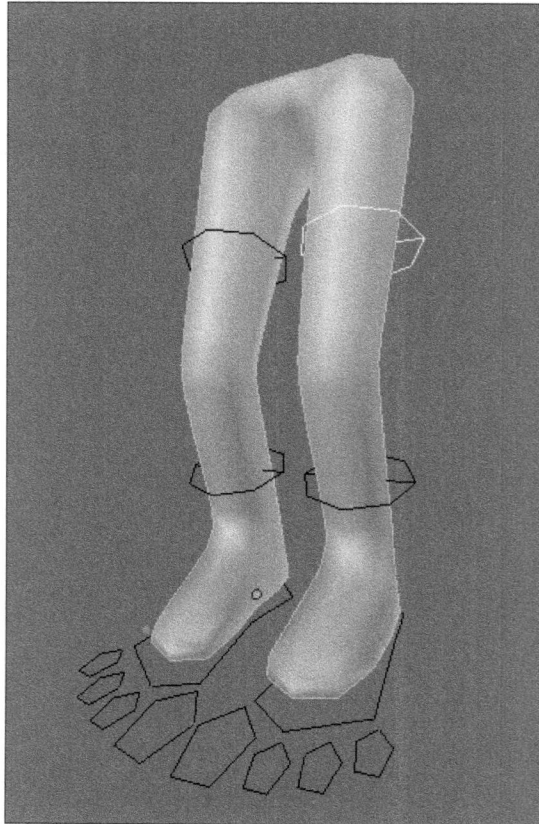

Now, the colors! We can use them to distinguish the bones in various ways: a color for the left limbs and other for the right ones, a color for IK and other for FK and so on. The important here is to make it easier for the animator to visually understand the difference between bones. Let's make the left ones red and the right ones green.

9. Select the left leg bones and press *Ctrl + G*. Choose **Add Selected to Bone Group**. This will create a new group of bones called just **Group**.

10. Go to the **Properties** window and select the **Object Data** tab. Under **Bone Groups**, you'll see a group called **Group**. Select it and change its name to `Leg_Left` on the **Name** field.

11. Under the **Color Set** list, select **01 – Theme Color Set** and click on the **Assign** button to make these bones red. Repeat the task for the bones on the right-hand side leg, choosing an appropriate name and selecting the entry **04 – Theme Color Set** to make them blue.

> The next screenshot shows our rig with shapes and different colors applied along with the settings on the **Properties** window (the color images can be downloaded from the publisher's website or viewed in the digital version of this book). The file 001-Legs-complete.blend has our finished recipe for your reference.

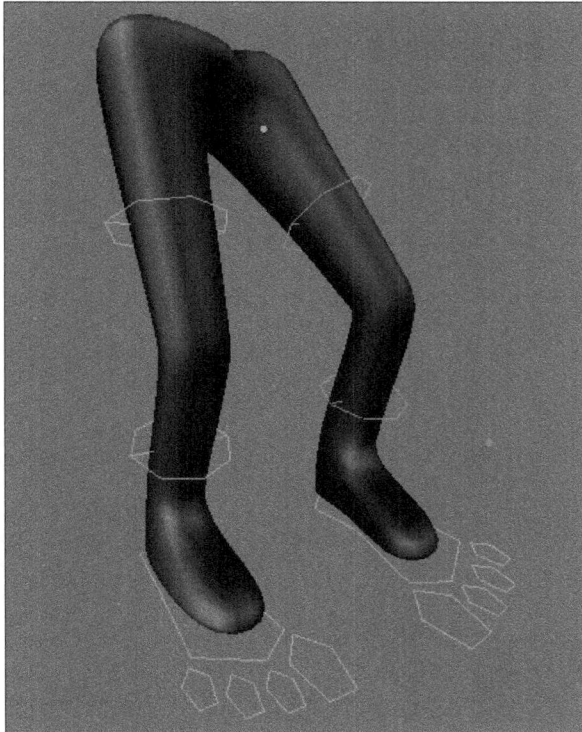

## How it works...

By setting custom shapes and colors for your bones, you can offer a much more intuitive interface for your controls, making the task of animation easier. You should create shapes that are larger than the mesh deformed by the armature, so that you can see the bones without using the clutter caused by the X-Ray property.

You should look for shapes that are simple and that show information about the control. In our example, we created an octagon with an edge through its middle. This edge shows visually the local X axis of the bone, making it easier for the animator to understand the default transformation of it. Feet, hands, and eyes controllers are often made using figurative shapes similar to the one in this example.

## There's more

Along with getting an organized 3D View, you should also be able to easily manage your entire scene. Blender has a special type of window, the **Outliner**, which allows us to see every object in our scenes organized hierarchically. But the **Outliner** alone doesn't do all the tricks: you have to create and name your objects properly in order to stay organized.

### Pay attention to the Outliner

The Outliner is a great tool in Blender to see the hierarchy of objects in your file. But when you create a rig with lots of custom shapes, the Outliner list can easily become full of objects you won't use. To remove the clutter of it, it's recommended to create an object (normally an "Empty" named "Shapes") to be parent of all Shape objects. This way, you can easily browse on the Outliner without dozens of shape objects. It's also useful to make this Empty object child of the Armature object, so all shapes are hierarchically related to the rig.

To prevent these objects from showing up in your render, a good practice is to select them all (*A*), move (*M*) them to the last layer and hide (*H*) them from your scene. The next screenshot shows the Outliner of this recipe's scene. Notice that the shapes are hidden (the disabled "eye" icon) and will not be rendered (the disabled "camera" icon):

## See also

*Chapter 1: Get Rigging*

# Using corrective shape keys

The ability to create bones that deform a mesh is great, but that alone doesn't solve all our rigging problems. Some may argue that it's possible to create perfect deformations in every movement of your character just with lots of extra bones and even more detailed weight painting, but that's too time consuming. We want our rigs ready to be animated in a short amount of time. We care about our character looking good on screen, not the purity of the technique.

That's why we can solve some trickier rigging problems with corrective Shape Keys. **Shape Keys** are saved states of our character's mesh, with the position of each vertex stored in the computer's memory. We're going to create some custom deformations in our character to correct specific issues caused by our rig. The example will take care of one of the most common source of deformation problems: the bending of arms.

## Getting ready

Open up the file 001-ShapeKeys.blend from this book's support files. You'll see an arm with two bones already set to deform the mesh. Try rotating the forearm on its X local axis for 130°. You'll notice that the vertices located near the elbow don't deform like a real arm would: there are noticeable intersections and the biceps should be contracted.

Even with the feature called **Preserve Volume** in the **Armature** modifier panel that uses the dual quaternion method to deform meshes in a more realistic way, some things such as muscles and specific skin deformations still need to be fixed manually. We're going to create a Shape Key here to act as the extreme deformation of this mesh when the character bends its arm to the maximum angle of 130°. Look at the next screenshot to see the before (left) and after the driven corrective Shape Key, where the biceps muscle gets contracted and the skin gets compressed between the arm and forearm.

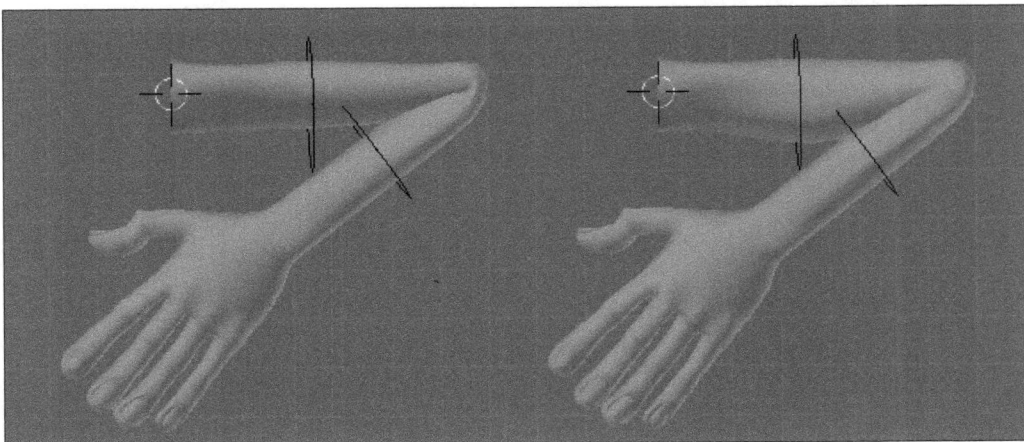

1. Keep the forearm bone rotated on its X axis for 130°. Select the mesh and enter Edit Mode (*Tab*). You'll see that the arm goes back to its original position, as seen in the next screenshot:

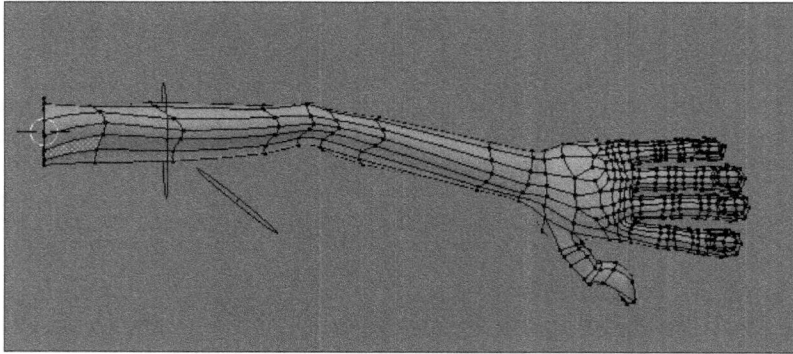

We can tell Blender to keep the armature's deformation on the mesh while we edit its vertices, so that it's easier to create the corrective Shape Key.

2. Go to the **Modifiers** tab under the **Properties** window and locate the armature modifier. Next to the eye button, enable the one with the tooltip **Use modifier while in edit mode**. It will bring us another button next to it. Enable it too. Now we can edit the mesh after the deformation performed by the armature. The following screenshot shows the arm with our desired behavior and the **Armature** modifier panel with the highlighted options:

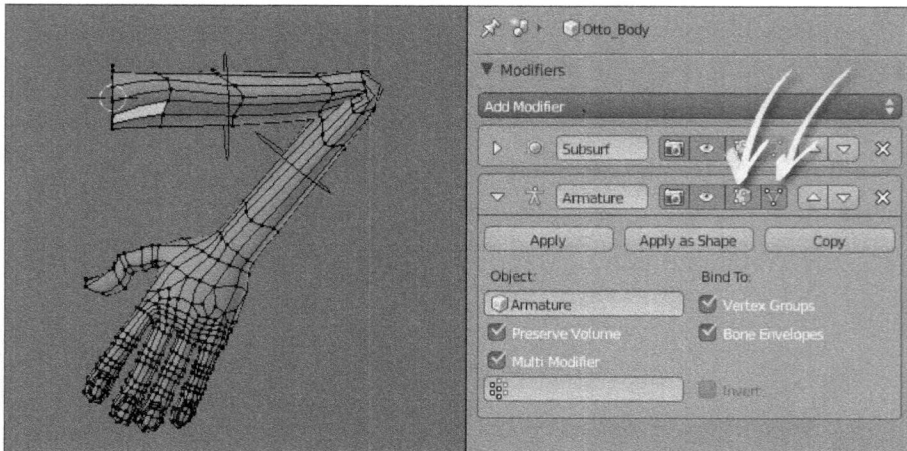

3.  Go back to Object Mode (*Tab*), go to the **Object Data** panel under the **Properties** window, and find the section called **Shape Keys**. Click twice on the plus sign to create two Shape Keys: one called **Basis**, which is the base state of our mesh, and other called **Key 1**, which is the one we will work on.

4.  Change the last Shape Key name to `Arm_Left`. This is important when dealing with complete characters and lots of Shape Keys.

    We're going to use both the sculpting tool and the Edit Mode to build our corrective shape. In order to be able to work on a Shape Key in Sculpt Mode, we have to pin this shape.

5.  With the **Arm_Left** key selected, click on the pin icon, just below the **Shape Keys** list. You should disable it when you're done sculpting. The next screenshot shows the **Shape Keys** section and the pin button highlighted:

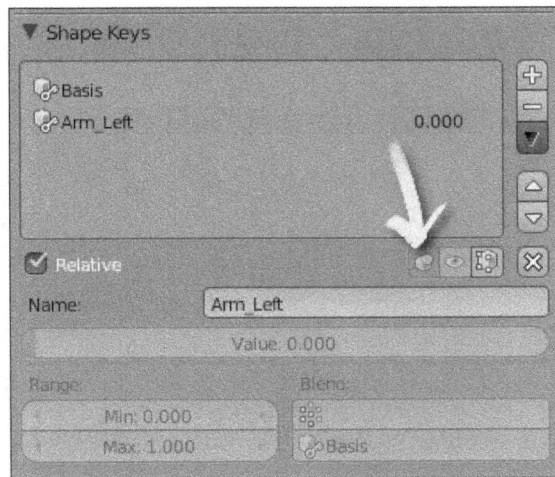

6. Sculpting in Blender is pretty straightforward: select the mesh, pick Sculpt Mode in the 3D view mode list on the window header, and start sculpting the mesh. Under the **Tool Shelf** (*T*) you can select the appropriate mode of sculpting, such as Inflate, Grab, or Smooth, for instance. Use the **Inflate** tool for growing the biceps, such as in the following screenshot:

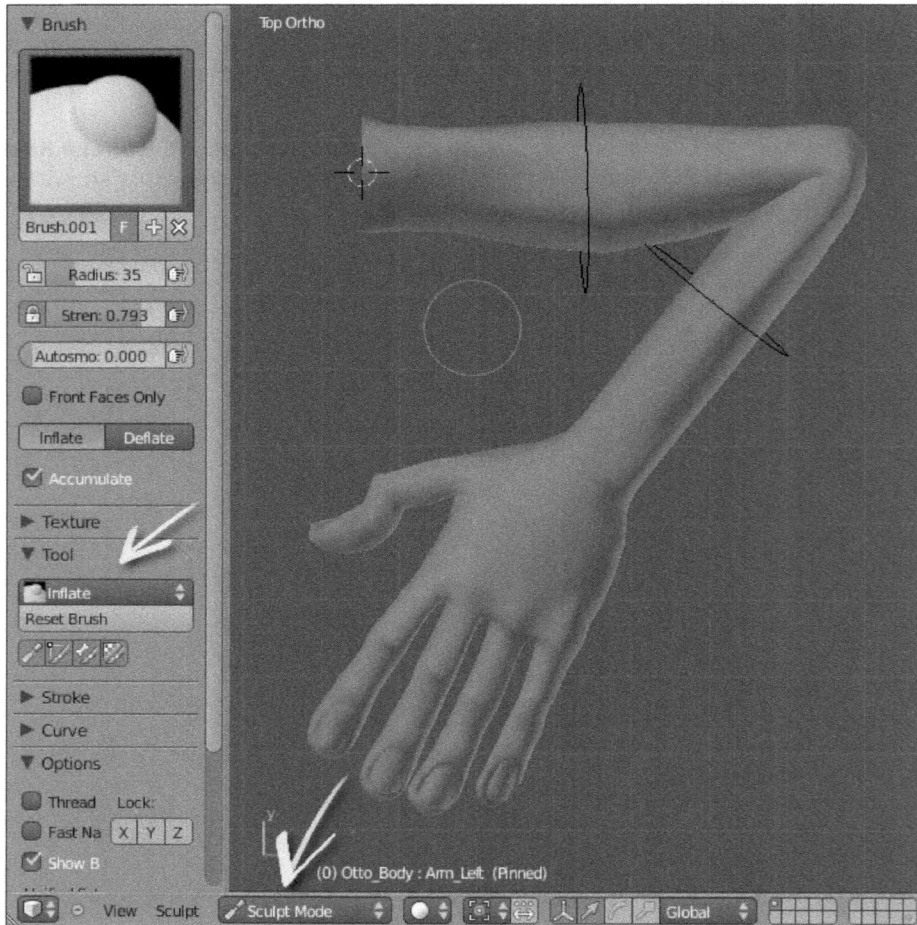

6. Since not everything will look right just with sculpting, disable the Pin button for the Shape Key you've enabled at step 5, enter into Edit Mode, and tweak the vertices until you're happy with the result of the arm bending shape. Go back to Object Mode when you're done.

Now comes the magic part: now that you have two shapes for your arm, we need to set a driver, so the rotation of the forearm bone on its X local axis triggers the morphing between those keys.

7. Below the Shape Key's name in the Object Data tab is a slider called **Value**. Right-click on it and select **Add Driver**. This will turn the slider into a pink color, which is how Blender shows you that this channel is driven by another object, expression, or property. The next screenshot demonstrates that:

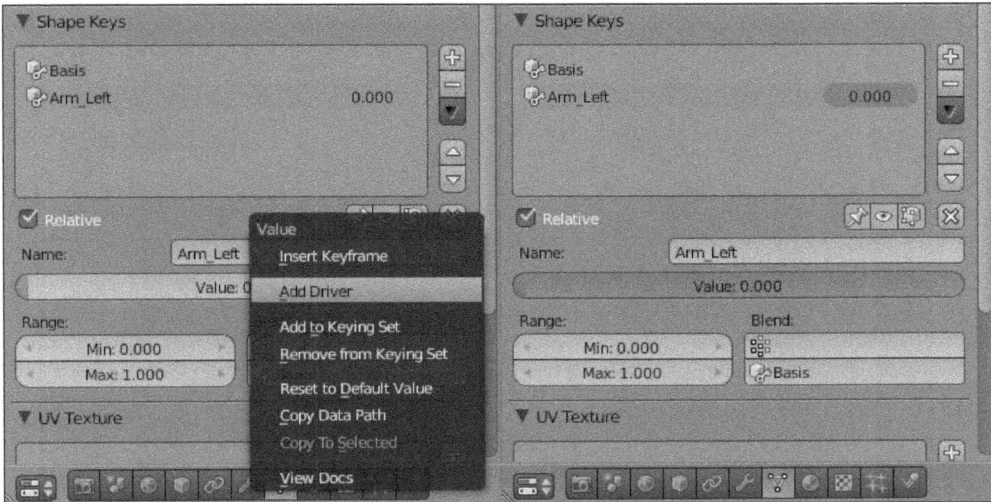

8. Open a Graph Editor window to set up the forearm bone as the driver for this shape. Select **Drivers** from the **Modes** list in the header.

9. On the left panel, click in **Value (Arm_Left)** in order to see the pink line in the editor. On the **Properties** (N) panel, leave the driver type as **Scripted Expression** and change the **Expr** value to `var`.

10. In the box just below the **Add Variable Button**, leave **Transform Channel** on the first item; select **Armature** from the **Ob/Bone** selector and also the bone **forearm** in the box that will appear after choosing the armature; select **X Rotation** in the last list and check the **Local Space** box. This will tell Blender to take into account the local X rotation of the forearm bone to control the blending between the **Basis** and **Arm_Left** shape keys.

11. Rotate the forearm bone on its X axis to see the transformation. The biceps and skin get changed when you rotate the forearm, but the transformation happens earlier than we would expect.

12. To fix that, look for the **Generator** box inside the **Modifiers** section on the **Properties** panel. Change the Y value to `-1` so that the blending between the Shape Keys starts only when the arm bending is closer to its final position. The next screenshot shows the driver and its values set:

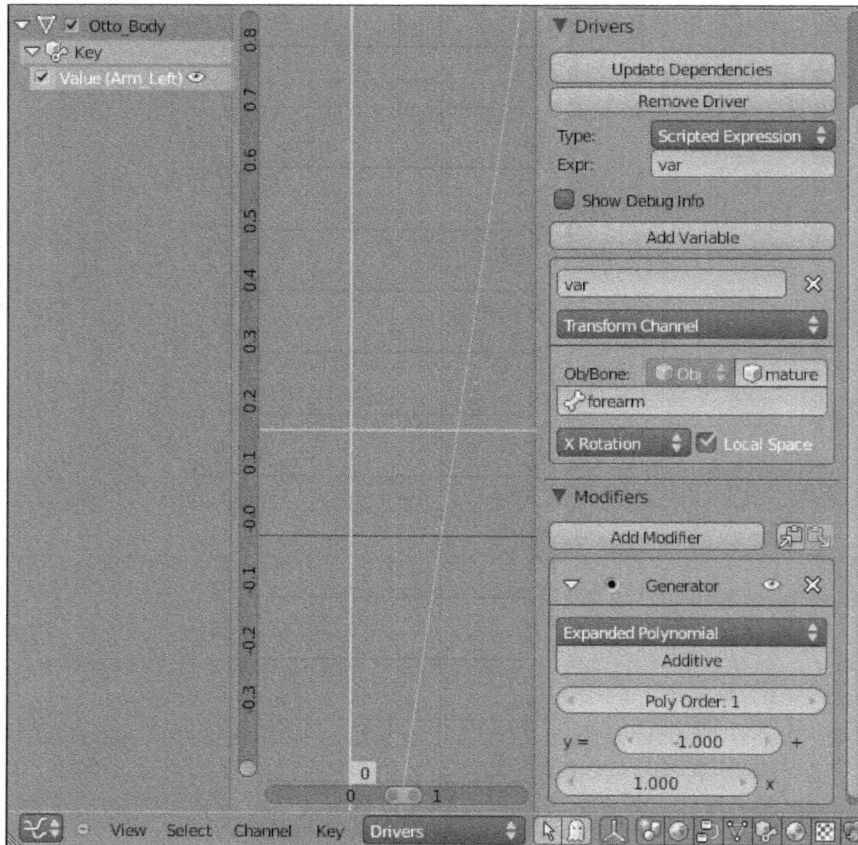

The file `001-ShapeKeys-complete.blend` has this finished recipe for your reference.

## How it works...

Using a basic rig as starting point, you move the bones around and look for strange deformations, which would occur mostly in joints. When you find such deformations, its time to use them as a base to build new Shape Keys that correct the mesh in such situations. By using drivers, you can use the same bone values that caused the bad deformations to trigger the corrective Shape Key.

In this recipe you've learned how to create simple drivers in Blender. You'll notice throughout this book that most rigging features rely on them at some point. Fortunately they are not difficult to create.

## Drivers

The use of drivers in Blender 2.5 changed significantly from previous versions. Now, almost every property in Blender can be animated, driven, and used as a driver for other properties. It's just a matter of right-clicking over the property that you want to control and selecting **Add Driver**, then setting it up on the Graph Editor window. You can even make complex drivers using scripted expressions that can take into account more than one property and math expressions, for example.

*Chapter 4*: *Adding expressions using Shape Keys*

# Making an IK-FK switcher

When creating rigs, we often face situations where we need to alter between two states or properties. The most iconic case is to alter from Inverse Kinematics (IK) to Forward Kinematics (FK) back and forth for a limb.

Forward Kinematics is the default state of regular chains of bones. When you move, rotate, or scale a bone in FK mode, all of its children bones inherit the same transformation. Therefore, we can say that the movement of a chain of bones in FK is driven by its base bone. It is often used for arm controllers when the character does **not** have its hands on a fixed position (such as doing push-ups).

Inverse Kinematics, on the other hand (no pun intended), works the opposite way: the movement of a chain of bones in IK is driven by its tip. It is often used for leg controllers, when the position of the foot bone drives the leg bones above it, and for arm controllers when the character does have its hands on a fixed position.

Since we may need to alter between IK and FK for an arm, for example, we can create specific controls to achieve that. These controls are normally made with bones that don't deform the mesh with some custom shapes applied to them.

## Getting ready

Open the file `001-IK_FK_Switcher.blend` from the book's support files. The file has an arm mesh with three chains properly named and grouped: one for the mesh deformation (green), one to act as the IK chain (blue), and another for the FK chain (red), as we can see in the following screenshot:

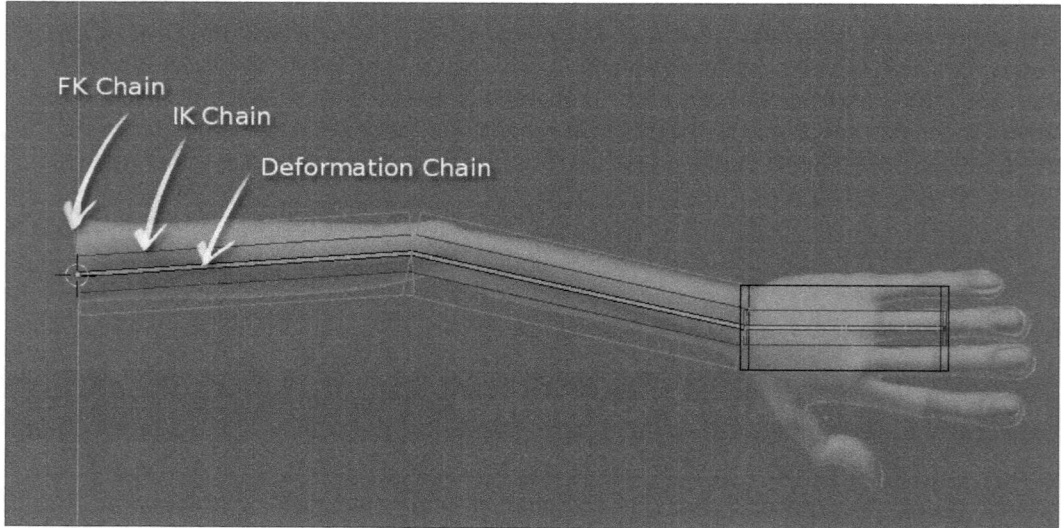

The three chains have the exact same position, scale, rotation, and orientation on the 3D scene. This is crucial to make our setup work as expected.

There is also a fourth chain with only one bone to act as the switcher interface. The bones are presented in B-Bone wireframe visualization with X-Ray enabled, which allows us to view them through the arm mesh and with different widths, since they are all on the same position.

Each bone on the deformation chain has two **Copy Rotation** constraints applied to it: one pointing to its relative bone on the IK chain and other to the one on the FK chain.

**Constraints** are restrictions applied to objects or bones. There are currently more than 20 types of constraints built in Blender with a variety of purposes. The Copy Rotation constraint used here is pretty straightforward: the constrained bone (on the deformation chain) will copy the rotation of a target (a bone on the IK or FK chain). To add a Copy Rotation constraint to a bone in Pose Mode, first select the target bone (the one which will have the rotation copied), hold *Shift*, select the bone which will receive the constraint, press *Ctrl + Shift + C*, and choose Copy Rotation on the pop-up menu.

The constraints on each bone act in opposite ways, so we need a way to alter their influence in order to make only one operational at a time. We're going to use the switcher bone to drive the influence of each constraint: when the IK chain has full influence over the deformation chain, the FK will have none, and vice versa.

Select each of the green deformer bones and take a look at the **Bone Constraints** tab in the **Properties** window. You'll see that each bone has two **Copy Rotation** constraints already set: one for the IK chain with an influence of 1, and other to the FK chain, with zero influence. If you move the bone called **IK_hand**, you'll see that the green chain will follow it properly, while the FK chain in red stands still, as shown in the following screenshot:

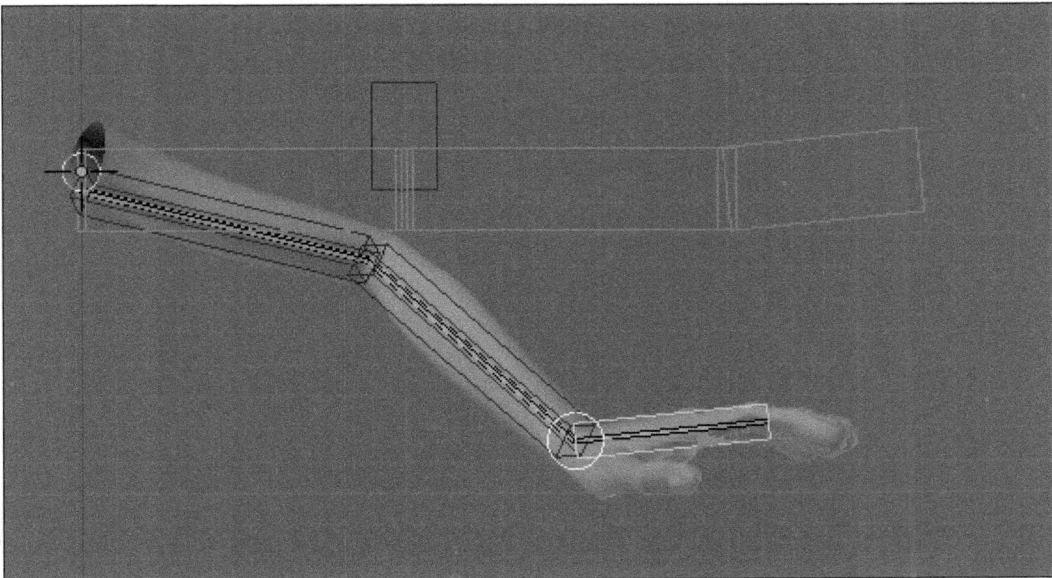

**How to do it...**

1. Select the bone **D_arm** and go to its **Bone Constraints** tab under the **Properties** window. Under the first constraint, named **IK_arm**, right-click on the **Influence** slider and select **Add Driver** as seen in the next screenshot. You'll see that the Graph Editor window above the 3D View gets updated and the **Influence** slider turns into a pink color:

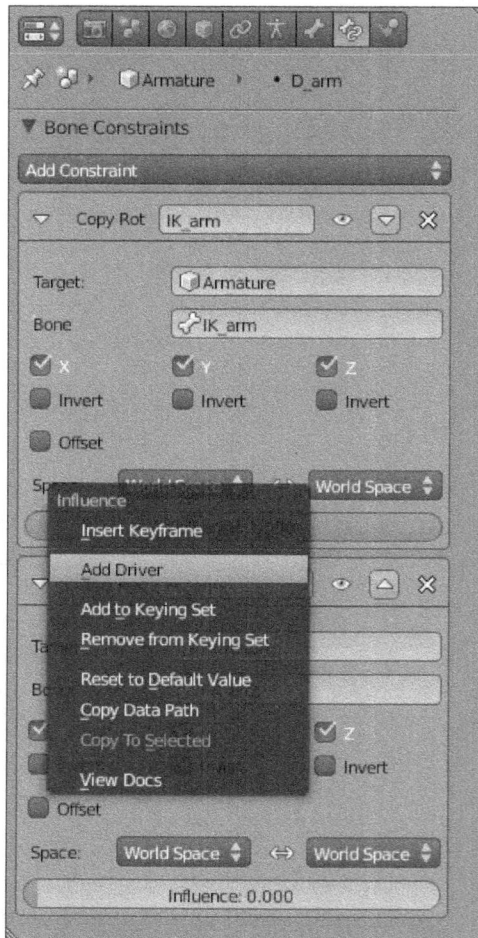

2. Under the Graph Editor, click on the driver on the left-hand side panel. Its properties will be shown on the **Properties Panel** (*N*). Navigate to the **Drivers** session, leave it as **Scripted Expression**, and change the **Expr** field to var.

3. Below the **Add Variable** button, leave the first list value as **Transform Channel**, select the **Armature** object on the **Ob/Bone** field and the bone called **IK_FK_switcher**.

4. Since we need this switcher bone to act as a horizontal slider, keep the **X Location** value and just enable **Local Space**. The next image shows our driver set:

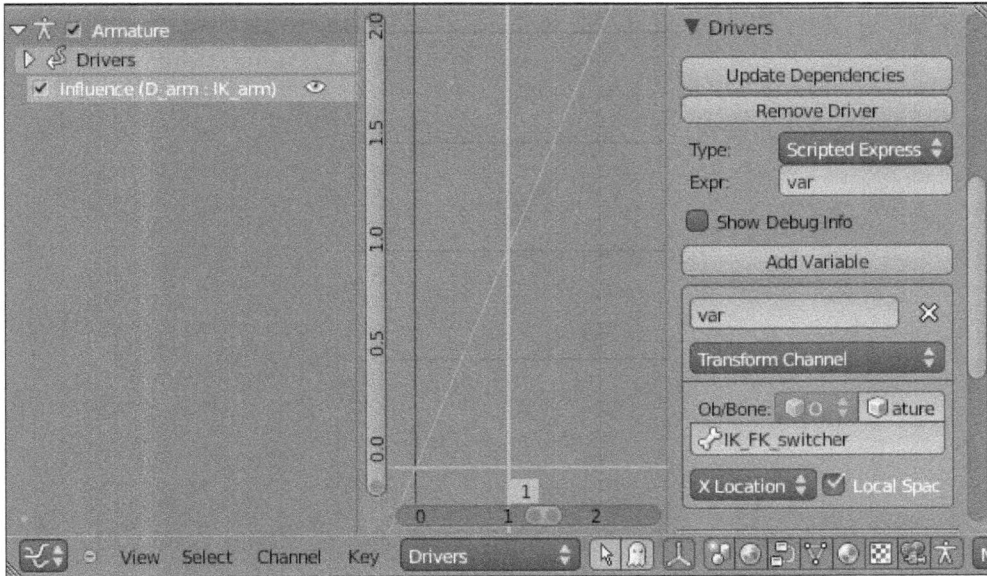

5. Go back to the **Bone Constraints** tab under the **Properties** window. Now, instead of creating the driver from scratch, let's use one of the new useful features in Blender 2.5: right-click on the pink **Influence** slider on the **IK_arm** constraint and select **Copy Driver**. Next, right-click on the **Influence** slider from the **FK_arm** constraint and select **Paste Driver**. Now, both constraints will have the same driver.

6. Since we need this FK driver to act contrary to the IK, head over the Graph Editor and click on the FK driver (named **Influence (D_arm: FK_arm)**). On the **Properties Panel** (*N*) at the right, you'll see that all values were copied from the first driver. Since we need an inverted mapping, just change the **Expr** field value to **1-var**. That's all we need to do create the inverted driver. The next screenshot shows the driver setup values:

Regular drivers act on an ascendant curve with linear mapping, meaning that a value of zero on the driver object will make the driven channel have the same value. When creating switchers, we need an ascendant and one descendant mapping. This way we can increase the amount of influence of one driver while decreasing the concurrent one. As a tip, leave your desired driver in the default state with a descendant mapping.

7. Now you should use the drivers set for the **D_arm** bone constraints as reference to the remaining bones on the deformation chain. You can use the process described in step 5 to copy the driver from the **IK_arm** constraint and paste it to the **IK_forearm** and **IK_hand** constraints. Do the same to the FK constraints and you're done. No need to change anything in the drivers values.

8. When you finish setting up the remaining drivers, move the FK and IK bones to different locations and switch the IK-FK slider: you'll see that the deformation bones (and the arm) alter between chains as you move the slider. The next screenshot shows the switcher in an intermediate position, where the deformation bones (and the arm) act under the influences of both IK (blue, medium width) and FK (red, fatter) chains.

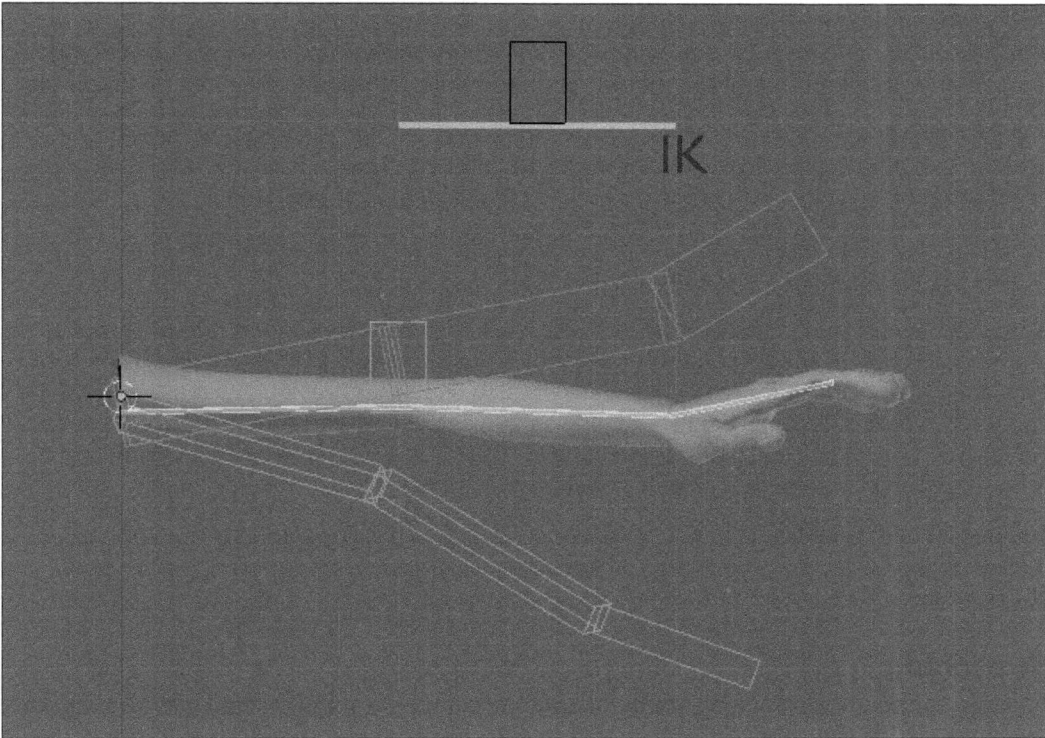

The file `001-IKFK-Switcher-complete.blend` has this complete example for your reference.

## How it works...

The logic behind a switcher is pretty simple, but the amount of chains and constraints may cause a little confusion. The deformation chain bones have two constraints each: one **Copy Rotation** with target to the FK chain and another one to the IK chain. The drivers are set in a inverse way: if IK has an ascending mapping on the Graph Editor, the FK must have a descending one. The controller bone does the rest: adding to one property reduces the opposite at the same amount.

## There's more

The switcher that we've just created is basically an interface to control a feature in our rig, and the principle behind it can (and should) be used to control various other rigging features beyond IK-FK. As a rigger, you should be ready to use all features that Blender offers you to make your rig easier to use and understand.

## Custom interfaces

With custom shapes and colors, we can create special interfaces as the slider used in this recipe. As we saw here, a single controller bone can drive more than one property in your rig.

In addition to these colors and shapes, user interface bones should also have constraints applied. In our example, the slider acts under a **Limit Location** constraint, which allows its transformation only on the local X axis, and just between the values 0 and 1.

More complex controls can act on some properties from its X location and other ones from its Z location, as drivers for facial controls.

Along with bones, your custom interfaces may have simple meshes to indicate the purpose of that control, such as the one on this recipe indicating the range and the IK and FK positions. It's a good idea to make such meshes un-selectable using the Outliner: just disable the pointer icon next to its name. This avoids unwanted selections, since the interface meshes act just as a visual guide. It's also interesting to make these interface meshes children of the Armature object to make them hierarchically related to it.

Blender 2.5 also enables us to add buttons and sliders to the application user interface through Python scripts. Although they are not difficult to create, they are beyond the scope of this book.

## Stretching

The Copy Rotation constraints are not the only ones to be used when creating IK-FK switchers. You can also add **StretchTo** constraints to the deformation chain bones in order to make them stretch and match the sizes of FK or IK chains without changing the models' volume.

The **StretchTo** constraints should be added on a similar way: two for each bone of the deformation chain. Each constraint should be mapped to the relevant bone of the IK or FK chain, and its influence slider must have a **Driver** pointing to the switcher bone. These stretching constraints should be used in conjunction with the **Copy Rotation** ones.

## See also

*Chapter 5: Hands down! The Limbs Controllers*

# Tips on weight painting your character

The process of weight painting is somewhat paradoxical: while it's one of the simplest in theory, it can be extremely difficult to get good results.

The complexity of getting good results will depend on how good your mesh topology is, and how you position and create your bones. Blender has an option to guess the bone weights when you bind a rig to a mesh, and it often bring us decent results. With this basic weights set, it's a matter of using the weight paint tools to define the deformation range of a bone into a mesh.

The logic behind weight painting is very simple: you pick a deformation bone and visually paint its influence on a mesh. Blender 2.5 offers some very neat features to allow us to turn this often tedious process into something quicker, such as allowing pressure sensitivity for tablets, mirroring weights, and custom brushes, just to name a few.

## Getting ready

Open the file `001-WeightPaint.blend` from this book's support files. You'll see the base mesh of my character Otto along with a basic rig in X-Ray mode. The armature is in Object Mode, so you can enter in Pose Mode (*Ctrl + Tab*) and try to move some bones. You'll notice that these bones aren't deforming the mesh yet, so the armature still needs to be connected to the mesh. The next screenshot shows the character and the armature:

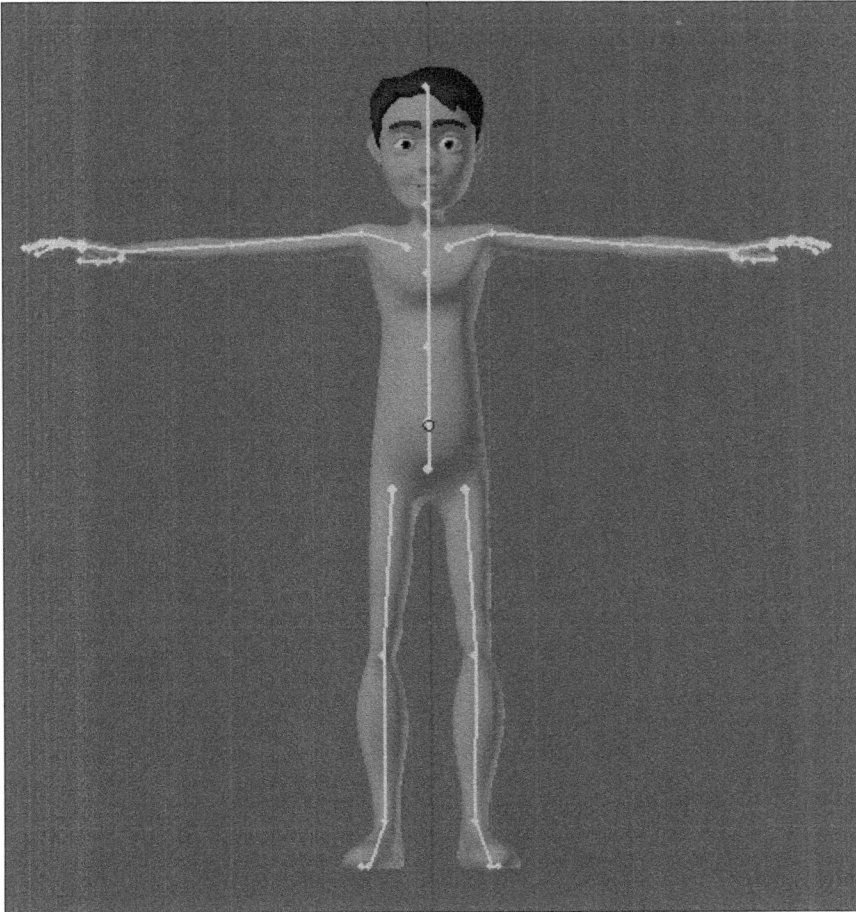

## How to do it...

1. Select the mesh, hold *Shift*, select the armature (or one of its bones, in the case the armature is in Pose Mode) and press *Ctrl + P*. Select **Armature Deform With Automatic Weights**. This will tell Blender to guess the influence of each bone on the mesh based on its size and position, painting the basic weights. This process is also often called **Bone Heat**, and (if you have created a good bone structure, matching the proportions of the mesh) brings us very reasonable results.

2. Enter in the armature's Pose Mode and try to move and rotate some bones. Notice that besides the automatic weights having being assigned quite reasonably, you may find some cases where the deformations need some adjustments.

3. Select the mesh again and enter in Weight Paint Mode (*Ctrl + Tab*). You'll see that the mesh color turns into a deep blue, and the last bone you selected in Pose Mode becomes selected again. The region affected by this bone gets colors in a gradient that goes from zero influence (blue) until 100% influence (red). The next screenshot shows different weight colors on the mesh after selecting the arm bone in Weight Paint Mode:

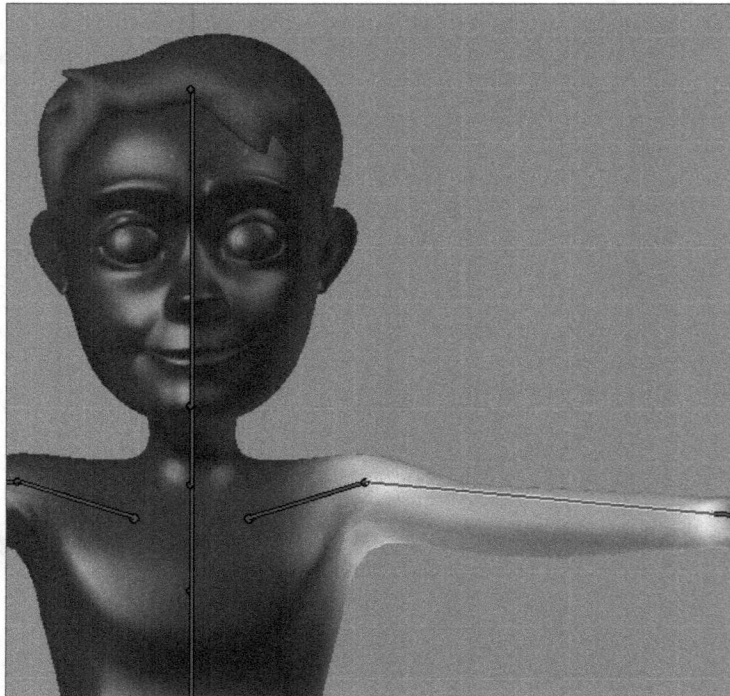

> If you want to change the default color gradient used in weight painting, you can do so by opening the **User Preferences** window (*Ctrl + Alt + U*). Navigate to the **System** tab, enable the **Custom Weight Paint Range** box and define your desired colors. To save this gradient for future sessions, press *Ctrl + U* to save the user preferences. Note that everything in your file (including meshes and armatures) will be saved too, so you might want to define a custom range in an empty file.

4. While in Weight Paint mode, you can still move the bones as you wish to test the influences you set in real time. Every time you select a bone, the mesh is updated to show the equivalent influence.

5. Make sure your **Toolbox** (*T*) is activated and select one of the painting tools available to adjust the weights on the **Tools** section. They act much like in 2D applications such as Gimp or Photoshop, allowing you to Add, Subtract, Blur, Darken, or Lighten weight colors. The Blur option, for example, is very useful to get smoother transitions on the weight colors.

6. If you use a graphics tablet, you can enable the pressure sensitivity on the **Brush Tools** section by clicking on the pointing hand besides the brush values. If you enable it, the sensitivity would pass values that go from zero to the value set on the slider. You can enable the sensitivity per value, so you can use a fixed value for size and a pressure driver for the brush strength, for example. The next screenshot indicates the options:

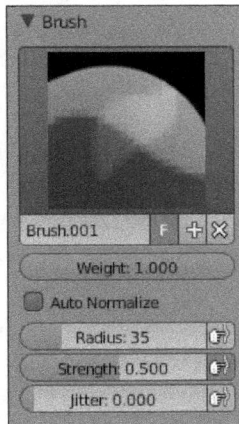

> The **Auto Normalize** option in the **Brush** section shown here makes sure that the sum of all weights applied to a mesh region is not greater than 1. This can be useful, but you may face problems if you're used to adding big weight values for different bones, since adding to one bone will subtract from the other.

7. To paint weight values on both sides of a character at the same time, enable the X Mirror option on the Toolshelf (*T*). You can paint the influences for the left limbs of your character, and the same weights will be applied for the right ones. This will work only when your bones have suffixes such as **.L** or **.R** to a proper identification.

8. When painting weights on the torso or head, for example, it is not possible to assign mirrored weights by using only X Mirror because there are no mirrored bones to take information from. This is when you should use the **Topology Mirror** option: it uses the information from the underlying edge loops on the mesh to apply mirrored weights based on the X axis.

9. To avoid painting on unwanted parts of the mesh, you can enable the Face Selection mode to select only the parts of the mesh that you want to paint over. Click on the Face Selection icon on the window header and select your desired faces as you would do in Edit Mode. The *B* and *C* selection keyboard shortcuts work as expected. The next screenshot shows the mesh with the Face Selection mode activated and an indication to the relevant icon on the window header:

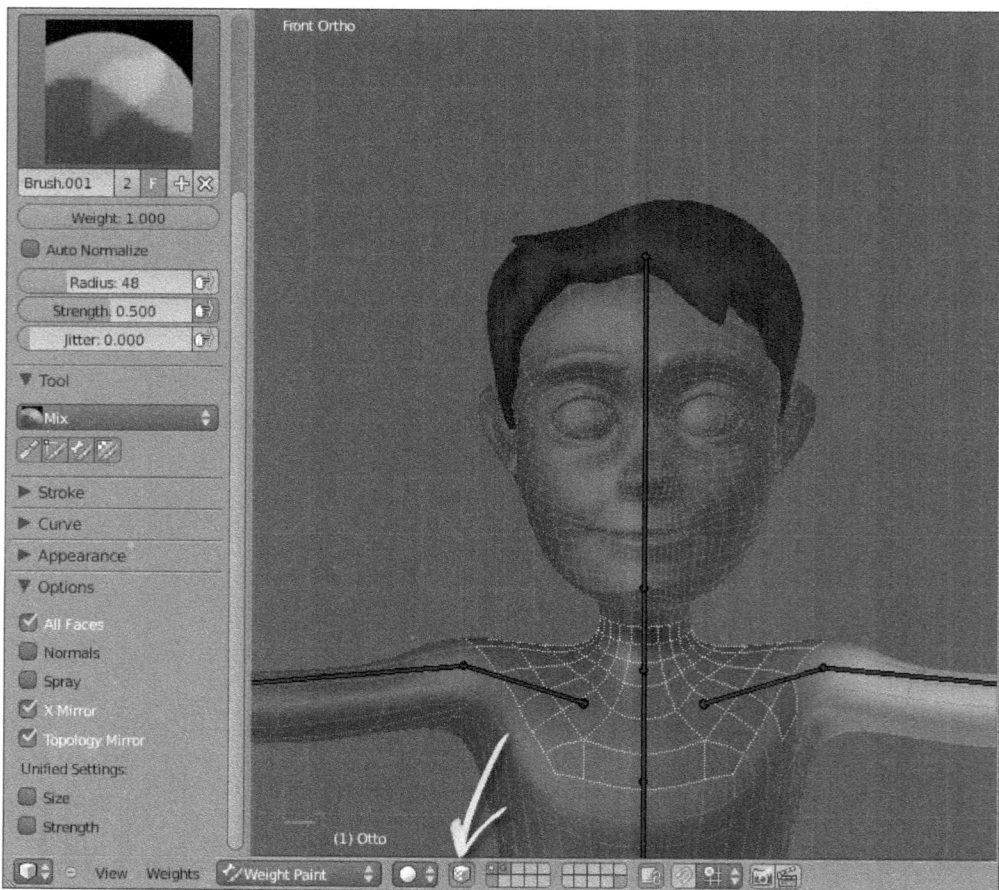

## How it works...

The logic behind weight painting is one of the simplest: based on a color scheme, you paint the influences of a bone on the mesh. After using the automatic weights calculated by Blender, you have some pretty neat tools to refine the results and get a proper deformation on your characters.

## There's more

Blender has some very useful tools to make the Weight Painting process quicker and easier. It is optimized for using with a graphics tablet, making the process even more intuitive, but it can be used nicely with a regular mouse.

### Brush hardness

Even if you don't have a graphics tablet, you can use a custom hardness setting for your brush when weight painting. The **Curve** section under the Toolbox (*T*) allows you to visually draw the curve that drives the pressure, as pictured in the next screenshot.

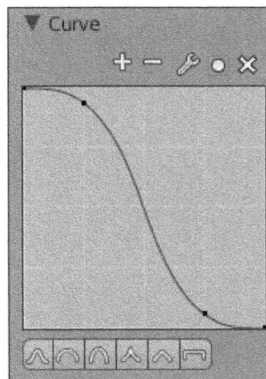

## See also

*Chapter 4: Poker Face? Facial Rigging*

*Chapter 5: Hands Down! The Limbs Controllers*

# 2
# Rigging the Torso

In this chapter, we will cover the following topics:

- ► How to create a stretchy spine
- ► Rigging the pelvis
- ► Making your character breathe
- ► Controlling the neck and head

## Introduction

Our first chapter was about some general and basic rigging practices that you can apply to most situations, regardless of their purpose: they can be used for characters and props, for example. From now on, the rigging chapters will talk about how to build our character by focusing on its body parts. This chapter is about our character's torso: we're going to see how to create hips, a spine, and a neck.

There are various ways of approaching this subject, and we're going to see a mix of solutions ranging from unique to adapted ideas by reverse-engineering some well known rigs available online, such as the ManCandy rig, Ludwig, or the Blender Foundation's open movie characters. While these solutions are not the only way to go, you can achieve quite satisfactory results and its building processes are far from being rocket science.

Aside from what you'll learn from here, it's important for you to take a look at how some of those rigs were built. You'll see some similarities, but also some new ideas to apply to your own characters. In this book you will learn enough to build your own characters, but it's always refreshing to see some new approaches. It's pretty rare to see two rigs built the exact same way.

# How to create a stretchy spine

A human spine, also called vertebral column, is a bony structure that consists of several vertebrae (24 or 33, if you consider the pelvic region). It acts as our main axis and allows us a lot of flexibility to bend forward, sideways, and backward. And why is this important to know?

That number of vertebrae is something useful for us riggers. Not that we're going to create all those tiny bones to make our character's spine look real, but that information can be used within Blender. You can subdivide one physical bone for up to 32 logical segments (that can be seen in the B-Bone visualization mode), and this bone will make a curved deformation based on its parent and child bones. That allows us to get pretty good deformations on our character's spine while keeping the number of bones to a minimum.

This is good to get a realistic deformation, but in animation we often need the liberty to squash and stretch our character: and this is needed not only in cartoony animations, but to emphasize realistic poses too. We're going to see how to use some constraints to achieve that. We're going to talk about just the spine, without the pelvic region. The latter needs a different setup which is covered in another recipe in this book.

## How to do it...

1.  Open the file `002-SpineStretch.blend` from this book's support files. It's a mesh with some bones already set for the limbs, as you can see in the next screenshot. There's no weight painting yet, because it's waiting for you to create the stretchy spine.

> ### Downloading the example code
>
> You can download the example code files for all Packt books you have purchased from your account at `http://www.PacktPub.com`. If you purchased this book elsewhere, you can visit `http://www.PacktPub.com/support` and register to have the files e-mailed directly to you. Alternatively, the author also maintains a copy of the code on his website at `http://virgiliovasconcelos.com/blender-animation-cookbook/`.

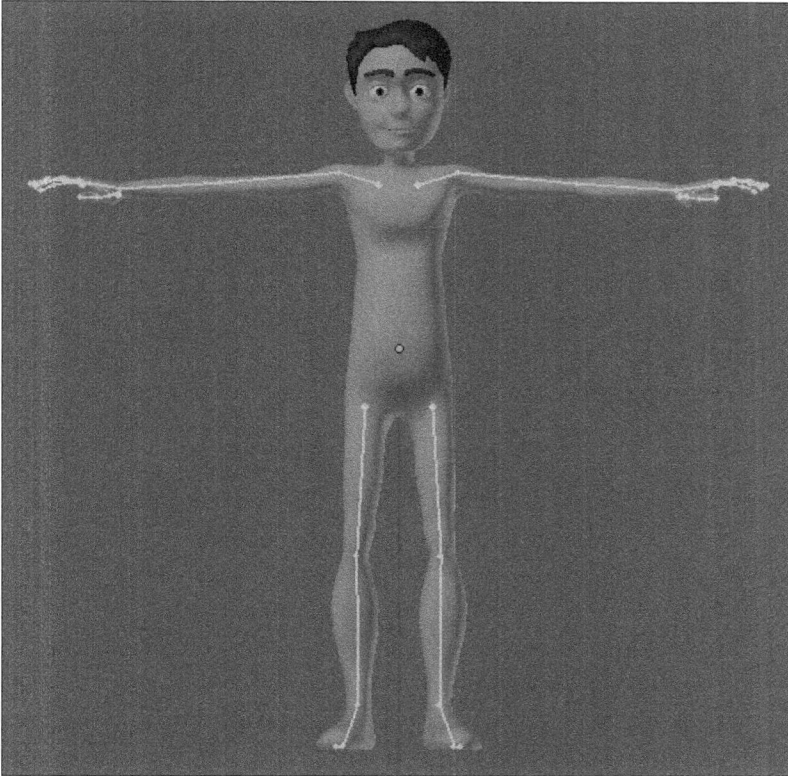

2. Select the armature and enter into its Edit Mode (*Tab*). Go to side view (*Numpad 3*); make sure the 3D cursor is located near the character's back, in the line of what would be his belly button. Press *Shift + A* to add a new bone. Move its tip to a place near the character's eyes.

3. Go to the **Properties** window, under the **Object Data** tab, and switch the armature's display mode to **B-Bone**. You'll see that this bone you just created is a bit fat, let's make it thinner using the **B-Bone** scale tool (*Ctrl + Alt + S*). With the bone still selected, press (*W*) and select **Subdivide**.

Do the same to the remaining bones so we end up with five bones. Still in side view, you can select and move (G) the individual joints to best fit the mesh, building that curved shape common in a human spine, ending with a bone to serve as the head, as seen in the next screenshot:

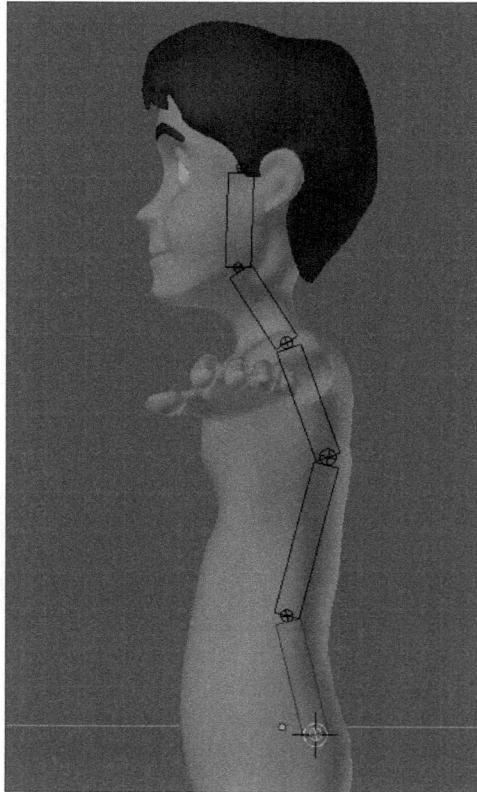

4.  Name these bones as D_Spine1, D_Spine2, D_Spine3, D_Neck, and D_Head.

5.  You may think just five bones aren't enough to build a good spine. And here's when the great rigging tools in Blender come to help us. Select the D_Neck bone, go to the Properties Window, under the **Bone** tab and increase the value of **Segments** in the **Deform** section to 6. You will not notice any difference yet.

Below the **Segments** field there are the **Ease In** and **Ease Out** sliders. These control the amount of curved deformation on the bone at its base and its tip, respectively, and can range from 0 (no curve) to 2.

6. Select the next bone below in the chain (D_Spine3) and change its **Segments** value to 8. Do the same to the remaining bones below, with values of 8 and 6, respectively. To see the results, go out of Edit Mode (*Tab*). You should end up with a nice curvy spine as seen in the following screenshot:

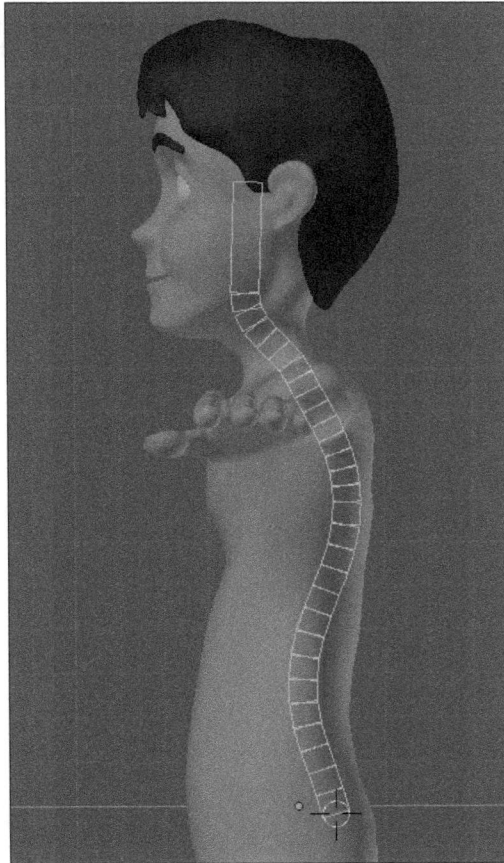

Since these bones are already set to deform the mesh, we could just add some shapes to them and move our character's torso to get a nice spine movement. But that's not enough for us, since we also want the ability to make this character stretch.

7. Go back into Edit Mode, select the bones in this chain, press *Shift + W*, and select **No Scale**. This will make sure that the stretching of the parent bone will not be transferred to its children. This can also be accomplished under the Properties Window, by disabling the **Inherit Scale** option of each bone.

8. Still in Edit Mode, select all the spine bones and duplicate *(Shift + D)* them. Press *Esc* to make them stay at the same location of the original chain, followed by *Ctrl + Alt + S* to make them fatter (to allow us to distinguish both chains). When in Pose Mode, these bones would also appear subdivided, which can make our view quite cluttered. Change back the **Segments** property of each bone to 1 and disable their deform property on the same panel under the Properties Window. Name these new bones as Spine1, Spine2, Spine3, Neck, and Head, go out of Edit Mode (Tab) and you should have something that looks similar to the next screenshot:

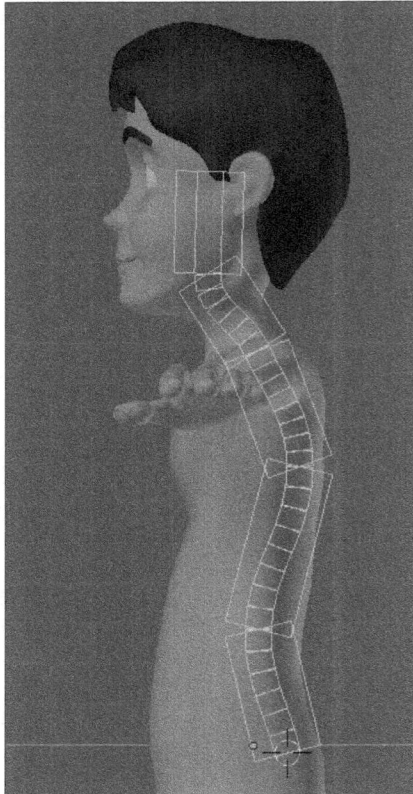

9. Now let's create the appropriate constraints. Enter in Pose Mode (*Ctrl + Tab*), select the bone Spine1, hold *Shift*, and select D_Spine1. Press *Shift + Ctrl + C* to bring up the **Constraints** menu. Select the **Copy Location** constraint. This will make the deformation chain move when you move the Spine_1 bone.

> The **Copy Location** constraint here is added because there is no pelvic bone in this example, since it's creation involves a different approach which we'll see in the next recipe, *Rigging the pelvis*. With the pelvic bone below the first spinal bone, its location will drive the location of the rest of the chain, since it will be the chain's root bone. Thus, this constraint won't be needed with the addition of the pelvis. Make sure that you check out our next recipe, dedicated to creating the pelvic bone.

10. With those bones still selected, bring up the **Constraints** menu again and select the **Stretch To** constraint. You'll see that the deformation chain will seem to disappear, but don't panic.

11. Go to the **Properties Panel**, under the **Bone Constraints** tab and look for the **Stretch To** constraint you have just created. Change the value of the **Head** or **Tail** slider to 1, so the constraint would be evaluated considering the tip of the Spine_1 bone instead of its base. Things will look different now, but not yet correct. Press the **Reset** button to recalculate the constraints and make things look normal again. This constraint will cause the first deformation bone to be stretched when you scale (S) the Spine_1 bone. Try it and see the results. The following screenshot shows the constraint values:

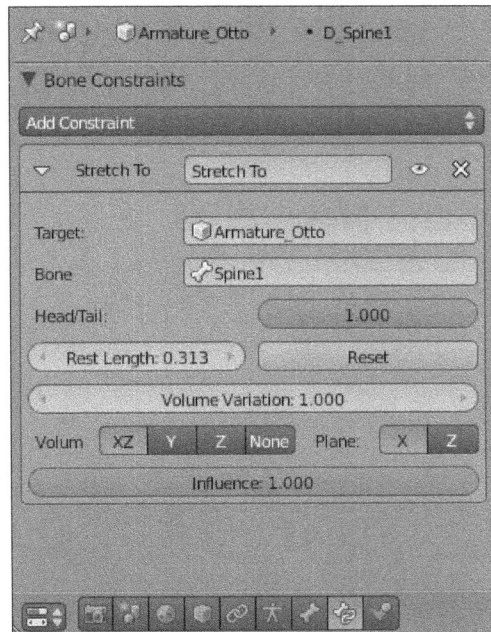

This constraint should be enough for stretching, and we may think it could replace the **Copy Rotation** constraint. That's not true, since the **StretchTo** constraint does not apply rotations on the bone's longitudinal Y axis. So, let's add a **Copy Rotation** constraint.

12. On the 3D View, with the Spine1 and D_Spine1 selected (in that order, that's important!), press *Ctrl + Shift + C* and choose the **Copy Rotation** constraint. Since the two bones have the exact same size and position in 3D space, you don't need to change any of the constraint's settings.

13. You should add the **Stretch To** and **Copy Rotation** constraints to the remaining controller bones exactly the same way you did with the D_Spine1 bone in steps 9 to 12.

14. As the icing on the cake, disable the X and Z scaling transformation on the controller bones. Select each, go to the **Transform Panel** (*N*), and press the lock button near the X and Z sliders under **Scale**. Now, when you select any of these controller bones and press *S*, the scale is just applied on their Y axis, making the deforming ones stretch properly. Remember that the controller bones also work as expected when rotated (*R*). The next screenshot shows the locking applied:

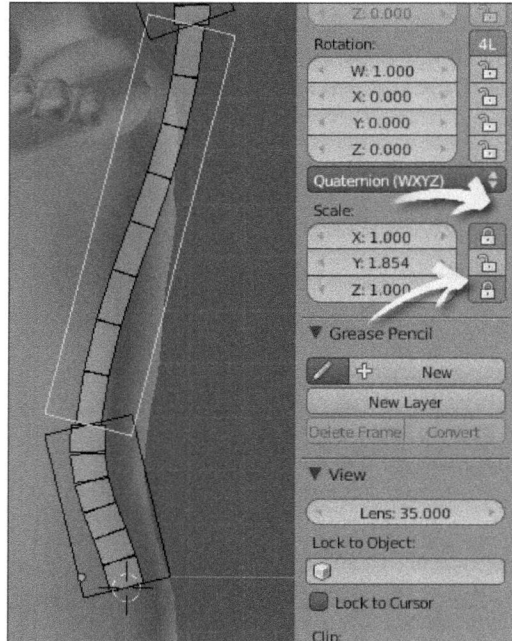

15. Enter into Edit Mode (*Tab*), select the Shoulder.L bone, hold *Shift*, and select both Shoulder.R and Spine3 (in this order; that's important). Press *Ctrl + P* and choose **Keep Offset** to make both shoulder controllers children of the Spine3 bone and disable its scale inheriting either through *Shift + W* or the **Bone** tab on the **Properties** panel.

When you finish setting these constraints and applying the rig to the mesh through weight painting (refer to the recipe *Tips on weight painting your character* in *Chapter 1, Get Rigging* if in doubt), you can achieve something stretchy, as you can see in the next screenshot:

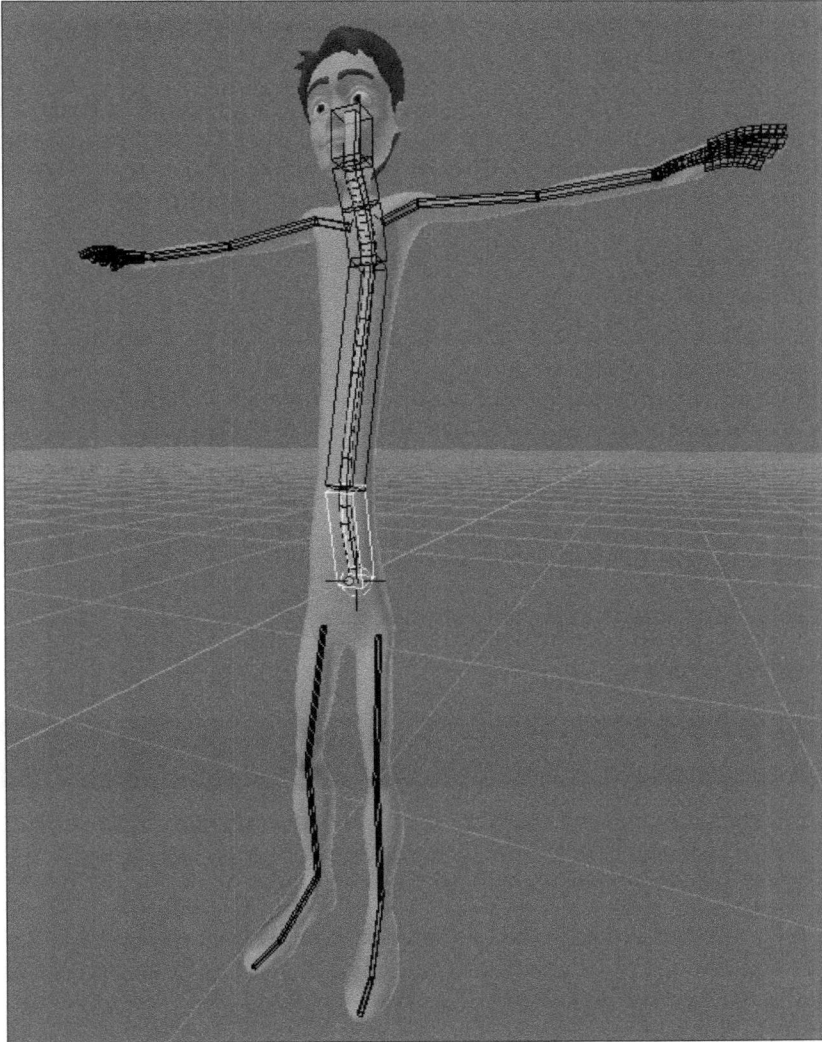

The file `002-SpineStretch-complete.blend` has this complete recipe, for your reference in case of doubts.

## How it works...

When creating spine rigs in Blender, there's no need to create lots of bones, since Blender allows us to logically subdivide each one to get soft and curved deformations. The amount of curved deformation can also be controlled through the **Ease In** and **Ease Out** sliders, and it also works well with stretching.

When you scale a bone on its local Y axis in Pose Mode, it doesn't retain its volume, thus the mesh deformed by it would be scaled without the stretching feeling. You must create controller bones to act as targets to the **Stretch To** constraint, so when they're scaled, the constrained bones will stretch and deform the mesh with its volume preserved.

## There's more...

You should notice that the spine controllers will be hidden inside the character's body when you turn off the armature's **X-Ray** property. Therefore, you need to create some custom shapes for these controller bones in order to make your rig more usable. Refer to the recipe *Customizing shapes and colors for your bones* in *Chapter 1, Get Rigging*.

## See also

Chapter 1: *Tips on weight painting your character*

Chapter 1: *Customizing shapes and colors for your bones*

Chapter 2: *Rigging the pelvis*

# Rigging the pelvis

*If you want your character to move like Elvis, you'd better pay attention to its pelvis.* The technique we're going to see in this recipe is often called "inverted pelvis", and you'll understand why when you go through the next few paragraphs.

This approach is very useful to achieve more relaxed poses with your characters. The pelvis is usually the first bone in the spine chain and, because of the nature of the bone structure, its pivot point for transformation is not at the ideal position for the twist movement that we can do with the pelvis. That's because our actual center of gravity is closer to our belly button than it is to the base of the bone.

The next screenshot shows a balanced pose that is easier to achieve with this kind of setup:

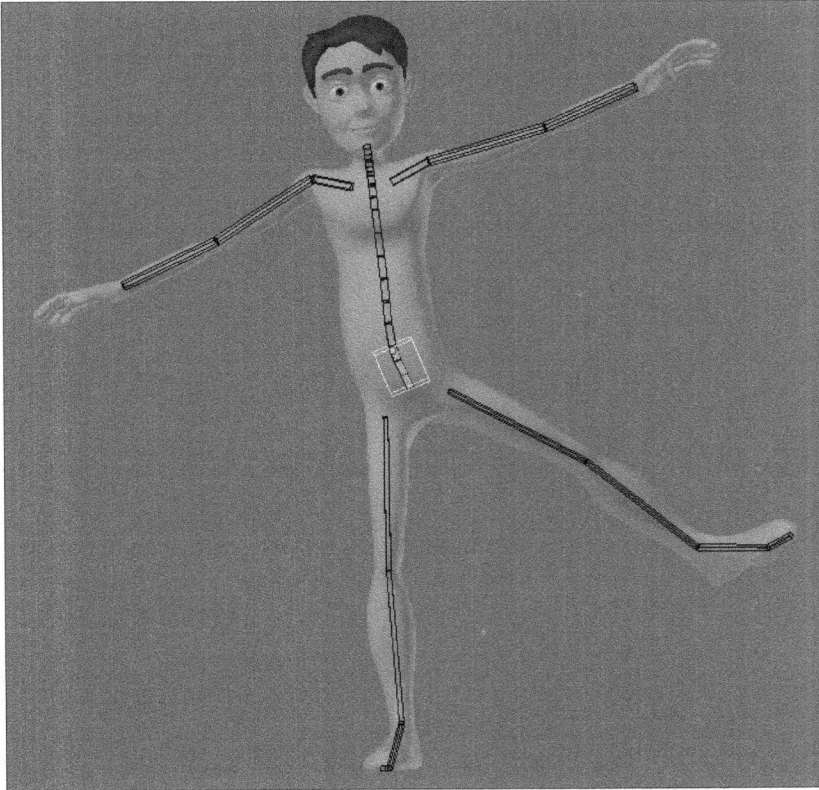

## How to do it...

1.  Open the file 002-Pelvis.blend from this book's support files. You'll see the character **Otto** with a basic deformation rig already applied as our starting point. If you select the D_Pelvis bone and rotate (R) it, you'll notice that the entire character moves along according to this transformation. That's because the pelvic bone is the parent of all other bones. What can we do to make him twist his pelvis to a more relaxed pose?

    > Since the armature's visualization mode is set to B-Bone, you'll see that all the spine bones are divided in segments in order to achieve a desirable curved deformation.

2. Go to the armature's Edit Mode (*Tab*), select the `D_Pelvis` bone, press *W*, and choose **Switch Direction**. Go back to Pose Mode and try to rotate *R* and move *G* it again. Besides having a good pivot point for this bone's rotation, some problems arose from it: the deformations are ugly, the legs and other spinal bones are no longer its children, and most importantly, the nice curved B-Bone deformation between the pelvis and spine bone is gone! That's not what we want.

   This second "wrong" step was intentional so that you can clearly understand what we need and what we must avoid.

   What we need is: the pelvis pivot point must be on its joint to the `D_Spine1` bone; a rotation on the pelvis or the spine must give the curved B-Bone deformations; the pelvis should be the parent of the legs and spine.

3. Now you should reopen the source file (or hit *Ctrl + Z* a couple of times until you revert to the original file) so we can start over and make it the right way.

4. With the original setup, enter the armature's Edit Mode (*Tab*), select the `D_Pelvis` bone, duplicate (*Shift + D*) it, and press *Esc* so it remains in its original position.

5. Change its width (*Ctrl + Alt + S*) so we can see both bones and name it just `Pelvis`.

6. Bring up the **Specials Menu** (*W*) and choose **Switch Direction**. Since this bone will act as a controller (thus not deforming the mesh directly), go to the Properties Window, under the **Bone** tab, change this bone's number of segments to 1 and disable its **Deform** property, as seen in the following screenshot:

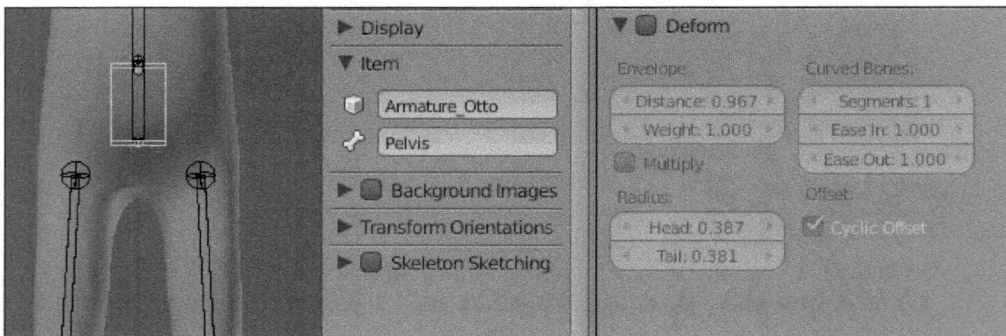

7. Still in Edit Mode, select the `D_Pelvis` bone, hold *Shift*, and select the **Pelvis** that you've just created. Press *Ctrl + P* to make it parent and choose **Keep Offset**.

8. Now, you must select the `D_Spine1` bone, go to the Properties Window, under the **Bone** tab, and disable both the **Inherit Rotation** and **Inherit Scale** options.

9. Go back to Pose Mode and rotate the `Pelvis` bone. Now you'll see that the spine doesn't rotate along, the center of gravity for rotation is near the belly button region and the soft curved B-Bones work as expected!

If you have already set up a stretchy spine as described in a previous recipe, you should now make the `Pelvis` bone parent of `Spine1`. You should also turn off **Inherit Rotation** for the bone `Spine1`, so the `Pelvis` bone acts like the torso's root bone for translation and still works correctly for the twist rotation.

> You may wonder why the legs rotate along the pelvis, when they should remain still. This is because this pelvis setup needs an **Inverse Kinematics (IK)** constraint for the legs, but that's the subject of another recipe called _Creating IK legs with a three-pivot foot_, in _Chapter 5, Hands Down! The Limbs Controllers_.

The file `002-Pelvis-complete.blend` has this complete recipe for your reference.

## How it works...

By using an inverted copy of the pelvic bone as a controller, we can set the pivot center of a rig around the belly button region. By inverting a copy, and not the original deformation bone, we can make sure that the soft curved deformations from Blender's B-Bones are applied as expected.

## There's more

If you've just read the previous recipe, maybe you're wondering: _what about stretching the pelvis?_

### Stretching the pelvis

Although our pelvic region doesn't stretch, it can be useful for cartoony rigs to have this option available. In order to do that, you must select the `Pelvis` bone, hold _Shift_, select `D_Pelvis`, press _Ctrl + Shift + C_, and select the **Stretch To Constraint**, just like the process described in the previous recipe. You also need to disable the **Inherit Scale** property from the `D_Pelvis` and `leg` bones in the **Bone** tab under the Properties Window.

For a better view of the rig, you should also lock the X and Z scaling for the `Pelvis` bone under the **Transform** panel (*N*). This setup allows you to achieve distortions similar to what you see in the next screenshot:

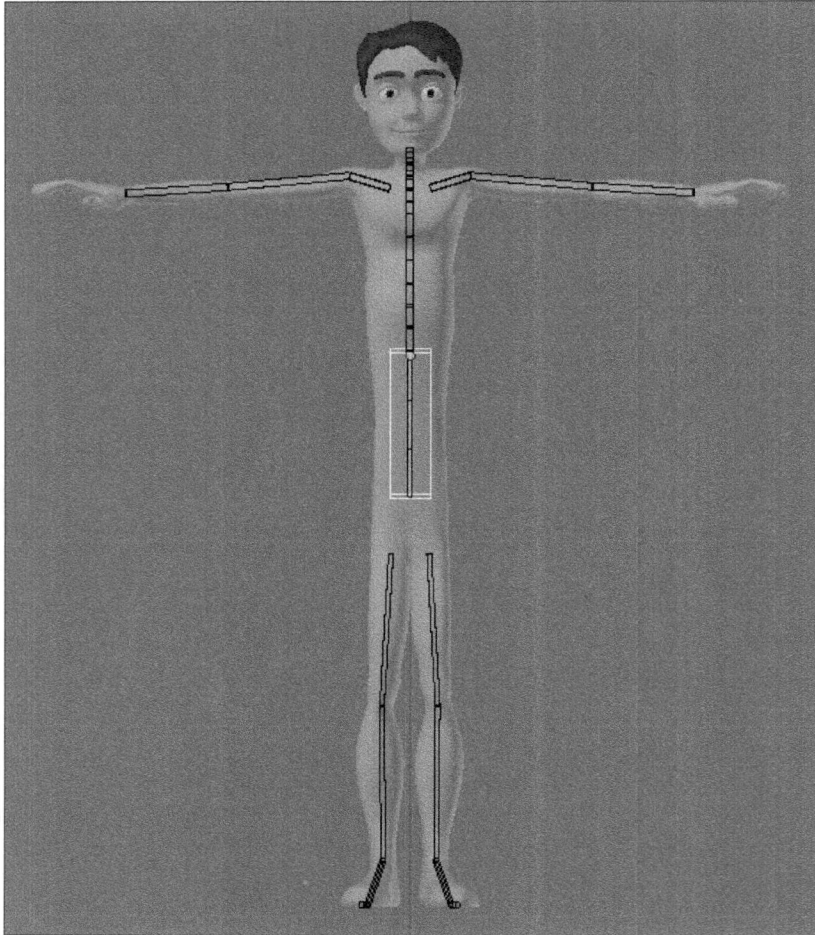

The file `002-Pelvis-complete.blend` is also set up for stretching. Try scaling the **Pelvis** bone and see for yourself!

## See also

*Chapter 2: How to create a stretchy spine*

*Chapter 5: Creating IK legs with a three-pivot foot*

# Making your character breathe

When you animate a character, the main goal is to make it look alive, isn't it? All techniques involved in the art of animation, regardless of the medium (paper, computers, clay...) have the same goal: help you make the audience believe that your character is a living being.

It can be very useful to add a controller to make your character look like its breathing. Although the breathing by itself isn't going to make your character believable, it can be added as a layer of visual complexity, contributing to the mood of a scene. If your character is nervous, scared, or has just finished a sprint for instance, you should probably make the breathing more noticeable.

## How to do it...

1. Open the file `002-Breathe.blend`. You'll see a character with a very basic rig and weight painting, and with a bone shaped like a pair of lungs, as seen in the next screenshot. This is our room to work, since adding bones and shapes is not our focus here. Take a look at *Chapter 1, Get Rigging* if you have any doubts on how to set up the character like this.

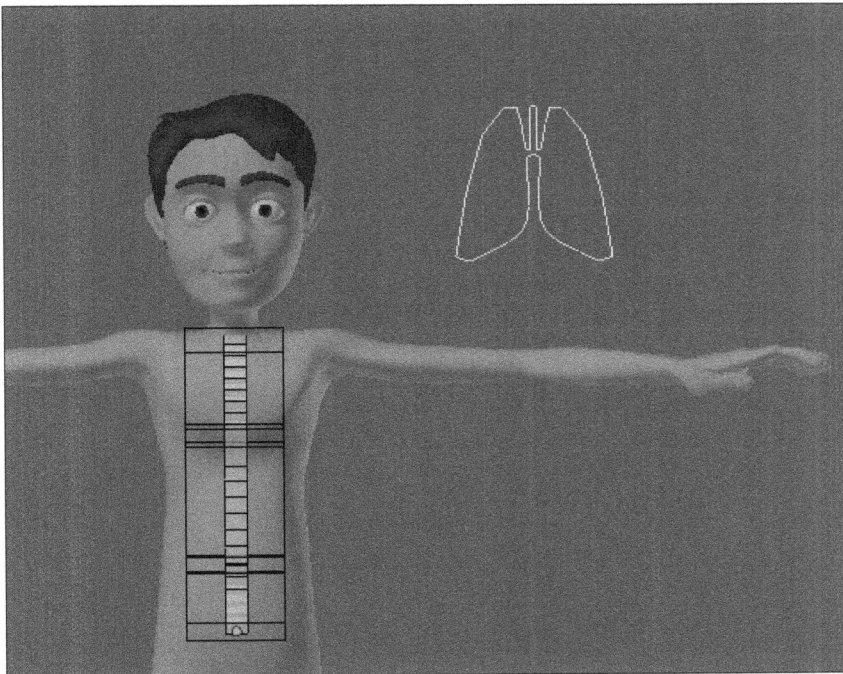

2.  Select the `Lungs` bone, hold *Shift*, and select the `D_Ribcage` bone. Bring the constraints menu with *Shift + Ctrl + C* and select the **Copy Scale** constraint.

3.  Go to the Properties Window, under the **Bone Constraints** tab. You'll see that there are two constraints assigned to that bone: the first is a **Stretch To** constraint, which allows the bone to be scaled while maintaining its volume. The second constraint is the one you have just created, and allows this deformation bone to be scaled following the transformation applied to the `Lungs` bone. Now let's just change its values in order to get a proper controller.

4.  Disable the **Y** option, since our character's imaginary lungs are just going to inflate and deflate, and the scaling would be applied only in the horizontal plane.

5.  Make sure you also set the two values of **Space** to **Local Space**, and bring down the influence slider to a value like 0.3. This will allow you to make bigger changes in the `Lungs` scale and still get subtle results. The following screenshot shows the constraint setup:

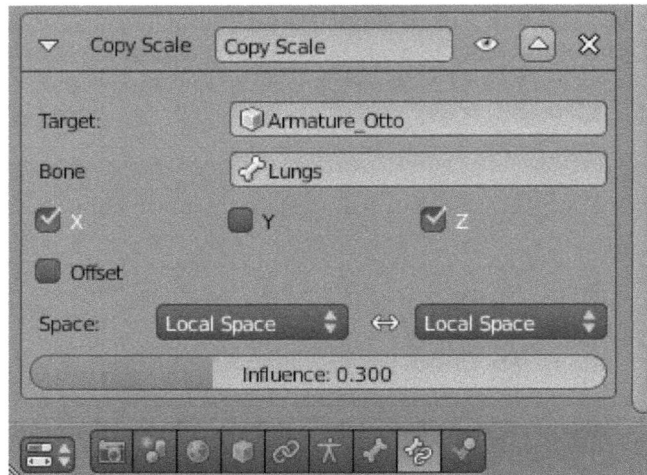

6.  Repeat this process from steps 2 to 5 on the bone called `D_Spine2`, but use a lower value for the **Influence** slider, like 0.1. These values may be different on your own characters, but the principle here is that the distortion on the mesh would be bigger on the ribs part of the mesh, and smaller on the belly. But you should feel free to even invert this, if you seek a funnier effect.

Now, scaling (S) up and down the **Lungs** controller will make your character look like it's breathing. The file `002-Breathe-complete.blend` has this finished recipe for your reference.

## How it works...

The breathing controller is nothing more than a bone which sets horizontal scaling on the ribs and belly bones. The secret is to have different (and low) **Influence** values for the constrained bones. When you scale the controller up, the character looks like it's breathing in. You should use this controller as a secondary one, just for adding details on top of an existing animation.

## There's more

In this recipe we saw something simple but important: more than one constraint can be applied to a bone at the same time. Not only that, but a bone can have multiple targets for its different constraints, making a rig considerably more complex as you add new constraints.

### Stacking constraints

This example is based on a rig with more than one constraint applied to the spine bones, showing that a single bone can have its properties changed by different controllers. You must notice that the constraints are stacked, and this means that the order in which they are applied is important. In our example, the breathing would be applied after the stretching. Fortunately the order isn't important in this unique example, but you may be wary of stacking too many constraints, since the results can be hard to predict.

## See also

*Chapter 2: How to create a stretchy spine*

*Chapter 1: Customizing shapes and colors for your bones*

# Controlling the neck and head

Our head movement can be broken down to basically two controllers: the head bone itself and the neck. It is possible to rotate the neck while keeping the head straight and vice-versa. For example, to move your head forward you have three options:

- ▶ You rotate just your head (like when you nod affirmatively to someone else's question).
- ▶ You rotate just your neck and keep your head up (like when you try to read those very tiny letters on a computer screen).

▶ You rotate both your neck and head (when you look to your belly button). You see these three positions in the following screenshot:

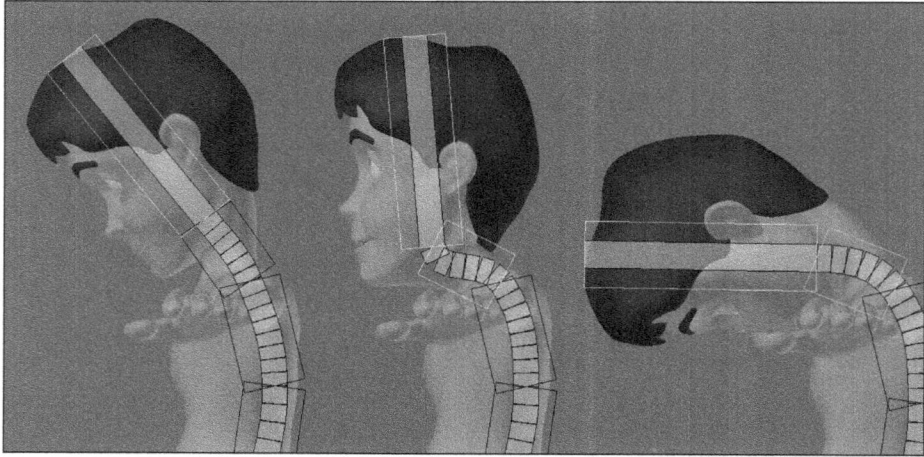

It is very useful in rigs to have the freedom to choose how your neck and head should behave when transforming their parent bones. You should be able, for example, bend your character's torso forward while keeping its neck and head looking forward, without inheriting their parents' rotation. This is often called hinge control. In this recipe we'll learn how to properly control the "hinge" property of the neck and head.

## How to do it...

1.  Open the file `002-Neck.blend` from this book's support files. You'll see the character **Otto** with an deformation already set and controller bones for its spine and pelvis, with support for stretching. There is also an interface called **Hinge**, with two controller bones already created. Everything up until here is covered in previous recipes, so you should take a look at them if you have any doubts on how to create the interface, pelvis, spine, or stretch controls.

The next screenshot shows our initial scene:

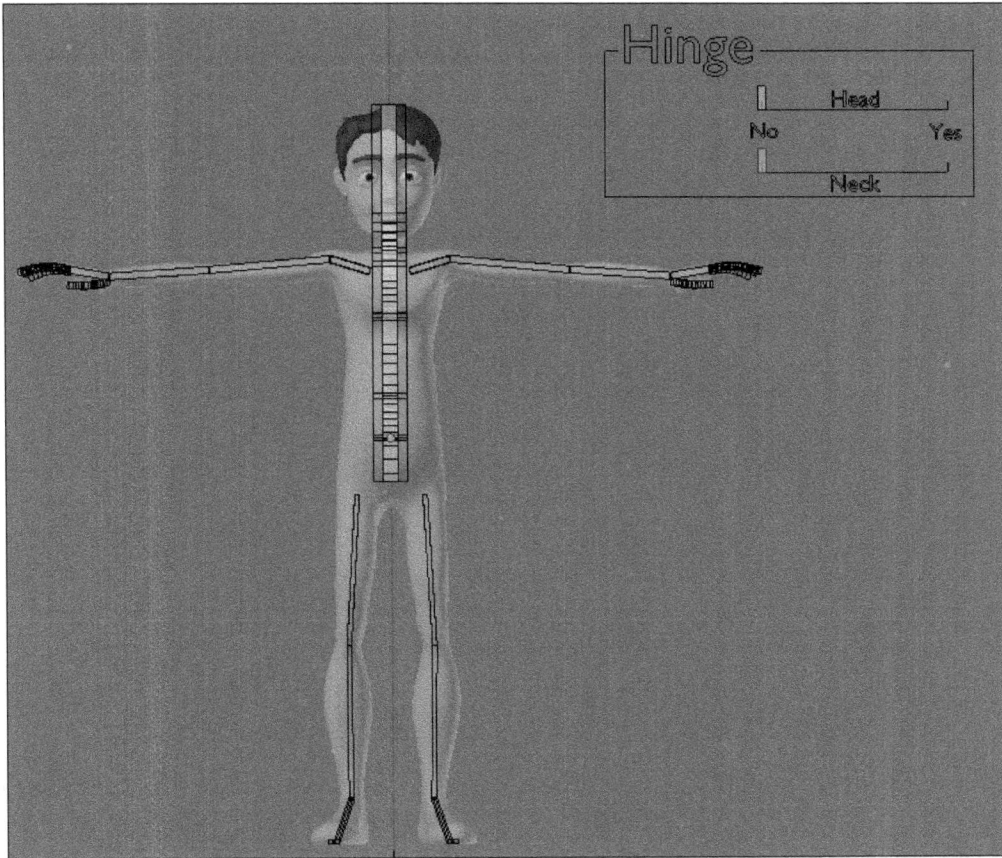

2.  The first thing we would do is set the hinge controller for the `Neck` bone. Select the `Neck` bone and go to the Properties Window, under the **Bone** tab. Right-click over its **Inherit Rotation** property and choose **Add Driver**. The checkbox field will get a pinkish hue.

> As you noticed on the previous step, in Blender, even checkbox values can have drivers applied or have its on or off state animated through a keyframe. This is achieved by right-clicking over them and selecting the appropriate option. Since checkboxes can have only True or False values, Blender translates driver values as `True=1` and every other value as `False`.

3. Open a Graph Editor window and pick the **Drivers** mode on its header. Click over the **Inherit Rotation (Neck)** driver on the left-hand side panel to view its details on the Properties Panel (*N*) on the right-hand side. Find the **Drivers** section on the Properties Panel. Leave the driver type as **Scripted Expression**, but change the **Expr** field value from True to 1-var.

4. On the box below the **Add Variable** button, set the Ob/Bone fields as Armature_ Otto and Hinge_Neck. Leave the **Type** value as **X Location** and enable the **Local Space** checkbox. The next screenshot shows the driver and its values:

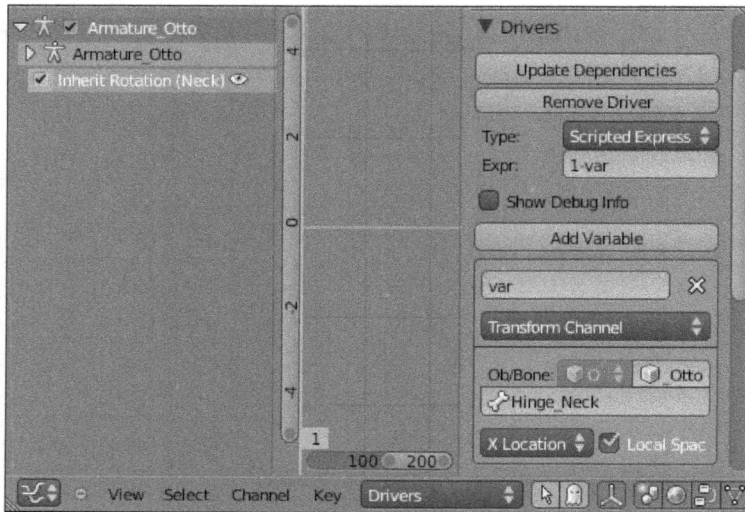

> The **Expr** field has the value of 1-var, used to invert the mapping of the bone driver. That's useful here, where our default behavior is to have the bones to inherit the rotation of their parents. Having these default behaviors properly planned is important when you just want to reset your UI sliders with *Alt + G* and have the rig working on its default state.

5. Repeat the process of steps 2 to 4 for the Head bone, making the driver for its **Inherit Rotation** property driven by the Hinge_Head bone.

6. In front view, rotate the Rib bone to the side. Move the sliders for the hinge controls, and you'll have three possible situations, demonstrated in the next screenshot:

   ❑ Both head and neck follow the torso

   ❑ The head doesn't follow the neck and torso (it's "hinged")

   ❑ The neck (and consequently the head) is "hinged"

The file 002-Neck-complete.blend has this finished recipe for your reference.

## How it works...

By adding drivers to the **Inherit Rotation** property of single bones, we can animate the "hinge" feature of the neck and head bones, allowing the animators to pose the characters with more freedom and flexibility. Blender 2.5 allows us to add drivers to user interface fields such as checkboxes, making it easier to animate the on/off state of virtually any feature in our rigs.

## There's more

The ability to animate and drive checkboxes in Blender 2.5 makes it easier to control features that only have on/off states. In previous versions, that wasn't possible and the rigger would have to try emulating that particular feature with fairly complex constraint setups.

### Not just the neck and head

You can use the same principle shown here to make hinge controllers for other parts of the body, notably the shoulders. When animating limbs with Forward Kinematics, it's often desirable a hinge setting in order to have more freedom when posing your characters.

## See also

*Chapter 2: How to create a stretchy spine*

*Chapter 1: Customizing shapes and colors for your bones*

*Chapter 5: Setting up the shoulders*

# 3
# Eying Animation

In this chapter, we will cover the following topics:

- ▶ How to control where your characters look at
- ▶ The eyelids controllers
- ▶ Controlling the pupils

## Introduction

There is a famous quote which says *The eyes are the window to the soul,* and its through them that we'll make our characters express most of their feelings. We must have a tight control over how our character's eyes appear and behave on screen, because that's where our viewers would naturally pay more attention to.

Subtle things such as the eyelids shape or the size of the pupil can make a big difference when you want to make the audience believe that your character is alive. We're going to see how to create rig features to enable a good amount of control for the animator. The objects for this small region of the body can be a bit tricky to set up, requiring lots of bones and constraints to achieve good expressions.

## How to control where your characters look at

Unless your characters have a very unique style, their eyes will have to look at something. Based on this idea, there is a common practice of making this "something" a bone where the eyes will always point to. This is very useful when animating, since you can position this bone to the exact place where your character should look at without further worries.

## How to do it...

1.  Open the file `003-Eyes.blend`. This file has a head mesh with two eyes ready for you to work on them. Notice that the eyes are separate objects from the head.

2.  Select the left eye object, press *Shift + S*, and choose **Cursor to Selected** to position the 3D cursor into the center of the object.

3.  Add an **Armature**: press *Shift + A* and select **Armature | Single Bone**. Go to Edit Mode (*Tab*) in side view (*Numpad 3*) and move the tip of the bone so that it points to the character's front, next to the eye's pupil, similar to the next screenshot. Activate the armature's **X-Ray** display mode in the Properties Window, under the **Object Data** tab, within the **Display** section to make things easier to see.

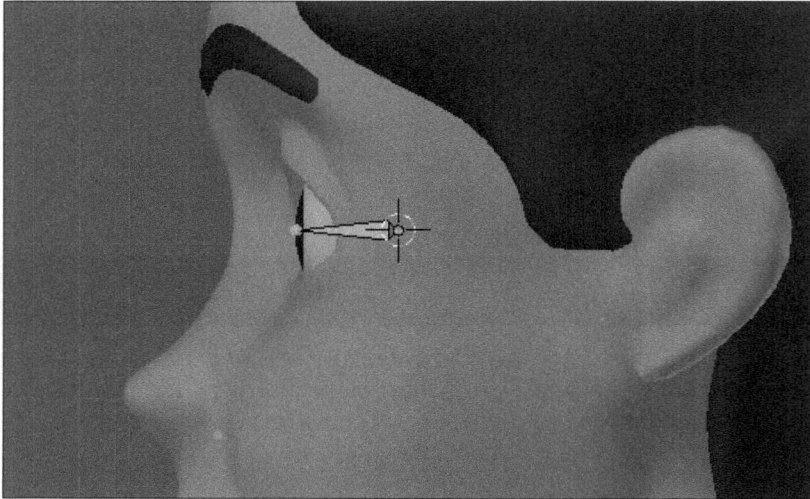

4.  Name this bone as `Eye.L` and extrude (*E*) its tip, creating a small bone in front of it. Name it as `T_Eye.L` ("T" stands for "target"), select it, press *Alt + P*, and choose **Clear Parent**, so it's no longer a child of the eye bone. You should also disable its **Deform** property by pressing *Shift + W* and selecting **Deform**. You should have the two bones positioned as seen in the following screenshot:

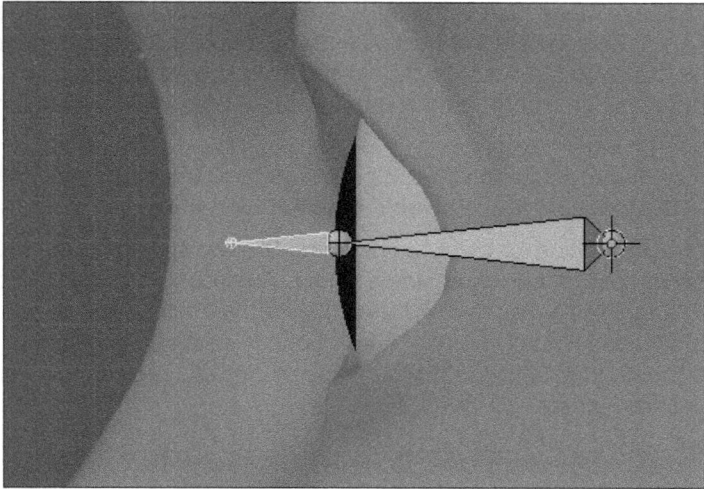

5.  Now let's add a IK constraint: enter Pose Mode (*Ctrl + Tab*), select the target bone, hold [*Shift*], select the `Eye.L` bone, press *Shift + I*, and select **Add IK to Active Bone**. If you move (*G*) the `T_Eye.L` bone around, you'll see that the `Eye.L` bone keeps pointing to it.

6.  Enter in the Armature's Edit Mode (*Tab*) again. Place the 3D cursor at the front of the character's head, between his eyes, and add another bone through *Shift + A*. Name this bone as `LookAt` and scale it down to about half its height. Select the target bone, hold *Shift*, select the `LookAt` bone, press *Ctrl + P*, and choose **Keep Offset**. Now the movement of the `LookAt` bone will drive the target, and you can see this new bone in the next screenshot:

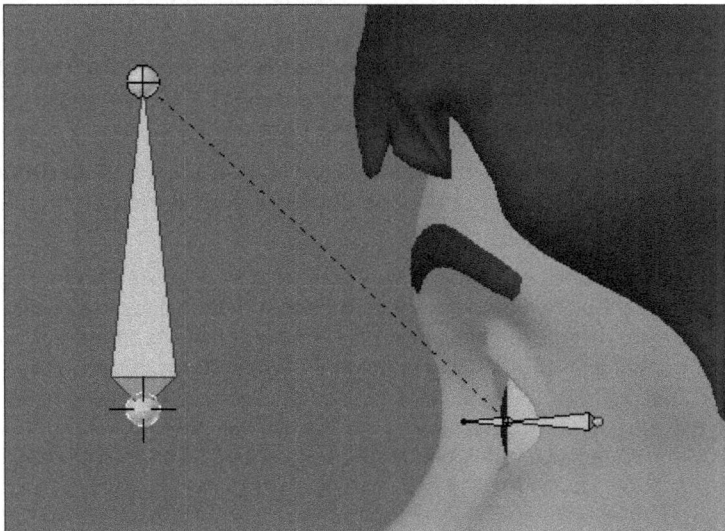

7. Go back to Pose Mode. Select the left eye mesh, hold *Shift*, select the `Eye.L` bone, press *Ctrl + P*, and choose **Set Parent to Bone**. Move the `LookAt` bone and you'll see that the left eye rotates accordingly, but you'll also notice that the eyeball rotates too much depending on where you place the `LookAt` bone. We need to limit the amount of its rotation.

8. Still in Pose Mode, select the `Eye.L` bone and go to the Properties Window. Under the **Bone** tab, navigate to the **Inverse Kinematics** section.

9. Enable the **Limit** fields for the **X** and **Z** limits. The two sliders on the right-hand side are for minimum and maximum angle values. An acceptable value for this setup is -20° and 20° for the X axis and -45° and 45° for the Z axis, and you can see a visual feedback of those limits while the `Eye.L` bone is selected: very useful for visualizing what are the rotation limits. In the next screenshot you can see the values set up and the limits shown on the 3D view:

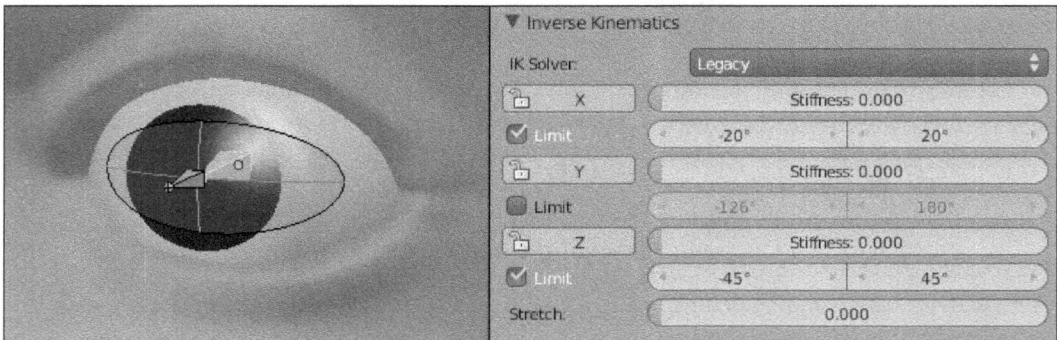

Now, when you move the `LookAt` bone, the eyeball rotates only until the pupil reaches the eye borders.

10. To the other eye, enter into the armature's Edit Mode, select the bones `T_Eye.L` and `Eye.L`, go to Front View (*Numpad 1*), duplicate (*Shift + D*), and move (*G*) them across the X axis until they are in the middle of the right eye.

11. With the bones still selected in Edit Mode, press *W* and select **Flip Names**, so Blender automatically detects the bones' suffixes and alters them to the correct side.

> When you append suffixes such as `.L` and `.R`, `.left` and `.right` to your bones, Blender understands that these bones are mirrored so you can make changes to one bone and have its "mirrored" one update as well when you enable the **X-Axis Mirror** option in the Toolshelf (*T*). These suffixes are not case sensitive, but you have to stick to one convention, since Blender will not understand this mirroring if you name one bone as `Eye.left` and the other `Eye.R` or `Eye.Right`.

12. Go back to Pose Mode, select the right eye mesh, hold *Shift*, select the `Eye.R` bone, press *Ctrl + P*, and choose **Set Parent to Bone**. Now, if you move the `LookAt` bone, both eyes should follow accordingly and within their limits.

13. The last thing that you should do is select the `LookAt` bone, go to the **Transform Panel** (*N*), and lock all **Rotation** and the **Y** and **Z** scale values. Leaving the **X** axis for scaling allows you to change the alignment of the eyes, as seen in the next screenshot, where the `LookAt` bone was scaled (S) down in Front View:

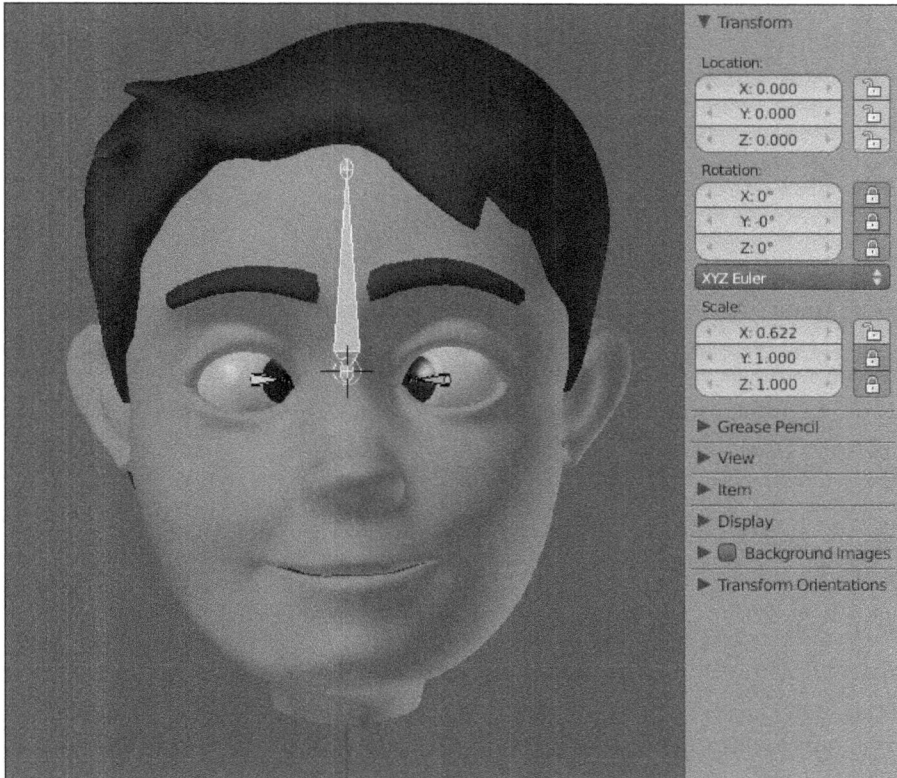

The file `003-Eyes-complete.blend` has this finished recipe for your reference.

## How it works...

By creating two IK chains with one parent bone to control their targets, you can easily make a `LookAt` controller. The IK chain consists of one bone located at the center of the eye and another bone to act as its target. By using a separate bone parent of both targets, you can make your character look at where you need. The use of an IK constraint on the eye bones allows you to set the rotation limits so the eyeballs don't rotate further than you expect them to.

## There's more...

When we look down or up, our eyelids follow the movement softly. This will be accomplished in the next recipe, dedicated only to the eyelids.

The `LookAt` controller is normally a child of another bone: some like it to be linked to the main head controller, so the eyes follow the head movement; some like it to be child of the Root bone, so the point where the character looks is independent of the head position. You can have the best of two worlds by setting a switcher to alter between these two "spaces". The concept of different spaces and how to create a controller to switch between them is covered in *Chapter 5, Hands Down! The Limbs Controllers*.

## See also

*Chapter 3: The eyelids controllers*

*Chapter 5: Different spaces for IK hands*

# The eyelids controllers

A blink of an eye. That's a pretty fast action, but the mechanics behind it may require some thinking by the rigger to be applied correctly. With careful weight painting, some constraints and bones correctly positioned, we can accomplish good results.

## How to do it...

1. Open the file `003-Eyelids.blend` from this book's support files. It's a head with some bones already set up for the eye's tracking. That's exactly what you would end up with in the previous recipe.

2. Select the armature and enter into Edit Mode (*Tab*). In side view (*Numpad 3*), select the base of the `Eye.L` bone, press *Shift + S*, and pick **Cursor to Selected** in order to move the 3D cursor to that position.

3. Add a new bone by pressing *Shift + A*, and move (*G*) its tip roughly to where the upper eyelid makes contact with the eye. Name that bone as `D_UpEyelid.L`. With its tip selected, extrude (*E*) to create another bone. Select it, name it as `T_UpEyelid.L`, remove its parent relationship by pressing *Alt + P* and choosing **Clear Parent**. Disable its **Deform** property by pressing *Shift + W* and choosing **Deform**. You should end up with a setup similar to the following screenshot:

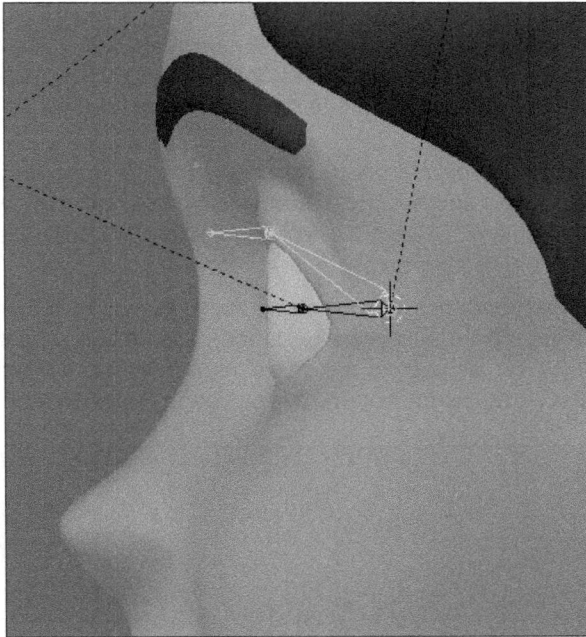

4.  Repeat step 3 to address the lower eyelid. Define the resulting bones' names as
    D_BottomEyelid.L and T_BottomEyelid.L.

5.  Go to Pose Mode (*Ctrl + Tab*). Select the T_UpEyelid.L, hold *Shift*, select the
    D_UpEyelid.L, press *Shift + I*, and choose **Add IK To Active Bone**. Do the same to
    the lower eyelid bones and you'll have one IK setup for each eyelid, as you can see in
    the next screenshot:

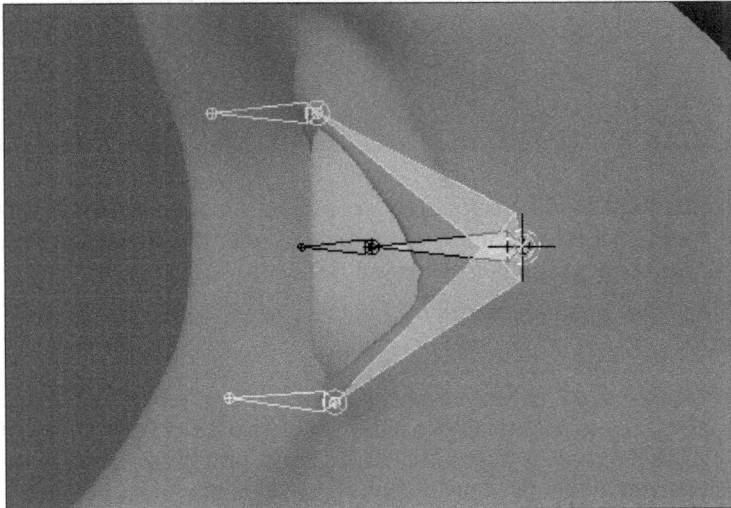

> If you named the bones correctly and try to move one of the eyelids' targets, you'll see that the eyelids follow the rig, since there are some basic bone weights applied to speed things up for you..

6. Go back to the armature's Edit Mode and place the 3D cursor in front of the bones you have created. Add another bone through *Shift + A*, call it M_Eyelids.L ("M" stands for "mechanism", since it's a helper bone to our setup). Disable its **Deform** property by selecting it after pressing *Shift + W*.

7. Parent (with offset) both eyelids' targets to the M_Eyelids.L bone. Still in Edit Mode, make sure the M_Eyelids.L bone has its base slightly above T_BottomEyelid.L as seen in the next screenshot. This will make the bottom eyelid move just a little when its parent is scaled in Pose Mode.

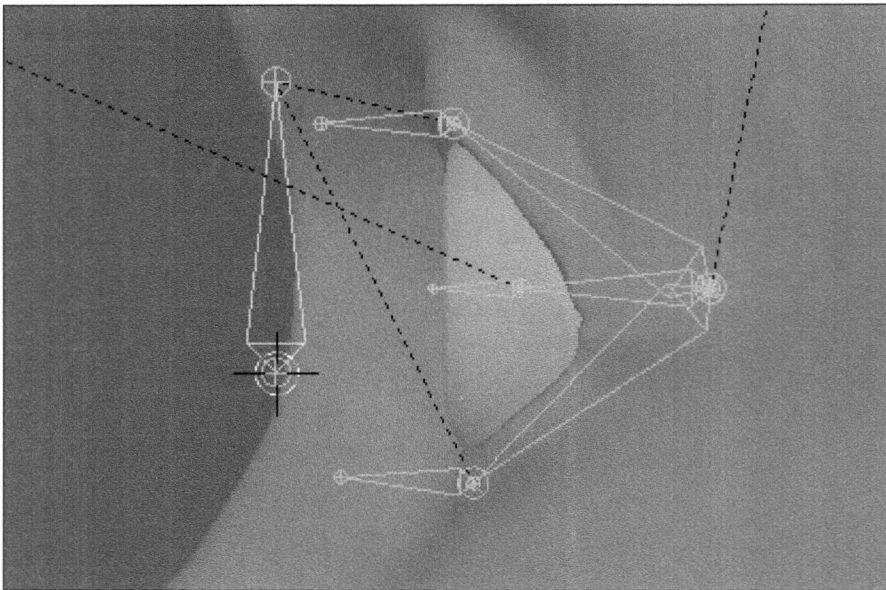

8. Now enter in Pose Mode. Select the M_Eyelids.L bone, lock all its rotation values, and the X and Z for both location and rotation, under the **Transform Panel** (*N*). If you scale (*S*) this bone down, the eyelids will close.

   These steps provide the basic functionality we need, but we should take things a bit further:

9. Enter the armature's Edit Mode again, go to front view, select and duplicate (*Shift + D*) the LookAt bone. Move it to the side, so it's in front of the left eye. Scale it down a bit, so it's smaller than the LookAt bone, and lock all its transform channels in the **Properties Panel** (*N*), leaving only the **Y** scale channel unlocked.

10. Name this bone as `Eyelids.L` and disable its **Deformation** property by hitting *Shift + W*. Make it a child of the `LookAt` bone (keeping its offset distance). This new bone will act as the controller for the eyelids, conveniently placed next to the main eye tracking bone as you can see in the next screenshot:

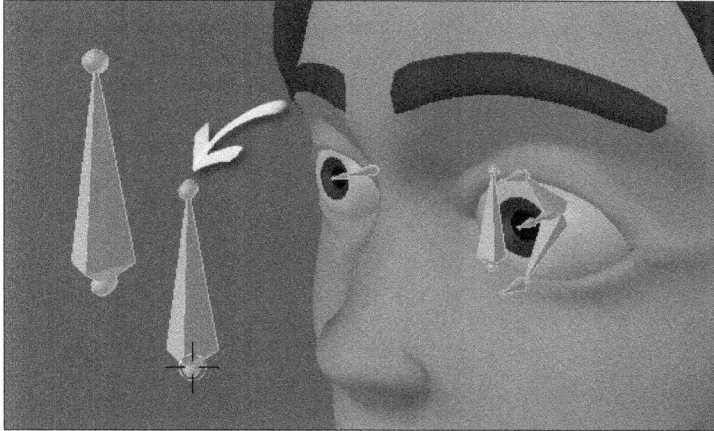

11. Go to Pose Mode, select the `Eyelids.L` bone, hold *Shift*, select the `M_Eyelids.L` bone, press *Ctrl + Shift + C* and pick **Copy Location**. Things will seem to break, but don't panic.

12. Navigate to the Properties Window, under the **Bone Constraints** tab, and change the values in the **Copy Location** constraint: disable **X** and **Z**, pick **Local With Parent** and **Local Space**, just like in the next screenshot, where you can see the constraint values:

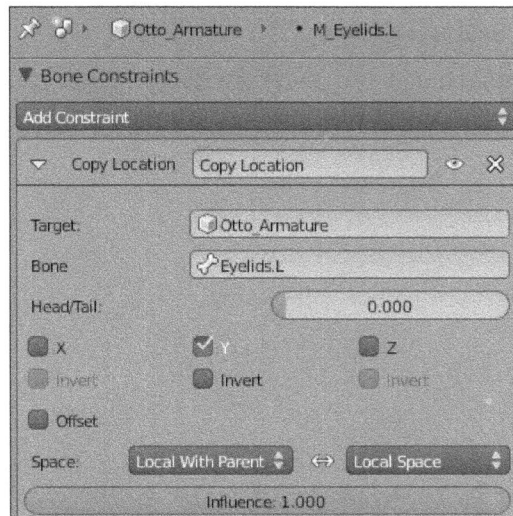

This would make the eyelids follow when you move the main eye controller, but their movements should be limited.

13. Select only the `M_Eyelids.L` bone, press *Ctrl + Shift + C*, and pick the **Limit Location** constraint. Find this constraint on the **Bone Constraints** tab in the Properties Window, check both the **Minimum Y** and **Maximum Y** fields and set the sliders to -.005 and 0.014, respectively. Finally, change the **Convert** field to **Local Space**, as you can see in the next screenshot:

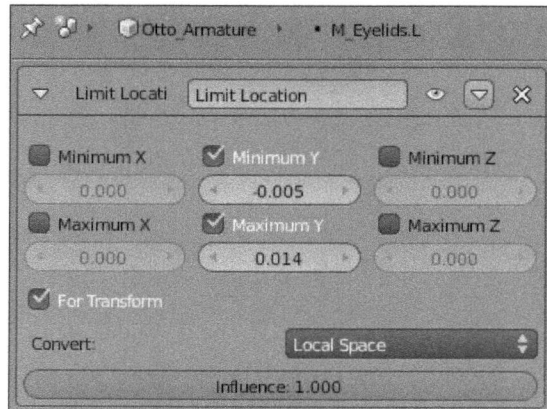

Now, try moving the `LookAt` bone. The eyelids will follow the eye up or down movements naturally.

14. To finish the left eyelids setup, select the `Eyelids.L` bone, hold *Shift*, select the `M_Eyelids.L` bone, press *Ctrl + Shift + C* and pick the **Transformation** constraint. Next, navigate to the Properties Window, in the **Bone Constraints** tab and locate the constraint that you've just created.

15. Check the **Extrapolate** field and, under the **Source** fields, click on the **Scale** button and change the **Y Min** and **Max** sliders to 0.5 and 1.0, respectively. Set all the remaining source axis sliders to 1.0.

16. Head over to the **Destination** fields, click on the **Scale** button, and set all sliders (except the **Y Max**, which should remain 0) to 1. You must also change both **Space** fields to **Local Space**. Refer to the next screenshot to see the values set in the panel:

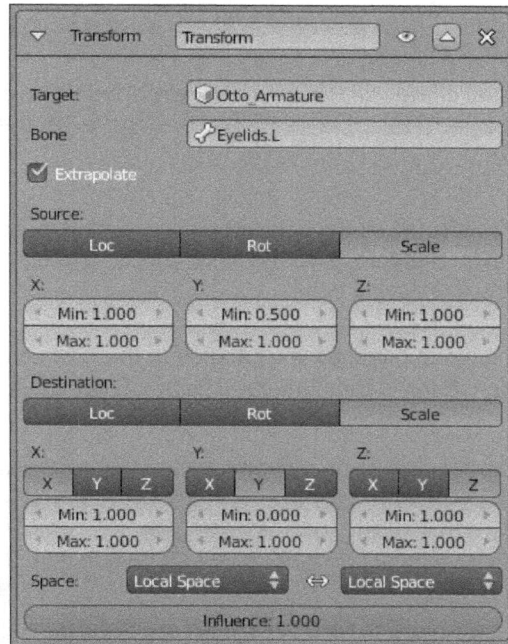

> These constraint values will make the left eye blink when you scale the Eyelids.L bone, without the need to scale it to 0 in order to close the lids, making the rig more usable. Another usability feature is having all eyes controllers in only one place, near the LookAt bone. This way you don't have to navigate much in order to adjust the character's eyes.

17. Now the finishing touches. Select the Eyelids.L bone and press *Ctrl + Shift + C*. Pick the **Limit Scale** constraint and navigate to the Properties Window, under the **Bone Constraints** tab.

18. In the **Constraint** panel, check both the **Minimum Y** and **Maximum Y** fields and define their values to 0.5 and 1.0, respectively. You also need to check the **For Transform** field and change the **Convert** value to **Local Space**. This will ensure that our eyelids controller will behave as expected.

19. Your left eye setup is now done. Enter in Edit Mode, select all the bones that you've created (D_UpEyelid.L, D_BottomEyelid.L, T_UpEyelid.L, T_BottomEyelid.L, M_Eyelids.L and Eyelids.L), duplicate (*Shift + D*) them, move (*G*) them to the right-hand side eye position, bring up the **Specials** menu (*W*), and select **Flip Names**. The right-hand side eye is now done, as a mirrored copy with all proper constraints applied!

20. To remove the visual clutter for the animator, you should leave only the LookAt, Eyelids.R, and Eyelids.L bones visible, and move (*M*) the remaining eye bones to an invisible layer.

> In a complete rig, all the bones you have just hid must be children of the main **Head** bone, so the eyes move accordingly when you move the character's head.

Your character will now be able to blink, as you can see in the next screenshot. If you have any doubts about this recipe, refer to the file 003-Eyelids-complete.blend to see the finished result.

## How it works...

The eyelids setup can be a little confusing due to the number of bones involved, but it's basically an IK setup for each lid, where the targets are driven by scaling a controller bone with some constraints to limit the amount of transformation.

## There's more...

You should also define some custom bone shapes to the eyelids controllers, so it's easier for the animator to understand what those bones are for and how they should be used. In the complete character rig that comes with the book support files, `Otto.blend`, the **Eyelids** have an eye shape with up and down arrows, inside the main `LookAt` shape, as seen in the next screenshot:

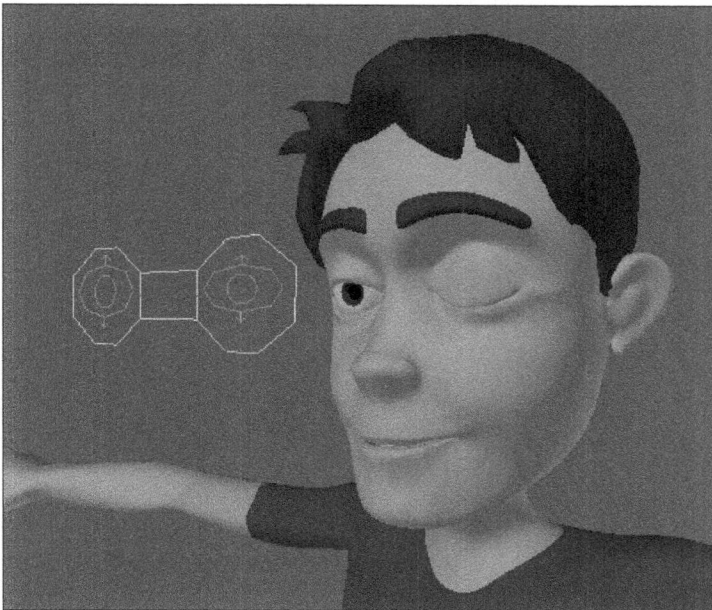

### More control to the eyelids

There are other ways of controlling eyelids that can be used alone or along with this technique to improve the amount of control you have over their shapes:

- ▶ You can use custom shape keys, modeling detailed shapes for each eyelid, and use drivers to set their influence
- ▶ You can use lattices to enhance the amount of deformation on each lid

Both techniques, although not focusing on eyelids but on general facial expressions, can be found in the next chapter.

**See also**

*Chapter 1: Tips on weight painting your character*

*Chapter 1: Customizing shapes and colors for your bones*

*Chapter 3: How to control where your characters looks at*

*Chapter 4: Adding expressions using Shape Keys*

*Chapter 4: Face controls with lattices*

# Controlling the pupils

The size of our pupils can say a lot about how we're feeling. Some methods of marketing research relate the size of the pupils to the attractiveness of TV commercials, for example.

Greater sizes can indicate that the person is attracted, happy, or just likes what it is seeing. Smaller usually denote the opposite, and that kind of control can be very useful in close up shots to help indicate how your character is feeling.

## How to do it...

1.  Open the file called `003-Pupils.blend` from the book's support files. You'll see a rig to control the eyes and eyelids, with shapes applied to the bones. That's our starting point, as you can see in the next screenshot:

2. First we need to create two **Shape Keys** for each eye. Select the `Eye.L` object, navigate to the **Properties Window**, in the **Object Data** tab, and locate the **Shape Keys** panel. Press the plus button to create the **Basis** shape. Click two more times to create our shapes. Select each on the panel and name them **Pupil_Small** and **Pupil_Big**, as seen in the following screenshot:

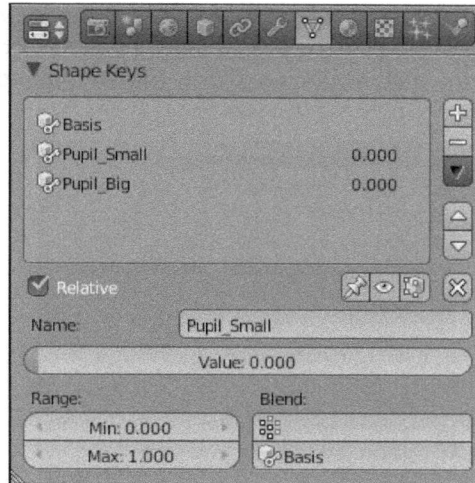

3. Select the **Pupils_Small** shape, go to the 3D View, and enter the eye mesh Edit Mode (*Tab*). Select the loop of vertices that define the pupil by holding *Alt*, right-clicking on one edge of this loop and scaling (S) it down, as seen in the following screenshot:

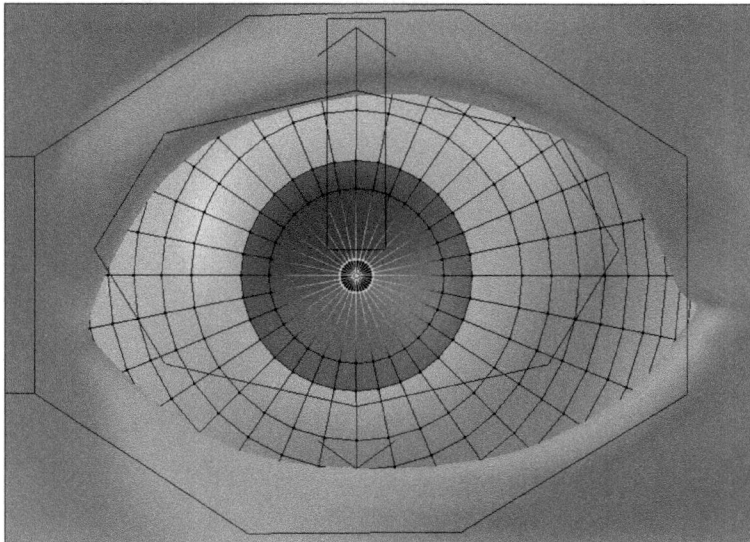

4. Go back to the **Shape Keys** panel, click on the **Pupils_Big** shape name to activate it. You'll see that the loop of vertices remain selected. Scale (S) them up so you get a dilated pupil.

We could just repeat the last three steps now to create similar shapes as the right eye, but we'll see a nice Blender feature to make our lives easier.

5. In Object Mode (*Tab*), select the left eye, hold *Shift*, and select the Eye.R object. Go to the **Shape Keys** panel in the Properties Window, click on the button with a down arrow below the minus button and pick **Transfer Shape Key**, as seen in the following screenshot:

This will transfer the active **Shape Key** (currently Pupil_Big) from the left eye object to the right eye, since they have the same topology.

6. Disable the **Pin** button for the transferred shape to the left of the "eye" button, just above the **Shape Key** name, as shown in the following screenshot:

7. Select the `Eye.L` object again, activate the `Pupil_Small` shape, and repeat steps 5 and 6 to transfer this **Shape Key** to the `Eye.R` mesh.

   Now that we have the necessary Shape Keys for each eye, it's just a matter of creating a driver controller for them.

8. Select the `Armature` object, enter in its Edit Mode (*Tab*). Make sure the **X-Axis Mirror** property is turned on in the Tool Shelf (*T*) panel.

9. Select the base of the `Eyelids.L` bone, extrude (*E*) it to roughly half the height of the eyelids controller. This will create a smaller bone in the same position of the `Eyelids.L` bone. You'll notice that another bone will be created at the base of the right eyelids controller, since we're in **X-Axis Mirror** mode, as you can see in the following screenshot:

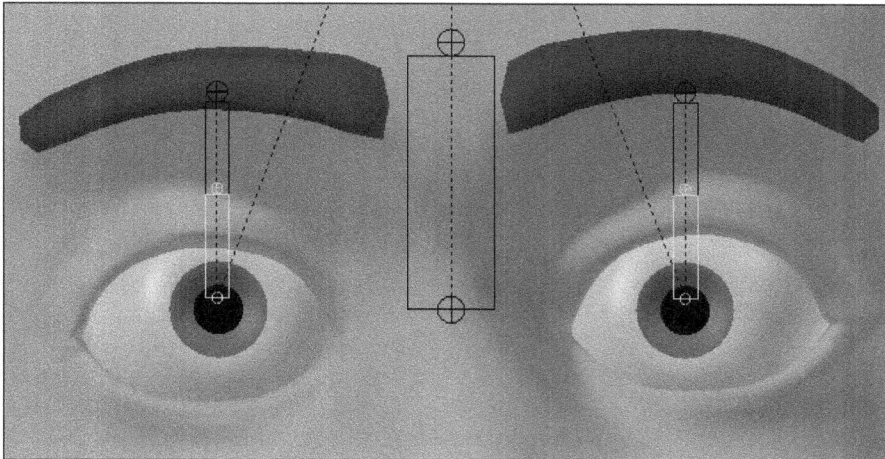

10. Select the bone you've just created, hold *Shift*, select the `Eyelids.L` bone and press *Ctrl + P* (Keep Offset) to make it child of the eyelids controller. Name the created bones as `Pupil.L` and `Pupil.R`.

11. Enter in Pose Mode and lock all the **Transform** channels of these bones, except the **Scale** in the **Y** axis. You should end up with a setup that looks similar to the next screenshot. It's a good idea to add a circle shape for the pupils controllers.

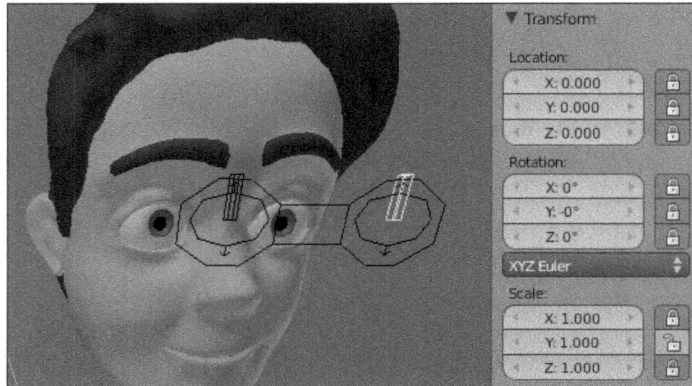

Now you should add a **Driver** for each **Shape Key**

12. Select the left eye mesh, go to the **Shape Keys** panel in the Properties Window, click on the **Pupil_Big** shape, right-click on its **Value** slider and choose **Add Driver**. The slider will get a pinkish hue.

13. Open a Graph Editor window, choose the **Drivers** mode on the window header, click on the **Value (Pupil_Big)** name in the left-hand side panel and change the following settings in the Properties (*N*) panel: in the **Drivers** section, change the **Expr** field to var on the box below the **Add Variable** button, change its type to **Transform Channel**; select the Otto_Armature object and the Pupil.L bone in the **Ob/Bone** fields; choose the **Y Scale** type and enable the **Local Space** field. The driver setup values are shown in the next screenshot, and the left eye pupil should dilate when you scale (S) up the Pupil.L bone:

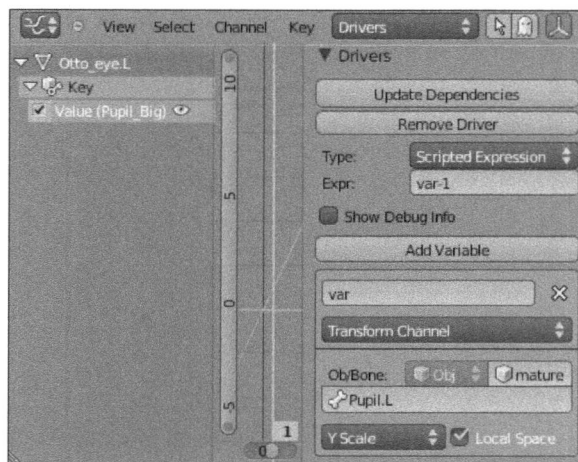

> The `var-1` value on the **Expr** field is because the default scaling value of objects and bones in Blender is equal to 1, in contrast to location and rotation which get default values of 0. This value allows us to get the desired result when scaling up the bone driver.

14. For the `Pupil_Small` shape you should repeat steps 12 and 13, with the only difference being that the **Expr** value should be set to `1-var`. The next screenshot shows the driver setup values, and the contracted pupil achieved by scaling down the `Pupil.L` bone:

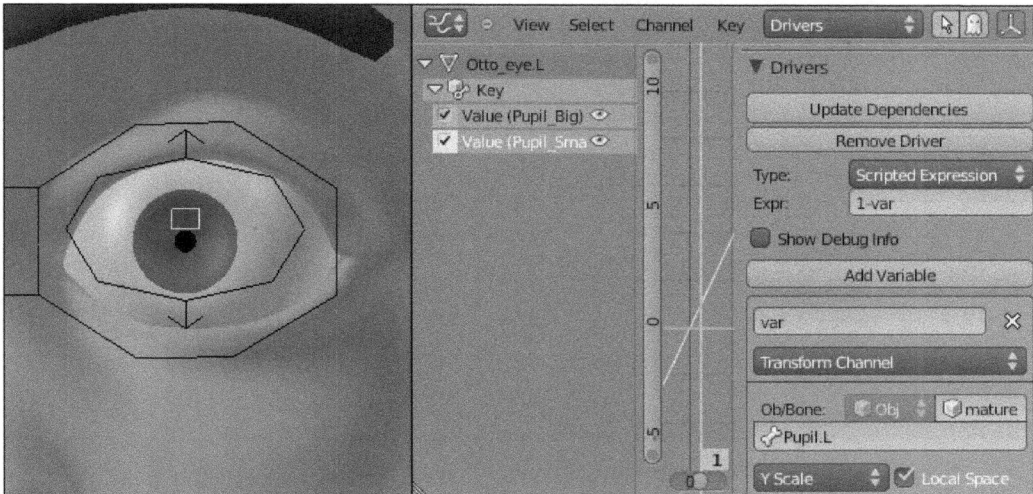

15. To apply the drivers on the right eye, you can copy the ones that you've set for the left eye. Select the left eye mesh, go to the **Shape Keys** panel in the Properties Window, select the desired shape, right-click on its pinkish **Value** slider and select **Copy Driver**, as seen in the next screenshot:

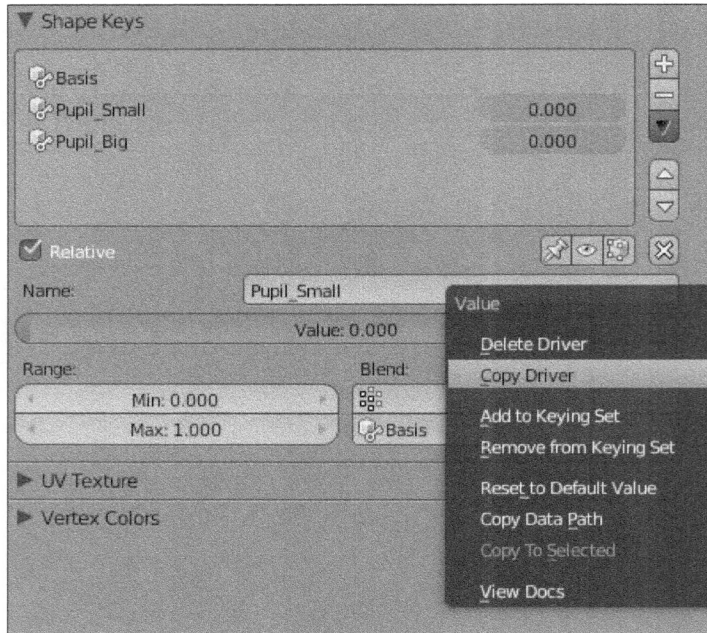

16. Then you should select the right eye and its equivalent shape in the same panel, right click on its **Value** slider and choose **Paste Driver**. The only thing that you need to do next is to change the target bone from Pupil.L to Pupil.R in the driver properties on the Graph Editor window. Repeat it for the other shape and you're done with the pupil controllers!

The file 003-Pupils-complete.blend has this finished recipe for your reference.

## How it works...

By creating shape keys for the pupil sizes and assigning bone drivers to their values, you can control the amount of their dilation. To use the same controller for both contraction and dilation shapes, you must use inverted expression values for evaluation in the Graph Editor window.

## There's more...

Besides the fact that the human iris doesn't contract nor expand, you can apply the same techniques shown here to control their size. If used very carefully, this kind of control can help you express your character's emotional state. This is most applicable to cartoon characters, though.

## See also

*Chapter 1*: *Using corrective shape keys*

*Chapter 1*: *Making a IK-FK switcher*

*Chapter 3*: *How to control where your characters looks at*

*Chapter 3*: *The eyelids controllers*

# 4
# Poker Face?
# Facial Rigging

In this chapter, we will cover the following topics:

- ▶ Adding expressions using Shape Keys
- ▶ Face controls with lattices
- ▶ Creating the jaw controller
- ▶ Controlling your tongue

## Introduction

The face is the most complex part of the human body to set up. We spend our entire lives looking at human faces, and we're pretty good at detecting the subtlest changes and what they mean emotionally. It's a tough job trying to replicate this amount of complexity in CG: from the carefully built mesh topology to the detailed shading, texturing, and—of course—the animation controllers and movements.

The more you try to build a realistic human face in CG, the more details you have to add in order to avoid the **uncanny valley** effect. This terms refers to a hypothesis in the field of robotics which holds that the human observers tend to be repulsed by something that looks and moves barely like a human being: if it's not exactly like a human nor a clear abstraction of it (like a cartoon character), the observers notice that there's something "wrong" or "strange" to the character—often referred to as "zombie like".

There are books dedicated to the subject of facial rigging, and it wouldn't be feasible to try and cover all the details in this cookbook. We're going to learn some general guidelines and techniques which are applied to a cartoon character that would help you get acceptable results, though. *Grosso modo*, it's the amount of detail and refinement used with these techniques that will lead you to better results.

A good thing to do is using a mixed approach when rigging faces: you should use Shape Keys controllers for specific expressions (such as a smile), a free deformation tool (such as a Lattice or a MeshDeform modifier), and Armatures (as drivers or to accomplish pivotal deformations, such as the jaw movement) to deform the character's mesh as you wish. In this chapter, we'll see how to create these kinds of controllers.

# Adding expressions using Shape Keys

Shape Keys, as you may already know, are saved states of your mesh that can be blended from one to another. For creating facial expressions, which can drastically change the shape of your character's face (like from a smile to an angry face), these are indispensable in the rigger's toolbox.

As a rule of thumb, you should use Shape Keys whenever a facial expression is too specific or complicated to achieve with regular bones. For instance, while smiling, the facial muscles create specific forms for your mouth and cheeks, creating skin folds (even your eyes and ears can move in a smile). Reproducing this kind of deformation with bones can be very hard, so you'd better model the specific shapes to accomplish this expression.

## How to do it...

1. Open the file `004-Face.blend`. It has our character head model, ready for the creation of shape keys.

2. Select it, go to the Properties window, under the **Object Data** tab and look for the **Shape Keys** section. Click on the plus sign icon to add the **Basis** shape on which the others will be based on. Click on the same button again to create the first shape and name it `Mouth_cornerUp.L`, as you can see in the next screenshot:

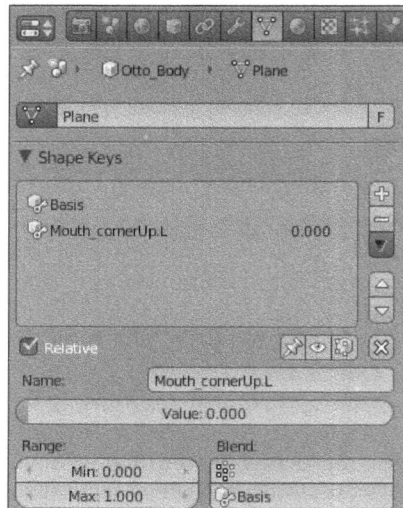

3. Enter in the mesh's Edit Mode (*Tab*) and model the shape of a half smile at the left side of the mouth. You can move (*G*) the vertices, edges, and faces as you wish, using modeling tools such as the Proportional Editing (*O*) mode. The next screenshot demonstrates our modeled shape. Notice the modeled skin fold, giving shape to a smile line around the mouth. This kind of deformation would be difficult to accomplish with bones.

4. To create the right side of the expression, you can model it yourself or mirror the current one. In order to accomplish the latter, set the Mouth_cornerUp.L shape slider value to 1, add another shape key through the plus sign, click on the down arrow button, and select **Mirror Shape Key**, as seen in the next screenshot. Then you can name this shape properly as Mouth_cornerUp.R and tweak its shape if you wish.

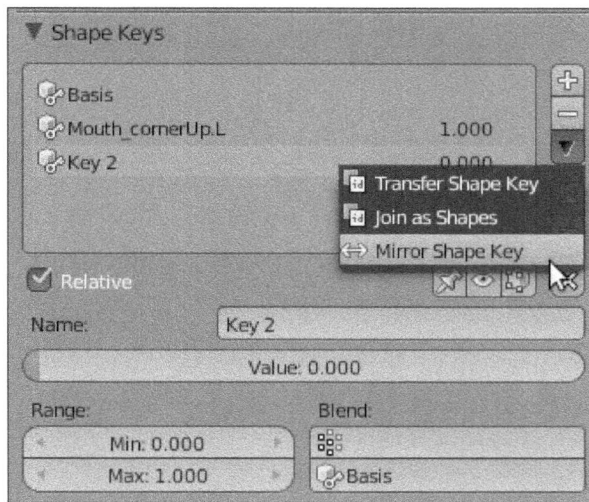

Another approach to this bilateral symmetry is to model the full expression with both its sides and create two vertex groups (one for each side of the face, such as `Face.L` and `Face.R`). Then you can duplicate that shape and set each copy to affect only one of these vertex groups. Each Shape Key has a field to select a vertex group: if one is selected, its weights would be used as a "mask" for the influence of the Shape Key; if none is selected, the entire mesh will be influenced by it.

After you create this shape, go on to model new shapes for different facial expressions. Building a Shape Key library is a somewhat long and repetitive task, so you should only model the shapes that are required to achieve a good variety of facial expressions. For instance, the main character from the Blender Foundation's short movie *Sintel* required more than 50 shapes.

Along with facial expressions, some professionals also choose to model phonemes (such as the character saying the letters "a", "o", "e", "m", "f", and so on). That's very useful, but you should use these phoneme shapes only as an addition to your existing library, since the emotional state of your character (thus his facial expression) will probably be different regardless of the spoken words.

You can have a look at some commonly used shapes in the following list and what they look like in the next screenshot:

1. Mouth_cornerUp (left and right)
2. Mouth_cornerSide (left and right)
3. Mouth_cornerDown (left and right)
4. Mouth_wide (top and bottom lips)
5. Mouth_curled (top and bottom lips)
6. Mouth_puck (only one shape)
7. Mouth_sneer (left and right)
8. Cheek_puff (left and right)
9. Cheek_suck (left and right)
10. Brow_mad (left and right)
11. Brow_sad (left and right)
12. Brow_surprise (left and right)

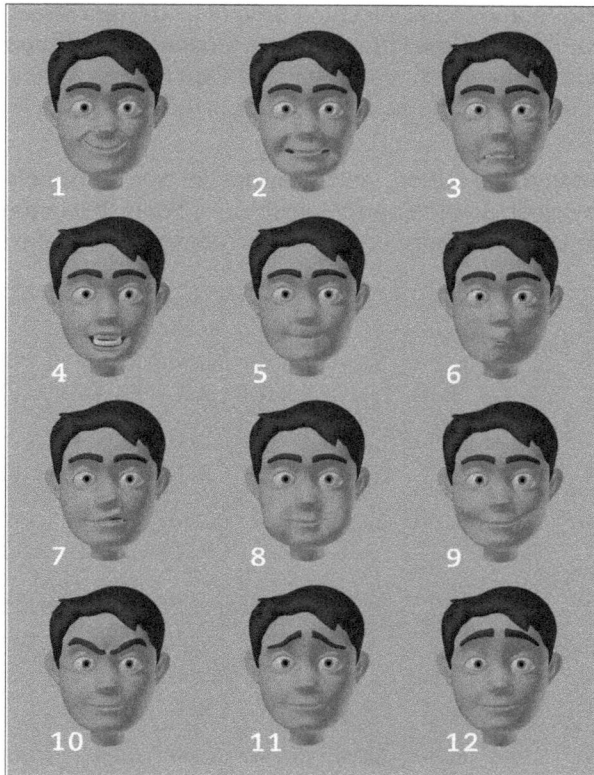

To stay organized, you should adopt some naming conventions for the shapes. Use prefixes such as Mouth_, Eyebrow_ and the suffixes .L and .R.

After you model all your needed shape keys, it's time to create the appropriate drivers. This is a matter of creating some controller bones and mapping their channels (location, rotation, scale, and so on) to the amount of influence of each shape key. The good thing is that one bone can drive more than one shape key.

5.  Let's create the drivers for the left corner of the mouth: open the file 004-Face-shapes.blend. This file has the head mesh with all shapes already modeled and an armature with the bones properly named and positioned after the face parts.

6.  Select the head mesh, go to the **Object Data** tab in the Properties window, and navigate to the **Shape Keys** panel. Select the Mouth_cornerUp.L shape, right-click over the **Value** slider and choose **Add Driver**. Do the same for the Mouth_cornerSide.L and Mouth_cornerDown.L shapes. We'll map these drivers to different channels and values of the Mouth_corner.L bone.

7. Go to a Graph Editor window, select the **Drivers** mode, and select the driver `Mouth_cornerUp.L` on the left side of the window. In the **Properties** panel (*N*), find the **Drivers** tab and enter `var*10` in the **Expr** field. This will make a small amount of movement on the `Mouth_corner.L` bone to give a high level of influence on the shape.

8. Below the **Add Variable** button, leave the variable type as **Transform Channel**, select the **Armature** object, and the `Mouth_corner.L` bone. Select the **Y Location** channel and check the **Local Space** field. The next screenshot shows the setup values:

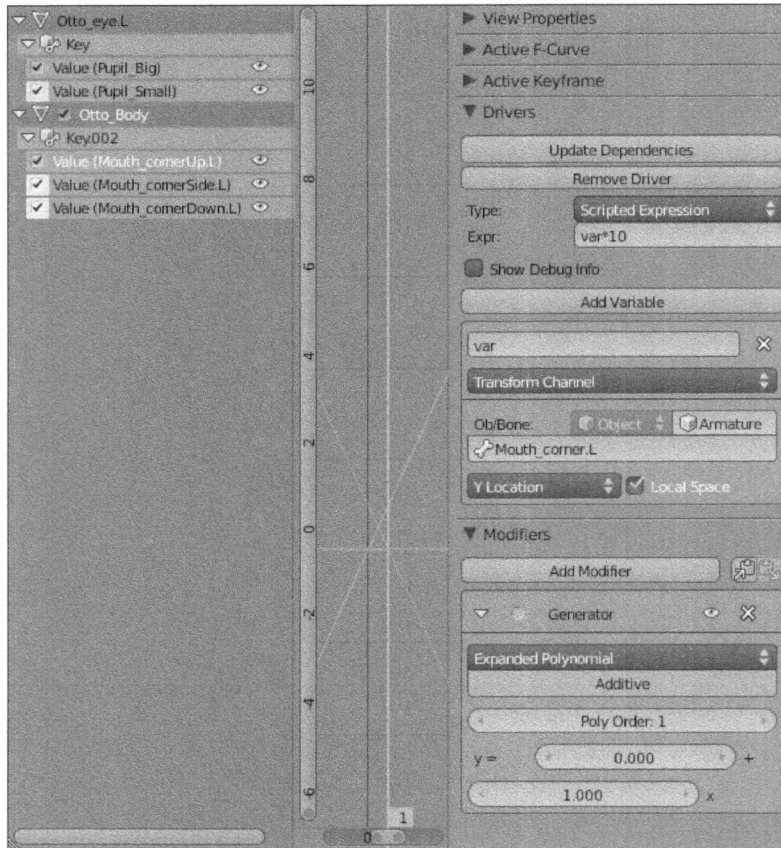

9. Now you should repeat steps 6 and 7 for the `Mouth_cornerSide.L` and `Mouth_cornerDown.L` drivers, with a few changes: for the `Mouth_cornerSide.L` you should use the **X Location** channel and set the remaining values exactly as you did before; for the `Mouth_cornerDown.L` the only difference to the `Mouth_cornerUp.L` driver is the **Expr** value, which should be inverted with the `var*-10` expression.

When you finish setting up these three drivers, the controller will act like this: when moved up, the `Mouth_cornerUp` shape is triggered; when translated to the side, the `Mouth_cornerSide.L` shape is activated; and when moved down, it will trigger the `Mouth_cornerDown.L` shape. The cool thing about this is that you can mix related shapes when moving the controller in a diagonal direction.

Using the principles and procedures shown here you can now set up the remaining drivers using the other bones. As a guideline, you should map:

- ❏ The `Cheek_puff.L` and `Cheek_suck.L` shapes to the `Cheek.L` bone, using the positive and negative X local location channels, respectively. The opposite goes for the right-hand side.

- ❏ The `Mouth_wide.top` shape to the `Mouth_lip.Top` bone, using the up Y local location channel.

- ❏ The `Mouth_curled.top` shape to the `Mouth_lip.Top` bone, using the down Y local location channel.

- ❏ The `Mouth_sneer.L` shape to the `Mouth_lip.Top` bone, using the left X local location channel. Use the inverted expression to the right equivalent.

- ❏ The `Mouth_wide.bottom` shape to the `Mouth_lip.Bottom` bone, using the down Y local location channel.

- ❏ The `Mouth_curled.bottom` shape to the `Mouth_lip.Bottom` bone, using the up Y local location channel.

- ❏ The `Mouth_puck` shape to the `Mouth_lip.Bottom` bone, using the front Z local location channel.

- ❏ The `Eyebrow_mad.L`, `Eyebrow_sad.L`, and `Eyebrow_surprise.L` shapes to the `Eyebrow.L` bone, using the negative local X location, the positive local X location, and the local Y location respectively.

The complete setup can be found in the file `004-Face-complete.blend`, for your reference if you have any doubts regarding the drivers configuration. With this setup you can achieve facial expressions like the one you see in the following screenshot:

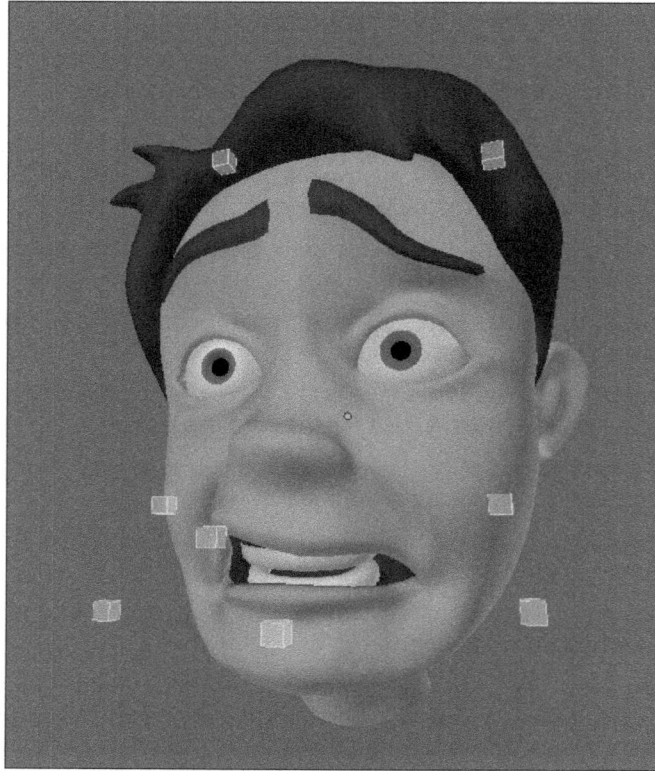

## How it works...

By carefully creating a library of shape keys, we can set up drivers and mix them to achieve good facial expressions. A single controller can (and should in some cases) drive more than one shape key. It's good to map opposite channels to opposite shapes so they don't overlap: this is the reason for mapping the `Mouth_cornerUp.L` shape to the positive local Y location and the `Mouth_cornerDown.L` to the negative local Y location of the same bone.

## There's more...

The facial expressions based on driven shape keys are good, but they aren't very flexible since the modeled shapes act like the extreme positions. In the next recipe we'll see how to use lattices to add more flexible deformations.

**See also**

*Chapter 4: Face controls with lattices*

# Face controls with lattices

The use of shape keys allows us to model some very specific facial expressions, notably those which produce deformations such as skin folds and creases. By building a shape key library you can interpolate between them to create very convincing facial expressions. The problem is that you're always limited to the size of your library, and building a huge one requires an equally huge amount of time and effort.

A good solution to achieve more freedom when building facial expressions is to add another layer of lattice-based controllers so that the animator can mold the face as desired in real time. This is easier, quicker, and makes your file lighter for not having an insane amount of modeled shapes. But the real benefit is that it allows you to achieve pretty good results.

With this mixed-technique approach we can get the best of each tool: modeling specific creases and wrinkles with shape keys; freely deforming the mesh in real time with lattices; and using bones where we need rotation (for the eyelids or the jaw, as we'll cover in the next recipe).

## How to do it...

1.  Open the file `004-Lattice.blend`. You'll see a face already set up with shape key controllers as the result of our previous recipe. This is our starting point.

    We're going to create some **Lattice** modifiers to deform our head mesh, but we'll make them deform only specific regions. We need one lattice to deform the face as a whole, one for fine tuning the upper lip, and another for the bottom lip. In order to achieve this, we need to create three vertex groups: one for each lattice.

> A lattice is a special object in 3D applications: visually, it's shape is similar to a subdivided mesh box, but it's not visible on the rendered image. It's purpose is to deform a mesh object based on the position of its control points. There is another modifier in Blender that allows us to achieve similar results: the **MeshDeform** modifier. Instead of using this special lattice object to deform our mesh, it uses another mesh (with fewer vertices) as the reference for the deformation.

2.  Select the head mesh and go to the **Vertex Groups** section, under the Properties window, in the **Object Data** tab. There will be some groups already created, but we need more. Add three groups by clicking on the plus button and name them `face`, `lips_bottom`, and `lips_top`, as seen in the following screenshot:

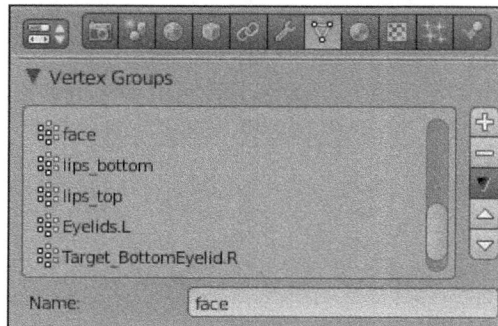

3.  On the 3D View, select the head mesh and activate the Weight Paint mode on the window header or through *Ctrl + Tab*. Make sure that the **face** vertex group is activated in the Properties window, set your painting tool to **Add** in the Toolbox panel (*T*), and start painting the influence zone of the face. When painting, leave the eyes and nose regions with no influence (blue, in Blender default colors; white in the grayscale image given next) and full influence (red, in Blender default colors; dark grey in the grayscale picture given next) from the chin to the forehead.

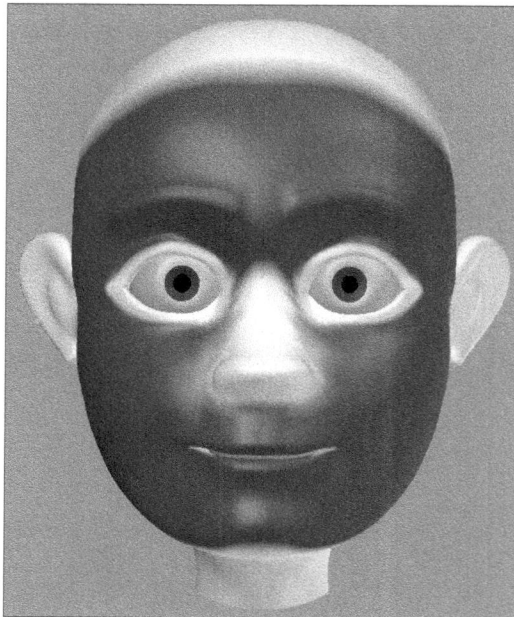

4. Repeat the process for the `lips_bottom` and `lips_top` vertex groups, painting its regions as seen in the next screenshot. Notice that the `lips_top` vertex group also adds the nose to its influence region (dark):

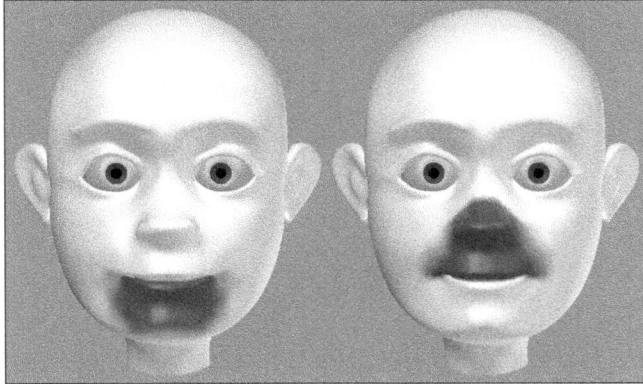

With the regions of influence properly painted, it's time to create the **Lattices** to deform our mesh.

5. Go back to Object Mode, position the 3D cursor in front of the face, go to front view (*Numpad 1*), press *Shift + A*, and choose **Lattice**.

6. In the **Object Data** tab, under the Properties window, set this lattice to have 5, 1, and 7 points on its U, V, and W coordinates respectively.

7. On the 3D view, scale (S) and position (G) the lattice so it fits the face size, similar to what you see in the next screenshot. Set its name as `Lattice_Face`.

Now that we have the **Lattice** and **Vertex Group** properly created, let's add the modifier.

8.  Select the head mesh, go to the Properties window in the **Modifiers** tab, and add a **Lattice Modifier**. Set the **Object** field value as **Lattice_Face** and choose **face** as the **Vertex Group**, as seen in the following screenshot:

If you enter into the lattice's Edit Mode and move any of its points, you'll see that the mesh is deformed accordingly. Now we just need to set some controllers to act on the **Lattice**. Since we already have an armature (on layer 2) to control the eyes and shape keys, it's a good idea to use it to also control the **Lattice** points.

9.  Select the armature, enter in its Edit Mode, and add a bone between the eyebrows and name it `Eyebrows_Center`. Move (*M*) it to an empty armature layer (such as layer 3), and make it the only armature's visible layer by pressing *Shift* + *M* and choosing that layer. This layer should have only bones that affect lattices, so you know where to find them. You should now have something similar to the next screenshot:

10. Select the **Lattice**, go to the Properties window in the **Modifiers** tab, and add a new **Hook** modifier. In the **Object** field, choose **Otto_Armature**; for the **Bone** field, pick **Eyebrows_Center**.

11. It's time to assign the lattice's points to that bone. Enter into the lattice's Edit Mode (*Tab*). You should notice that the **Hook** modifier panel in the Properties window had changed a bit. Now you have two new buttons called **Select** and **Assign** for that modifier.

12. Select the **Lattice** point near the `Eyebrows_Center` bone. Go to the **Hook** modifier panel and click on **Assign** and then **Reset** to recalculate the modifier.

13. Exit the Edit Mode, select, and move the `Eyebrows_center` bone. You'll see that the assigned point follows it and the face shape is deformed by the **Lattice**, as seen in the following screenshot:

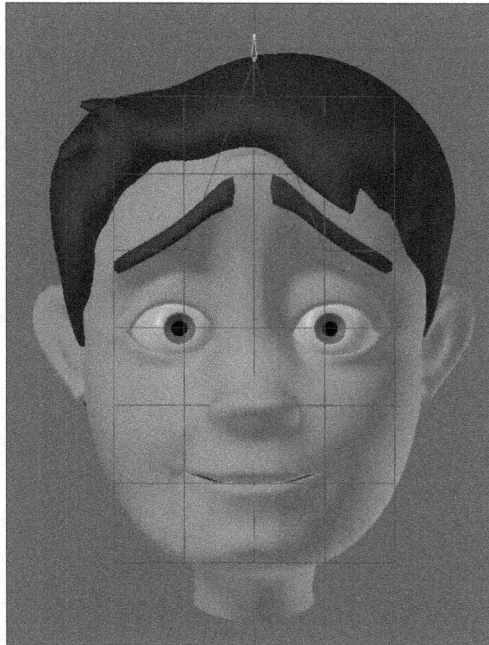

14. Repeat steps 9 till 13 to add new bones to the **Armature** and more **Hook** modifiers to control the other points of the **Lattice**. Once you're finished, you'll have a good amount of control over the face, even if you have a shape key applied.

15. After finishing with the first lattice, create two more: one for the bottom lip and another for the upper lip, with their sizes and number of control points relevant to the vertex groups you've created: **lips_bottom** and **lips_top** respectively.

16. Repeat the process from steps 5 to 14 for each **Lattice**, defining their deformation range to their relevant vertex group and creating more bones and hook modifiers as you wish. To follow the head movement, all lattices should be parented to the **Head** bone.

> This process can also be applied to have a finer control over the shapes shapes of eyelids, if you need more control than just opening and closing them.

After you finish assigning all the lattices, bones, and hook modifiers, you should end up with a very flexible rig, which allows you to freely deform the mesh on top of previously assigned shape keys. The following screenshot shows an example of it, and you can find the complete exercise in the file `004-Lattice-complete.blend`. The shape keys controllers are the square bones, while the lattice controllers are the cross-shaped ones:

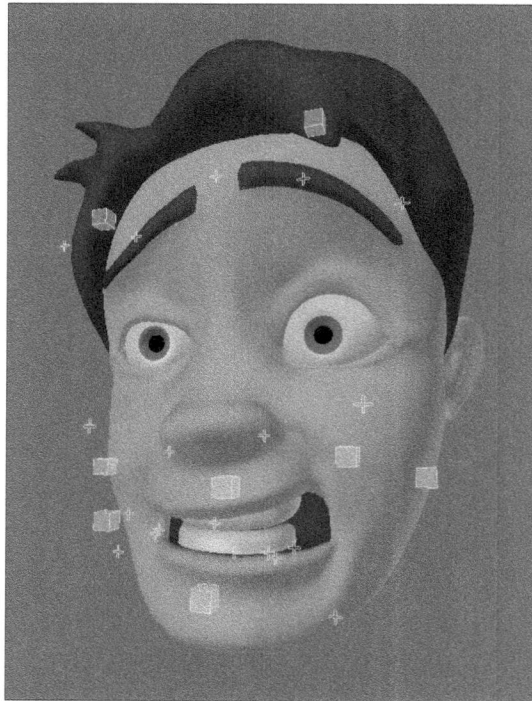

## How it works...

By assigning lattices to specific regions of the face through vertex groups, you can control them with bones through the **Hook** modifier, thus easily creating free deformations on top of any existing shape keys.

## There's more...

This method is good for creating smooth and subtle changes in the mesh, but you shouldn't be limited only to faces. Bouncy bellies in fat characters or muscles can also be tweaked with this technique.

## See also

*Chapter 4: Adding expressions using Shape Keys*

# Creating the jaw controller

The action of opening the mouth is defined by the jaw bone. Although at first it seems like a simple movement, a more careful look shows there's more to it. More than just rotating in one axis, the jaw moves towards the front, back, and to the sides as well, allowing us to make somewhat complex movements.

When creating the jaw controller, we should not only pay attention to its unique movements, but also to the hierarchy of bones, since we'll have controllers such as the lips and tongue that should follow its movements.

## How to do it...

1.  Open the file `004-Jaw.blend` from this book's support files. This file holds our character's head mesh along with some controllers for its eyes and facial expressions. You'll also see a visible **Lattice** for controlling the lower lip of our character, as a result of our previous recipe, as seen in the next screenshot:

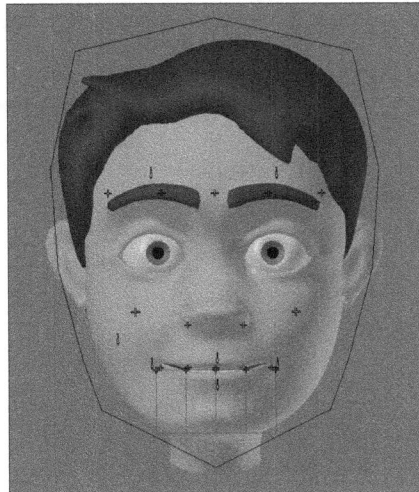

2. Select the **Armature**, enter into Edit Mode, and add a bone to act as the jaw. It should have its root on the jaw's imaginary axis of rotation, near the center of the head. Its tip should be located at the chin, as seen in the next screenshot (the other bones are hidden for clarity's sake). Name it D_Jaw. Since the mesh already has a vertex group with the same name, when you move this bone the mesh should be deformed accordingly.

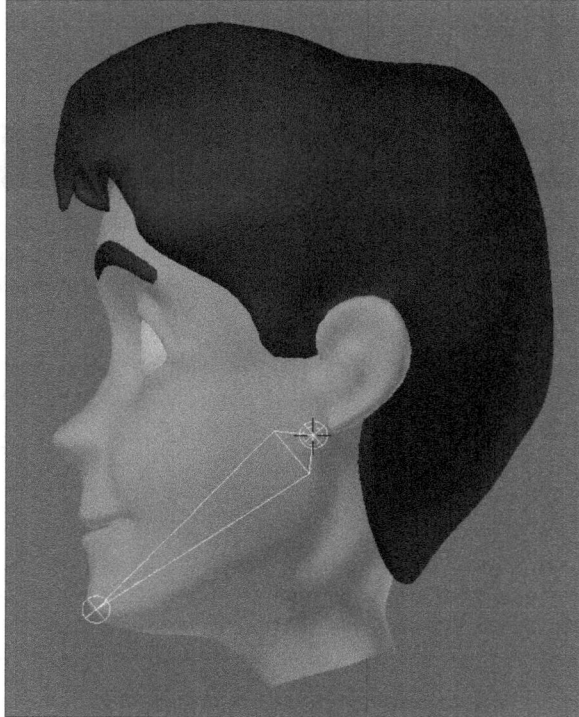

You should pay attention to the bones and objects hierarchy. All the bones that have names starting with Lip_Bottom and the Mouth_lip.Bottom should be parented (*Ctrl + P*) to the D_Jaw bone so that they follow its movement. In addition to these bones, you should also parent two more objects to the D_Jaw bone: Lattice_Jaw and Otto_Teeth.Bottom. Finally, the D_Jaw bone should be parented to the Head bone so that it follows the head movement.

This jaw bone would only deform the mesh, and won't be touched by the animator. Since it would perform some specific movements, we're going to control it using the **Action** constraint. The **Action** constraint is based on a series of preset animations, triggered by a controller.

3.  With the D_Jaw bone selected in Pose Mode, open a **DopeSheet** window, select the **Action Editor** mode on the window header, and add a new **Action** using the plus button. Call it jaw.

    Now you will move and rotate the D_Jaw bone, defining keyframes on this newly created action.

4.  For the first frame, just press *I* and choose **LocRot** in the **3D View** to define a keyframe to the rest position.

5.  Go up 10 frames (*up arrow*), rotate the jaw bone until the mouth is fully open, and set a keyframe (*I*) (choosing **LocRot**) there. Remember the keyed frames: 1 and 11. We're going to need these.

6.  Repeat step 4 for the remaining key poses, all spaced by 10 frames to make things easier:

    - ❏  Frame 21 with a rest position
    - ❏  Frame 31 with a fully closed mouth
    - ❏  Frame 41 with a rest position
    - ❏  Frame 51 with the jaw rotated left
    - ❏  Frame 61, rest again
    - ❏  Frame 71, rotated right
    - ❏  Frame 81, rest
    - ❏  Frame 91 with the jaw moved to the front
    - ❏  Frame 101, rest
    - ❏  And finally, 111 with the jaw moved back

> You don't need to create new positions for the resting poses. Just duplicate (*Shift + D*) the first key position, which holds the resting pose, and move the copies to frames 21, 41, 61, 81, and 101.

The next screenshot shows all the different key poses: rest (side), open, closed, front, back, rest (front), rotated right, and left.

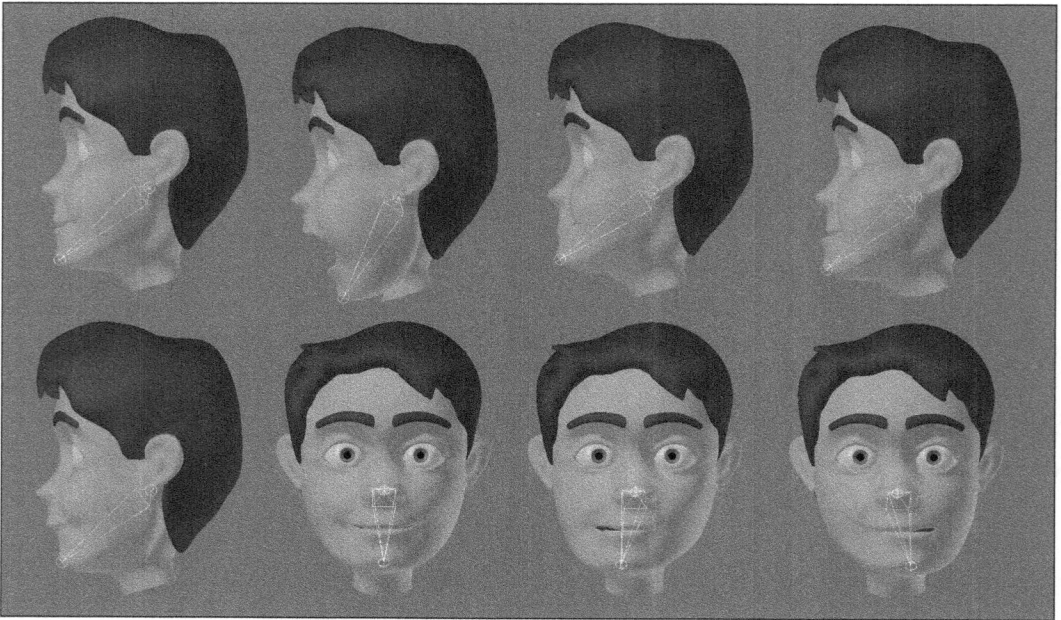

Now comes the fun part. We're going to set the controller for the jaw movements.

7. Create a new bone just in front of the chin. Make it smaller and call it just `Jaw`. With this bone still selected and in Pose Mode, hold *Shift*, select the `D_Jaw` bone, press *Ctrl + Shift + C* and select the **Action** constraint.

8. Go to the Properties window, under the **Bone Constraints** tab and change the settings for the constraint you've just created: select `jaw` for the **Action** field; `Location Y`, for **Transform Channel**; `Start:1, End:11` for the **Action Length**; `Min:0, Max:-0.1` for **Target Range**; and finally, `Local Space` in the **Convert** combo. This will make the character's mouth open when you move the controller down.

9. For the other movements, repeat the previous step and change only the values for **Action Length**, **Target Range**, and **Transform Channel**. You should create five more constraints so that the jaw closes with the controller up movement; go left, right, back, and front with the relevant controller transform channels. The settings for all six constraints are shown in the next screenshot:

| ▽ Action | Open ▽ ■ ✕ | ▽ Action | Left △ ▽ ■ ✕ | ▽ Action | Front △ ▽ ■ ✕ |
|---|---|---|---|---|---|
| Target: | Otto Armature | Target: | Otto Armature | Target: | Otto Armature |
| Bone: | Jaw | Bone: | Jaw | Bone: | Jaw |
| Action: | jaw | Action: | jaw | Action: | jaw |
| Transform Channel: | Location Y | Transform Channel: | Location X | Transform Channel: | Location Z |
| Action Length: | Target Range: | Action Length: | Target Range: | Action Length: | Target Range: |
| Start: 1 | Min: 0.000 | Start: 41 | Min: 0.000 | Start: 81 | Min: 0.000 |
| End: 11 | Max: -0.100 | End: 51 | Max: 0.100 | End: 91 | Max: 0.100 |
| Convert: | Local Space | Convert: | Local Space | Convert: | Local Space |
| | Influence: 1.000 | | Influence: 1.000 | | Influence: 1.000 |

| ▽ Action | Close △ ▽ ■ ✕ | ▽ Action | Right △ ▽ ■ ✕ | ▽ Action | Back △ ■ ✕ |
|---|---|---|---|---|---|
| Target: | Otto Armature | Target: | Otto Armature | Target: | Otto Armature |
| Bone: | Jaw | Bone: | Jaw | Bone: | Jaw |
| Action: | jaw | Action: | jaw | Action: | jaw |
| Transform Channel: | Location Y | Transform Channel: | Location X | Transform Channel: | Location Z |
| Action Length: | Target Range: | Action Length: | Target Range: | Action Length: | Target Range: |
| Start: 21 | Min: 0.000 | Start: 61 | Min: 0.000 | Start: 101 | Min: 0.000 |
| End: 31 | Max: 0.100 | End: 71 | Max: -0.100 | End: 111 | Max: -0.100 |
| Convert: | Local Space | Convert: | Local Space | Convert: | Local Space |
| | Influence: 1.000 | | Influence: 1.000 | | Influence: 1.000 |

Now you can move the **Jaw** controller freely and the character will move accordingly. The complete example is in the file `004-Jaw-complete.blend`, so you can refer to in case of any doubts.

## How it works...

By creating predefined positions for the jaw in a separate action, you can trigger parts of that animation with a controller and an **Action** constraint. Because the jaw movements are a bit more complex, involving rotation and translation, it's a good idea to use a separate controller and predefined keys.

## See also

*Chapter 5: Creating IK legs with a three-pivot foot*

# Controlling your tongue

The tongue is very important when animating your character, helping to create good facial expressions which are fundamental when animating dialogues. Although subtle in essence, it makes a big difference when animating your character while it's saying things such as "hello".

Not only when speaking, but what if your character wants to have an ice cream?

## How to do it...

1. Open the file `004-Tongue.blend` from this book's support files. You'll find our character's face rigged with shape keys, lattices, and a jaw controller as the result of previous recipes.

   If you move the **Jaw** controller down, you'll see that there's a mesh called **Otto_Tongue** inside the character's mouth. It is parented to the `D_Jaw` bone, so it follows the jaw movement.

2. Enter into the armature's Edit Mode and add a chain of two bones for the tongue, as you can see in the next screenshot. Name them `D_TongueBase` and `TongueTip` and make them both children of the `D_Jaw` bone: (*Ctrl + P*) | **Keep Offset**.

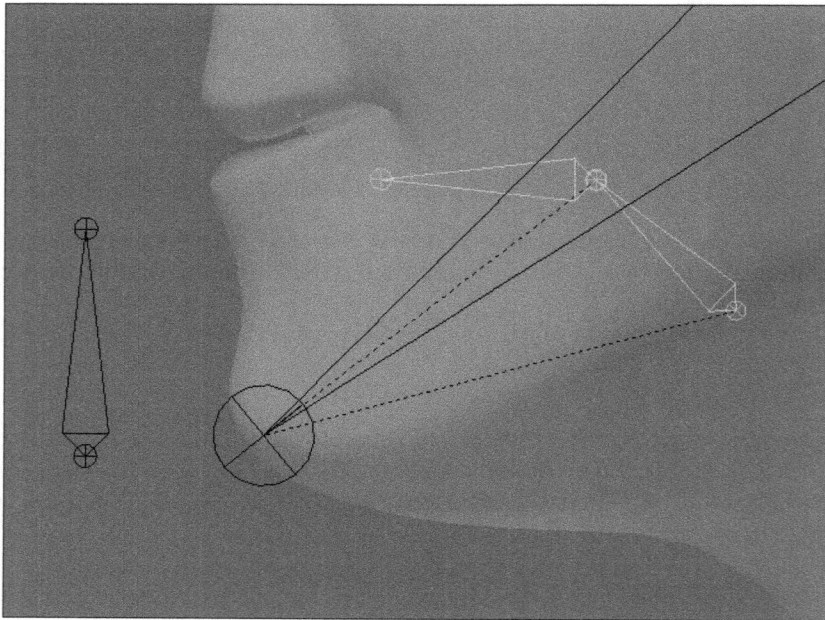

3. Enter into the armature's Pose Mode (*Ctrl + Tab*). Select the `TongueTip` bone, hold *Shift*, select the `D_TongueBase` bone, press *Ctrl + Shift + C*, and choose the **Stretch To** constraint. This will make the base stretch to the position of the `TongueTip` bone.

4. Select the `Otto_Tongue` object, hold *Shift*, select the `TongueTip` bone, press *Ctrl + P*, and choose **With Automatic Weights**. This will bind the tongue mesh to the armature. Adjust the influences of each bone using weight painting.

> In order to better visualize the tongue object and its bones, you can select the Otto_Body mesh and move it (*M*) to another layer. You can also hide (*H*) it (press *Alt + H* to unhide) or use a Mask Modifier, with the D_Head vertex group and the **Invert** option selected.

5.  Now you can apply a shape to the TongueTip bone and move (*M*) the D_TongueBase bone to a hidden armature layer. The tongue will be deformed to match the position and rotation of this bone, while inheriting the transformations from the D_Jaw bone.

    The file 004-Tongue-complete.blend has this finished recipe for your reference, in case of any doubts. You can see the resulting deformation in the next screenshot:

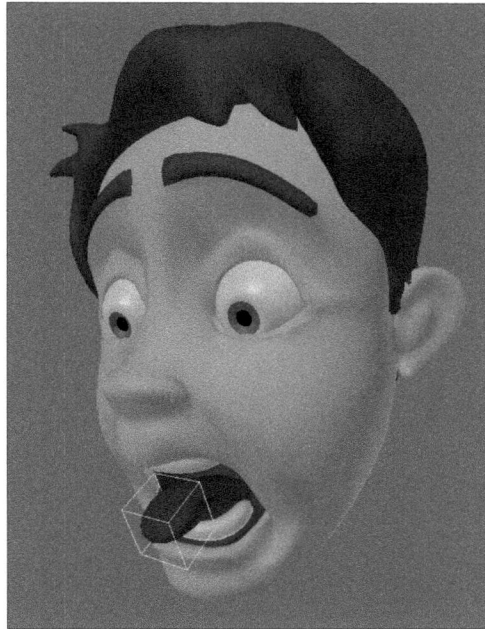

## How it works...

With a simple setup of two bones parented to the jaw and a **Stretch To** constraint, we can create a flexible yet convincing controller for our character's tongue.

## See also

*Chapter 4: Creating the jaw controller*

# 5

# Hands Down! The Limbs Controllers

In this chapter, we will cover the following topics:

- ▶ Controlling fingers
- ▶ Creating IK legs with a three-pivot foot
- ▶ Stretch those limbs!
- ▶ Setting up the shoulders
- ▶ Cartoon bending for arms and legs
- ▶ Different spaces for IK hands

## Introduction

In your animations, your characters will often need to walk, run, hold things, fight, jump, or just express their feelings. These, and countless other actions, can be achieved even in pantomime using arms, legs, and hands.

We've already seen some techniques to control our characters' eyes, face, head, and torso. Now it's time to take a look at how to create the limbs controllers and finish our basic set of character rigging recipes. Now, let's get hands on!

# Controlling fingers

The human hand is a pretty complex device. The range of actions it allows us to accomplish is pretty unique: we can make very subtle and delicate movements, necessary to create a piece of art, prepare food, write, build things, play instruments, and so on; we can also make broader movements to help us in our locomotion, fight, play sports, and even express our feelings through our hand movements. Our fingers play a huge part in what we can do with our hands.

Due to its innate complexity, with lots of joints and possible combinations of their use, our ideal rig should offer some general controllers together with the ability to fine-tune the results.

## How to do it...

1.  Open the file `005-Fingers.blend`. It has a hand mesh with some basic bones for deformation, ready for us to work on its constraints.

    You'll see a few chains of bones to deform this mesh: one for the hand and one for each finger. Pay attention to their orientation: the default rotation of joints the bone's local X axis. Since this is a left hand, all bones have the `.L` suffix at the end of their names. Refer to *Chapter 1, Get Rigging* if you have any doubts about how to define these orientations. The following screenshot shows this basic setup:

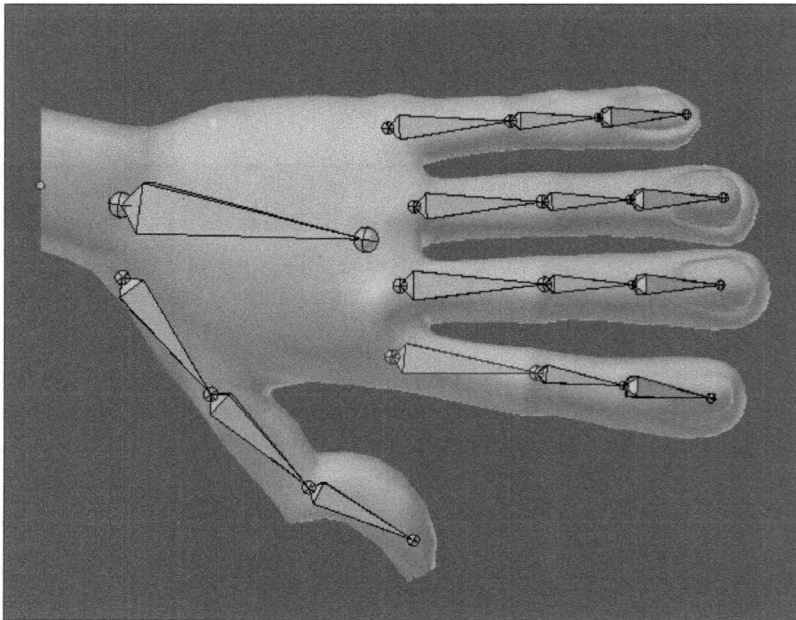

The bones already deform the mesh, so you can rotate them as you wish. The issue that arises is: if our character has five fingers, with three bones each, we'll have to pose 15 bones in order to animate only the fingers! That's neither practical, nor quick to animate. We need a quicker solution to easily pose each finger.

2. Enter into the armature's Edit Mode and create five more bones above each finger and roughly of the same size, pointing in the same direction as them. These will be our main controllers for each finger, and should be children of the D_Hand.L bone. Name them Thumb.L, Index.L, Middle.L, Ring.R, and Pinky.L. Select all these five bones and disable their **Deform** property after pressing *Shift + W*. Refer to the next screenshot to see the bones that we've created from the top and side views:

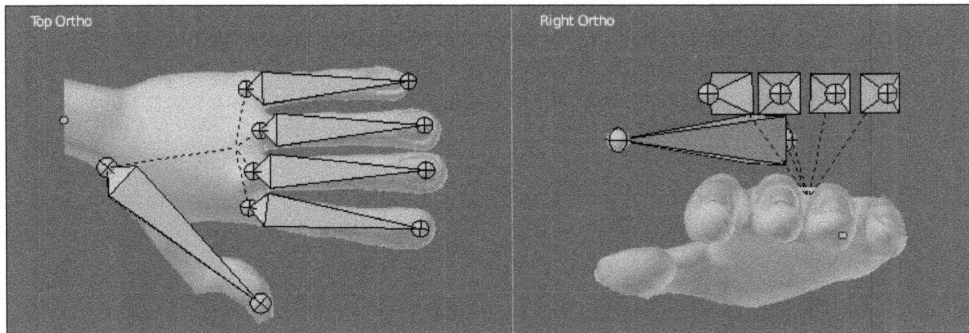

3. Enter into the armature's Pose Mode (*Ctrl + Tab*), select the Pinky.L bone, hold *Shift*, select the D_Pinky1.L bone, press *Ctrl + Shift + C*, and pick the **Copy Rotation** constraint. Under the **Bone Constraints** tab in the Properties window for the D_Pinky1.L bone, you'll see the constraint that we've just created. Disable the **Y** axis box (since fingers don't rotate on this axis), enable **Offset**, and change both **Space** combos to **Local Space**, as seen in the following screenshot:

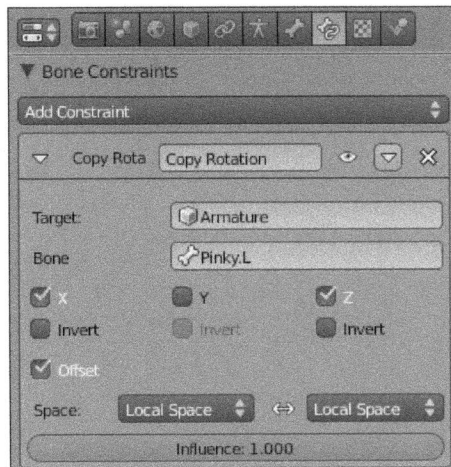

4. Repeat step 3 to add the **Copy Rotation** constraint to the D_Pinky2.L and D_Pinky3.L bones, but instead of disabling only the **Y** axis box, disable both **Y** and **Z**. This is because these joints only rotate on their local X axis.

5. The last step for this finger is adding another constraint to its first bone. Select the Pinky.L bone, hold *Shift*, select the D_Pinky1.L, press *Ctrl + Shift + C*, and choose the **Copy Location** constraint. Locate this constraint under the **Bone Constraints** tab in the Properties window and change both **Space** selectors to **Local Space**.

> The **Copy Location** constraint is necessary because our fingers don't just rotate from a fixed point. Our hand is a somewhat flexible device, so the base of our fingers can move to better adapt to the surface it's touching, or holding. By using the **Copy Location** constraint, you can **subtly** move the controller in order to get a nicer deformation on the character's hand.

6. To improve our controller, select the Pinky.L bone and disable its rotation on the **Y** axis and all scaling fields on the Properties panel (*N*) in the 3D view, as seen in the next screenshot:

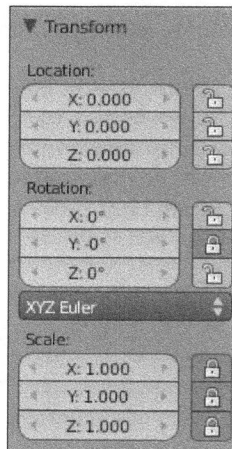

7. Repeat steps 3 to 6 to create the remaining fingers, and you'll be able to control them with only one controller for each, as you can see in the next screenshot:

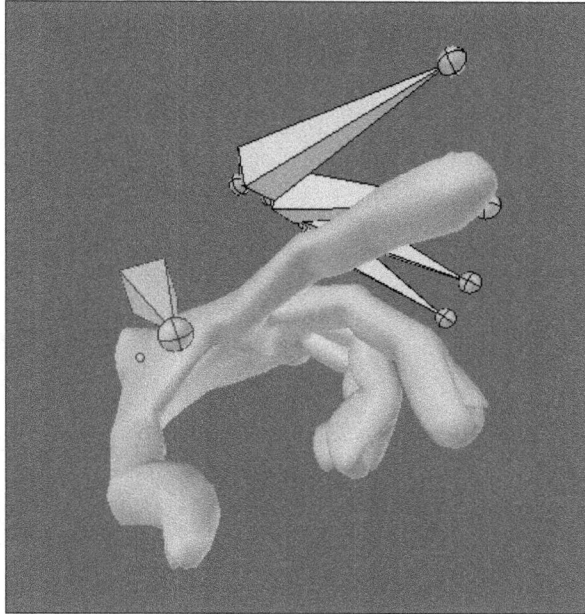

But wait, there's more!

These general finger controllers allow us to quickly pose the fingers in their closed and open states, but these are not the only possible positions for the fingers. You should be able, for instance, to bend only one joint of the fingers.

Since we've enabled the **Offset** option on each **Copy Rotation** constraint, we can build our custom finger pose on top of the transformation produced by the controller. In order to do this, simply select the desired bone and rotate it until you get what you want.

The deformation bones are inside the mesh, so we need to be able to see them properly without relying on the **X-Ray** property. In the provided file, there is a ready-to-use shape named `Fingers`, and you should assign it to each finger bone, from the **Bone** tab in the Properties window, on the **Custom Shape** field.

Once you assign this shape to all finger bones, you can disable the **X-Ray** property of the armature and make custom poses, as seen in the next screenshot:

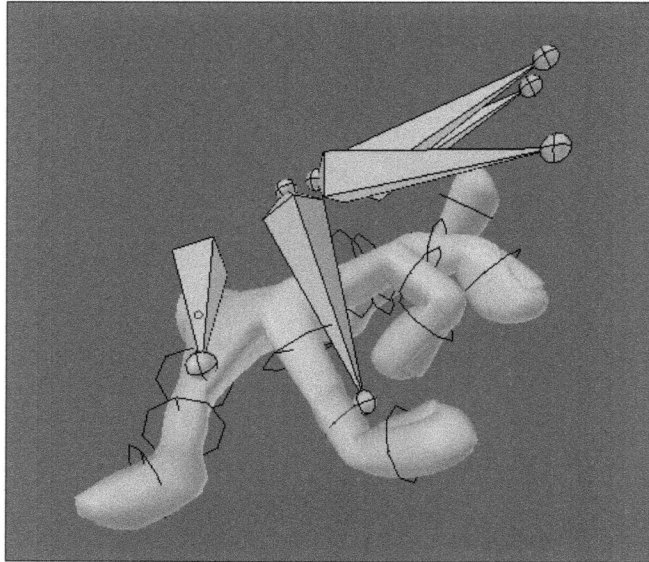

You can view the final result of this recipe in the file `005-Fingers-complete.blend` for your reference.

## How it works...

By assigning a **Copy Rotation** constraint to a separate controller, you can make the basic (and often used) poses for your character's fingers. The use of the **Offset** property on each constraint enables you to further refine each finger's pose on top of the transformation created by the constraints.

## There's more...

Since the finger bones are in a FK chain, if you want a cartoony stretching effect, you can use the same principles applied to the FK arms, legs, and torso covered in different recipes in this book.

## See also

Chapter 1: *Customizing shapes and colors for your bones*

Chapter 1: *Defining  good orientations for your bones*

# Creating IK legs with a three-pivot foot

Legs are often controlled with an **Inverse Kinematics** constraint. Why? Because of the very nature of the IK constraint, which controls a chain by the position of its tip, rather than by its root. Our character's legs position will often be controlled by where its feet are in relation to the ground. This is a somewhat general rule: whenever a limb (arm or leg) has its control point dictated by its tip (hand or foot), you should use an IK constraint.

That's the case we'll find very often for legs, so the feet remain still on the ground while your character moves. The big issue is that there's more than one pivot point to the foot movement: your character can stand over its ankle, ball of the foot, or the tip of its toes. We need an easy way to control the leg regardless of what pivot point is used.

> When the chain's control point resides on its root (such as the shoulders or hips), FK can be a good solution to achieve nice and fluid motion arcs.

## How to do it...

1.  Open the file `005-IK-Leg.blend`. It has a leg mesh with a deformation bone chain already set up for our work, as you can see in the next screenshot:

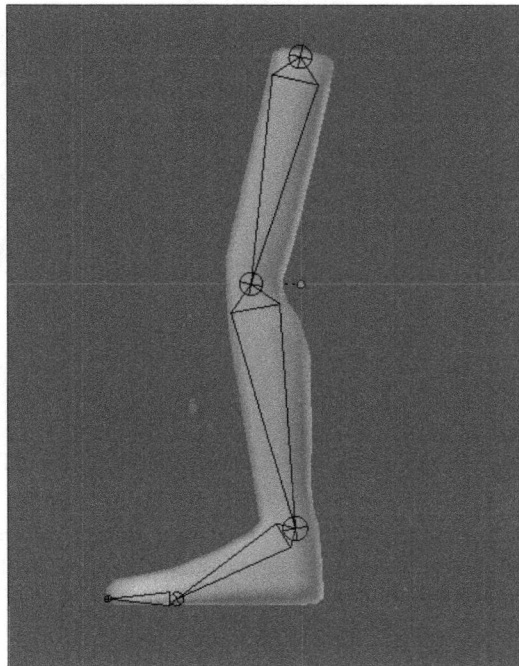

By default, all bone chains act in Forward Kinematics mode. If you rotate the D_Thigh.L bone, the whole leg will follow, as you would expect from an FK chain.

2. To create the IK motion, let's create another bone chain to drive our deformation ones. In the armature's Edit Mode, select the D_LowerLeg.L bone, hold *Shift*, select the D_Thigh bone and duplicate them using *Shift + D.* Press *Esc* so the duplicates remain in the same place.

3. Change to the B-Bone display mode in the **Object Data** tab under the Properties window and press *Ctrl + Alt + S* to change these bones' thickness so you can tell them apart from the deformation bones. Disable their **Deform** property (*Shift + W*) and rename them to IK_Thigh.L and IK_LowerLeg.

4. Select the IK_Thigh.L bone, hold *Shift*, select the D_Thigh.L bone, press *Ctrl + Shift + C* and select the **Copy Rotation** constraint. Repeat the same for the lower leg bones, then move (*M*) both D_LowerLeg.L and D_Thigh.L to a disabled armature layer in order to remove the visual clutter, since we won't touch them anymore.

5. Go back to the Octahedral bone display mode, select the tip of IK_LowerLeg.L, and extrude (*E*) it to the back of the foot. Name it T_Leg.L and clear its parent relationship (*Alt + P*). We need this because this bone will drive the leg movement, acting as the IK target. The IK target cannot have a parent-child relationship with the constrained bone chain. The next screenshot shows the created target:

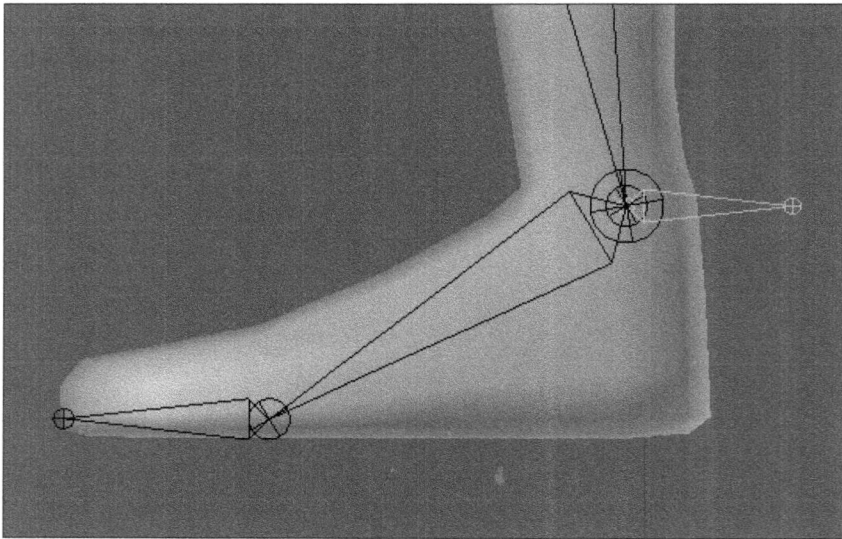

> The prefix T stands for Target bone. Next we'll see another one: M is for Mechanism bones, which shouldn't be touched by the animator; and P stands for Pole target for IK constrained chains.

6.  Go back to Pose Mode, select the `T_Leg.L` bone, hold *Shift*, select the `IK_LowerLeg.L` bone, and press *Shift + I* to add an IK constraint. Try moving the `T_Leg.L` bone around to see the IK constraint in action. Under the **Bone Constraints** tab, in the Properties window, change the **Chain Length** slider to 2, since we need the constraint to affect only the lower and upper leg bones.

    After moving the target bone, you'll see that the foot rotates too, since it's a child of the `D_LowerLeg.L` bone. We want it to remain still, rotating just when **we** want it to.

7.  Select the `D_Foot.L` bone, and disable its **Inherit Rotation** property in the Properties window, under the **Bone** tab. In the 3D view, select the `T_Leg.L` bone, hold *Shift*, select the `D_Foot.L` bone, press *Ctrl + Shift + C*, and pick the **Child Of** constraint. Things will look messy, but don't panic: go to the **Bone Constraints** tab under the Properties window and click on the **Set Inverse** button in the constraint section. Now the foot rotation will follow the target bone instead of inheriting the lower leg properties, as you can see in the next screenshot:

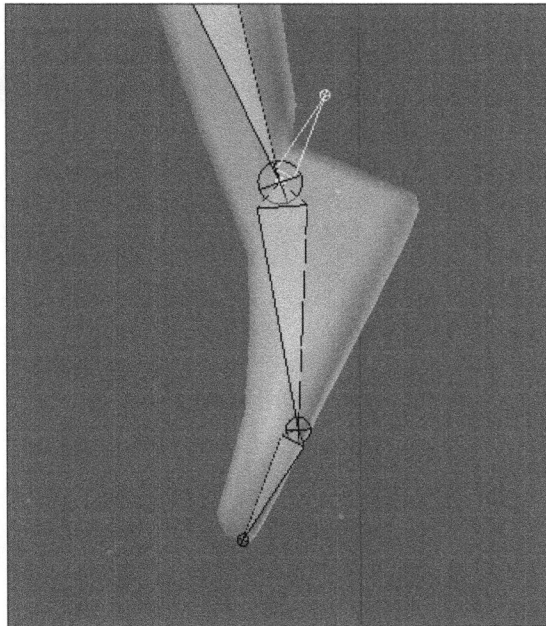

8. Now we need to set up three bones to act as pivots for the foot rotation. Go back to the armature's Edit Mode and add three bones, named M_Pivot1.L, M_Pivot2.L, and M_Pivot3.L, located at the ankle, ball of the foot, and tips of the toes, respectively, as you can see in the next screenshot:

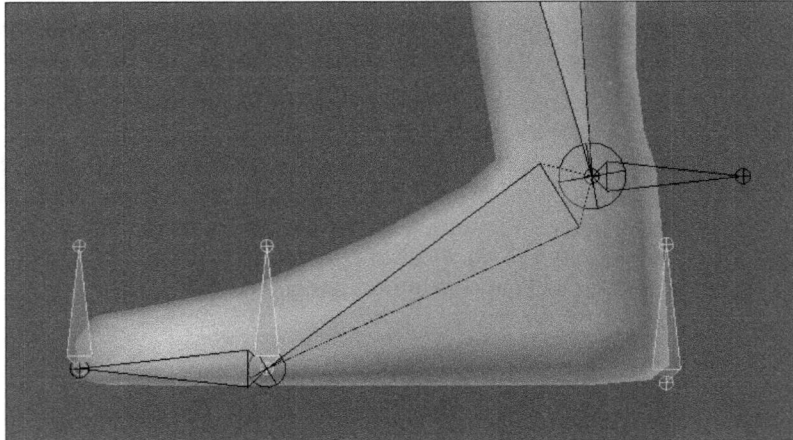

9. Still in Edit Mode, select the T_Leg.L bone, hold *Shift*, select the M_Pivot2.L bone, press *Ctrl + P*, and choose **Keep Offset** to make the target bone children of the second pivot. Repeat this process, now making the ankle pivot parent of the tip of the foot one (M_Pivot3.L); and the M_Pivot3.L parent of M_Pivot2.L.

This chain of parent relationships will result in the following: if you go back to Pose Mode, rotating the M_Pivot1.L bone will make the foot and leg rotate around the ankle; rotating the M_Pivot2.L bone will rotate them around the ball; and rotating the M_Pivot3.L bone will rotate them around the tip of the toes, as shown in the next screenshot:

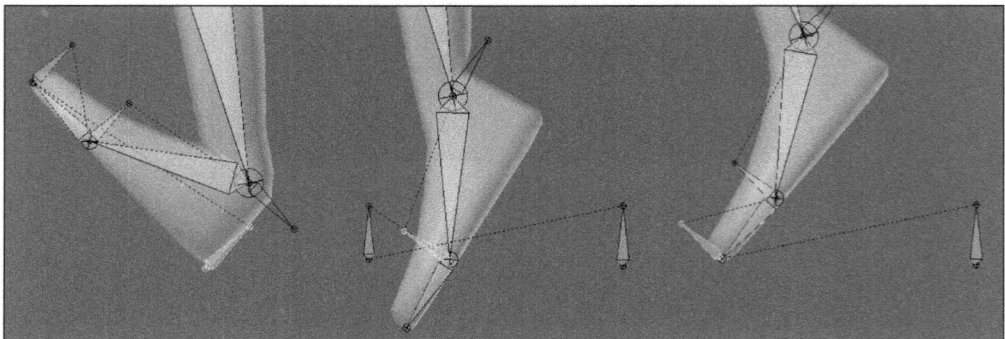

Now we just need a way to control these three pivots with only one bone, and you probably noticed that when we rotate the second pivot, the toes should have remained planted on the ground. Lets do that now.

Since this is a somewhat complex transformation requiring different rotations on different bones, we'll use an **Action** constraint. This is very useful for when we have definite yet complex transformations, because we can "record" that transformation in a separate **Action**.

10. Open a DopeSheet window, making sure the **Action Editor** type is selected. Click on **New** to add a new **Action**, and name it FootRoll. In the first frame of this action, select all three pivot bones plus the D_Toes.L bone and insert a keyframe (*I*) to define their rest rotation states.

11. Go up ten frames (*Up Arrow*), select the M_Pivot2.L bone, rotate it 60 degrees left in side view (*Numpad 3*), holding *Ctrl* for precision, and press *I* to set a new keyframe for its rotation. Select the D_Toes.L bone and rotate it up the same 60 degrees, so it goes back to its rest position, as seen in the following screenshot:

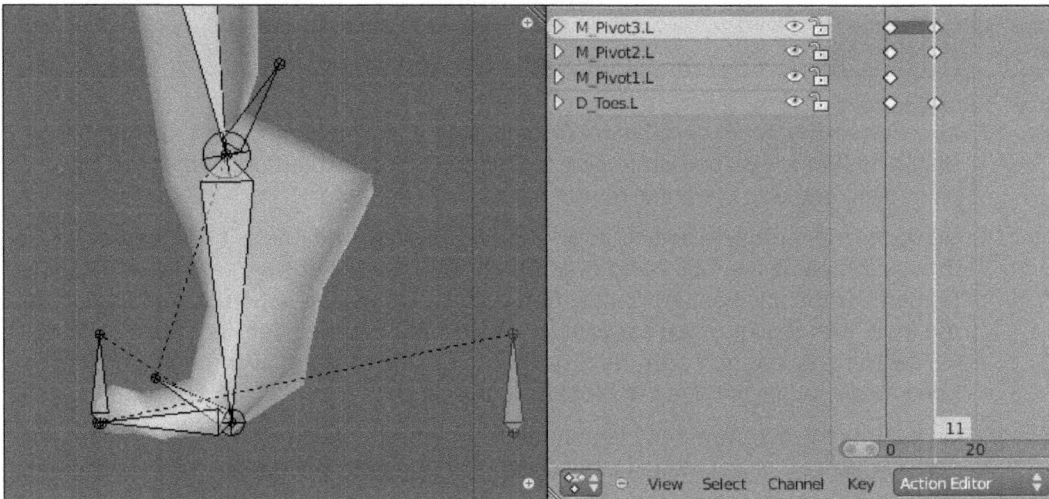

12. Select the `M_Pivot3.L` bone and set a keyframe for its rotation too. Go up further 10 frames, rotate the `M_Pivot3.L` bone 80 degrees to the left and insert a new keyframe for it. Rotate both the `M_Pivot2.L` and the `D_Toes.L` bones 60 degrees back to their original positions, so you get the foot up on its toes, as seen in the next screenshot:

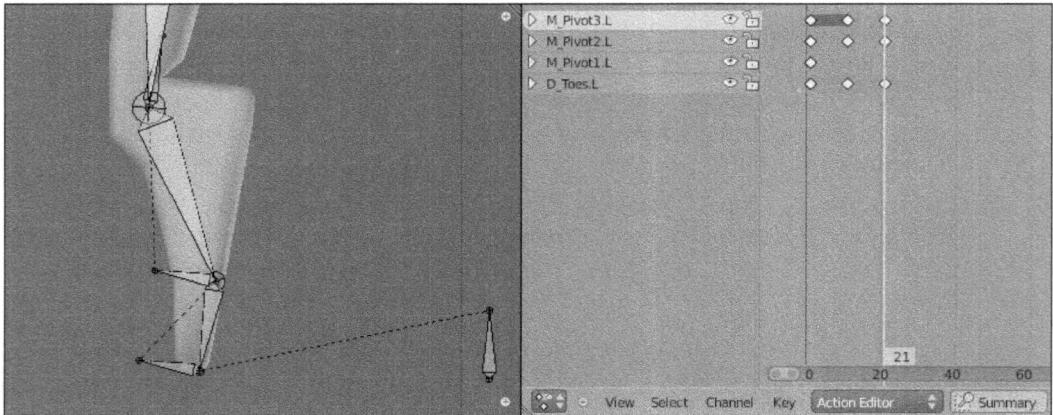

13. Almost there! Now, go up 10 more frames, select the keyframes from the first frame, duplicate (*Shift + D*), and drag them to frame 31. We're creating another resting position to precede the ankle rotation.

14. Go up 10 more frames, select the `M_Pivot1.L` bone and rotate it 45 degrees to the right, making the foot stand over the ankle. Set another keyframe for its rotation. Remember the position keyframes: from 1 to 21 we get the action of standing up on the toes, with the intermediate position of standing over the ball first; from 31 to 41 we get the final rotation over the `M_Pivot1.L` bone to stand over the ankle. We'll need these values to set up the foot roll controller.

15. Go back to the first frame of the animation, enter into the armature's Edit Mode, and add a new bone near the ankle, but pointing in the opposite direction as the foot. This will act as our controller. Name it `FootRoll.L` and go back to Pose Mode.

16. With the `FootRoll.L` bone still selected, hold *Shift*, select the `M_Pivot1.L` bone, press *Ctrl + Shift + C*, and choose the **Action** constraint. In the Properties window, under the **Bone Constraints** tab, choose **FootRoll** under the **Action** field; **Rotation X** under **Transform Channel**; **Start: 1, End: 21** in **Action Length**; **Min: 0, Max: 40** in **Target Range**; and finally, **Local Space** in **Convert**. Repeat this process for the `M_Pivot2.L`, `M_Pivot3.L`, and `D_Toes.L` bones.

If you rotate the controller up, you'll see our recorded action taking place, and the foot will stand on its toes nicely. We just need another constraint on the ankle bone, for the opposite action.

17. Select the `FootRoll.L` bone, hold *Shift*, select the `M_Pivot1.L` bone, press *Ctrl + Shift + C*, and choose the **Action** constraint. In this constraint panel, choose **FootRoll** under the **Action** field; **Rotation X** under **Transform Channel**; **Start: 31, End: 41** in **Action Length**; **Min: 0, Max: -60** in **Target Range**; and finally, **Local Space** in **Convert**. The next screenshot shows the values for both **Action** constraints:

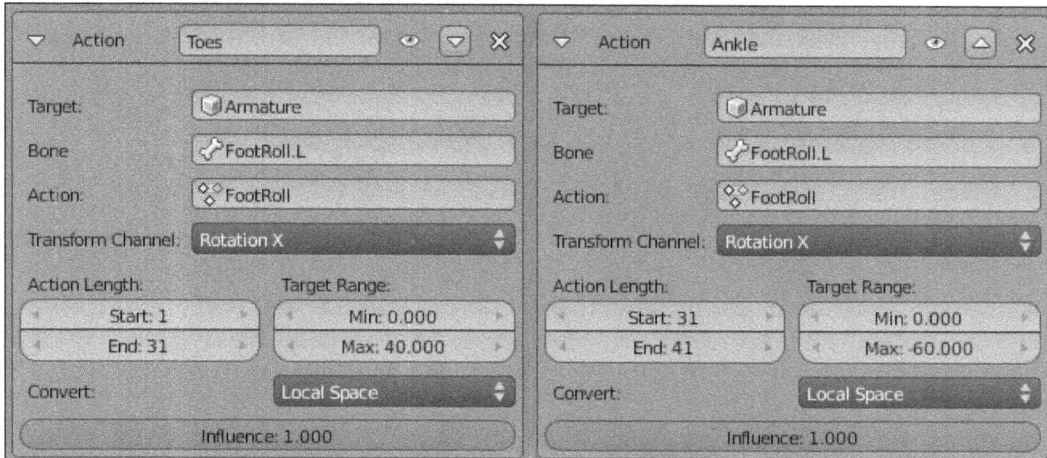

| Action | Toes | | Action | Ankle | |
|---|---|---|---|---|---|
| Target: | Armature | | Target: | Armature | |
| Bone | FootRoll.L | | Bone | FootRoll.L | |
| Action: | FootRoll | | Action: | FootRoll | |
| Transform Channel: | Rotation X | | Transform Channel: | Rotation X | |
| Action Length: | Target Range: | | Action Length: | Target Range: | |
| Start: 1 | Min: 0.000 | | Start: 31 | Min: 0.000 | |
| End: 31 | Max: 40.000 | | End: 41 | Max: -60.000 | |
| Convert: | Local Space | | Convert: | Local Space | |
| Influence: 1.000 | | | Influence: 1.000 | | |

> It's a good practice to give names to your constraints, so that you can easily remember what they are up to. That's also valid for modifiers: It's not uncommon to have various constraints and modifiers in your mesh and bones. In the previous screenshot we have two very similar constraints, and their names help us understand what they do.

To finish our leg rig we need only two more bones: the main foot controller and the IK pole, to control the direction of the knee bending. Let's add them.

18. Go back into the armature's Edit Mode and add a bone below the foot of roughly the same size of it, having its base near the ankle and tip near the toes. Name it `Foot.L`. Make it a parent of both `FootRoll.L` and `M_Pivot1.L`.

19. Still in Edit Mode and in side view (*Numpad 3*), select the knee joint and position the cursor there through (*Shift + S*) **| Cursor to Selected**. Add a new small bone there and drag it to the left, so it stays on the front of the leg. Name it `P_Leg.L` and make it a child of the `Foot.L` bone.

20. Back in Pose Mode, select the `IK_LowerLeg.L` bone and go to its **Bone Constraints** tab under the Properties window. In the IK constraint attached to it, define **Armature** as the value for the **Pole Target** field and `P_Leg.L` in the **Bone** field which will appear. The leg will bend to the side, which is definitely not what we want. To correct this, set the **Pole Angle** slider to 90 degrees.

> Remember to disable the **Deform** property (*Shift + W*) of all bones except those with the D prefix!

That's it! Now you can move all other bones to a disabled armature layer (*M*) and keep only the `Foot.L`, `FootRoll.L`, and `P_Leg.L` ones visible, since they're the only bones needed to control the leg. It's also a good idea to define custom shapes to them. The following screenshot shows the finished leg set up with only those three bones visible:

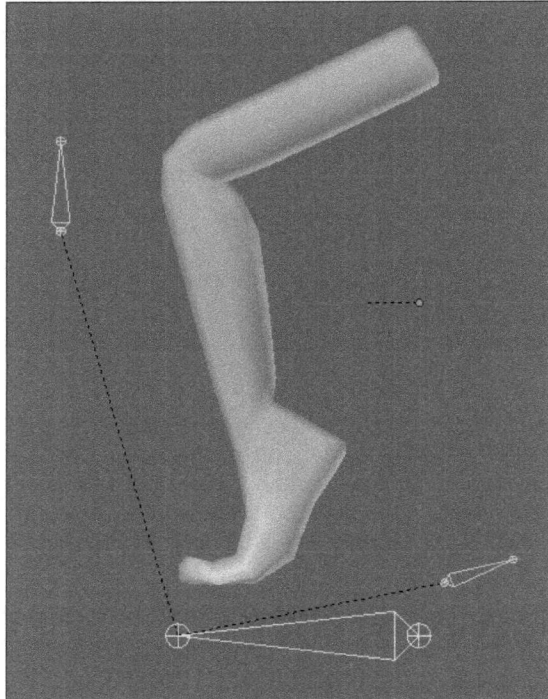

If you want to compare your results, there is a file with this complete recipe called `005-Leg-complete.blend`.

## How it works...

By using three helper bones to act as the foot pivots and a recorded action of the foot movement, we can use a single controller to move an IK leg based on three different points. By using a careful set of parent-children relationships, we can reduce the number of controllers of the leg to just three. It can be a bit tricky to set up, but it gives the animator a very easy and flexible rig to use.

## There's more...

IK arms work in a similar but much simpler way, since you don't need to create pivots nor actions: just create a bone to act as the hand controller, used as a target bone for the IK chain and to drive the rotation of the hand with a **Copy Rotation** constraint; and another bone to act as the pole target. That's all!

## See also

*Chapter 5: Stretch those limbs!*

# Stretch those limbs!

If you want to build a cartoon character rig, it's a good idea to enable it to squash and stretch. Even if your character is not cartoony, some animated shots may require a little stretching in order to achieve more convincing and clear poses. Depending on your project and schedule, it can be a good idea to enable this feature in all of your rigs.

## How to do it...

1.  Open the file `005-Stretch.blend`. It has an IK leg setup similar to the result of the previous recipe. Move the `Foot.L` bone around and see how it works. We need the leg to stretch to the position of the foot controller.

2.  Select the `IK_Thigh.L` bone and go to the **Bone** tab, under the Properties window. You'll see a panel called **Inverse Kinematics**. Change the **Stretch** field value to `0.1`. Do the same for the `IK_LowerLeg.L` bone.

    If you move the foot controller, you'll see that IK chain bones change their size, but the leg mesh doesn't follow. It happens because we have two chains: one for deforming the mesh and another for the IK movement. The deformation chains only have **Copy Rotation** constraints, so it won't follow the size of the IK chain bones.

You can see the results in the following screenshot:

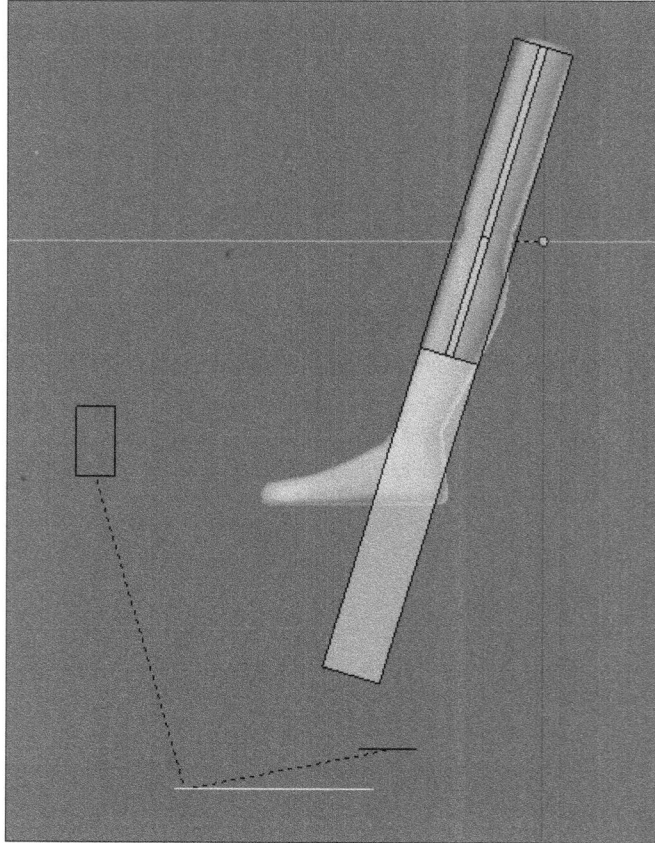

> If we were using only one chain to both deform and have the IK constraint, we would have a bigger problem: the stretching would not retain the mesh volume. This is one reason why we need separate bone chains. We need one to give the IK motion, while the other follows it maintaining its volume.

3. Select the Foot.L controller and reset its position (*Alt + G*) and rotation (*Alt + R*) if you have it anywhere else than its rest position. Go to the wireframe (*Z*) visualization mode in the 3D view, so you can view both chains of bones clearer.

To stretch our mesh we're going to keep the **Copy Rotation** constraints applied on the deform chain and add another one: the **Stretch To** constraint.

4. Select the IK_Thigh.L bone, hold *Shift*, select the D_Thigh.L bone, press (*Ctrl + Shift + C*), and choose the **Stretch To** constraint.

5. Things will seem very wrong and messy, but don't panic. Go to the Properties window, under the **Bone Constraints** tab for the D_Thigh.L bone, change the **Head/Tail** field value to 1, and click on the **Reset** button in the **Stretch To** constraint panel.

6. Repeat steps 4 and 5 for the D_LowerLeg.L bone.

7. Now, select both D_LowerLeg.L and D_Thigh.L bones and move (*M*) them to a disabled armature layer. Move the Foot.L controller around and you'll have a good stretchy IK leg. The next screenshot shows the result with the IK chain hidden for clarity:

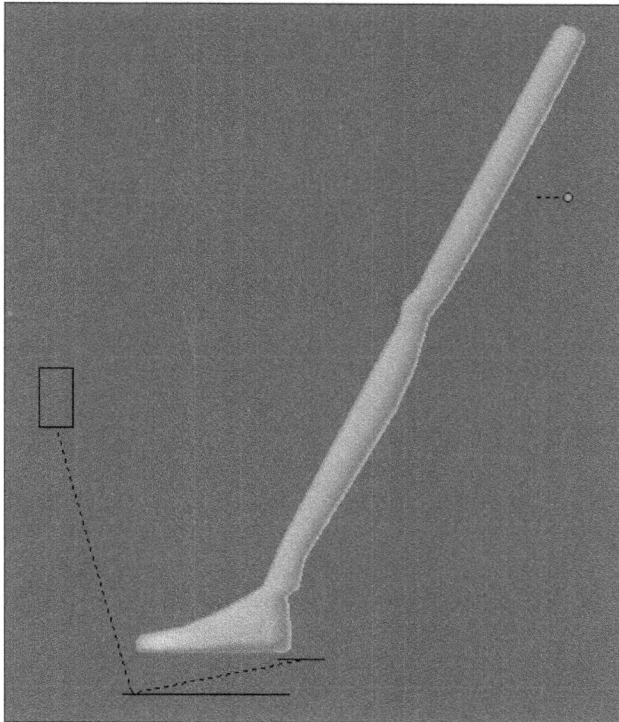

A good thing about this setup is the fact that you are able to adjust the amount of stretching in each segment of the limb. You can, for instance, select the IK_Thigh.L bone and scale it (*S*) up and down to achieve the desired amount of stretching and squashing.

8. This file has some ready-to-use shapes for the leg IK bones called SHAPE_Legs. Select the IK_Thigh.L bone, go to the Properties window, in the **Bone** tab and set the **Custom Shape** value in the **Display** panel to SHAPE_Legs.

9. Repeat step 8 for the IK_LowerLeg.L bone. After that, scaling up and down both bones gives you a flexible stretching setup, as you can see in the next screenshot:

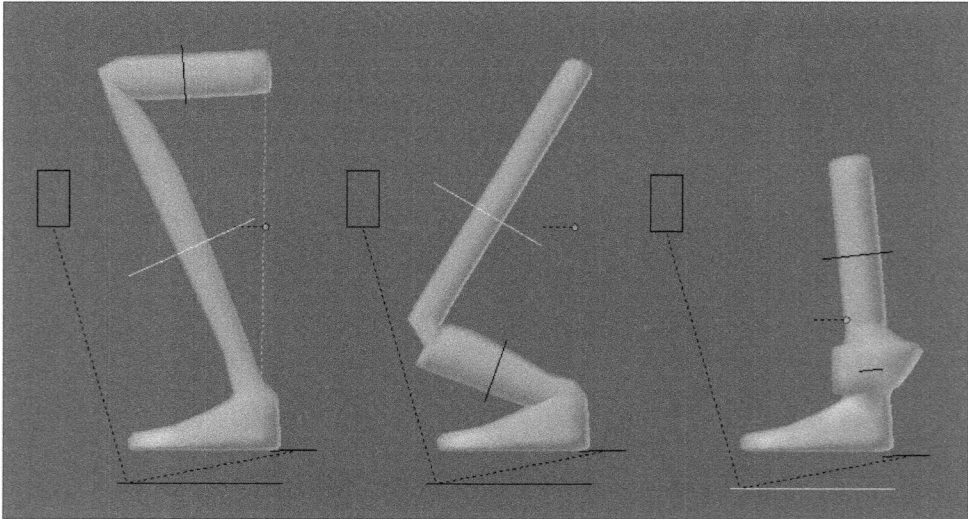

This process of adding **Stretch To** constraints to the leg bones can also be applied to IK arms and FK setups. Refer to the file 005-Stretch-complete.blend to the see the complete recipe for your reference.

## How it works...

By using separate bone chains for deformation and control, along with the **Stretch To** and **Copy Rotation** constraints applied on the deformation bones, you can make your character squash and stretch its limbs easily by scaling the controller bones.

## There's more...

And what if you want to turn the ability to squash and stretch on and off? Thanks to the new "everything can be animated" paradigm in Blender 2.5, it's just a matter of creating a driver to control the influence of the **Stretch** property on the IK chain:

1. Open the file 005-Stretch-toggle.blend, which has the result of this recipe with a bone to act as the driver.

2. Select the IK_LowerLeg.L bone, go to its **Bone** tab in the Properties window, right-click on the **Stretch** slider, and choose **Add Driver**, as shown in the next screenshot:

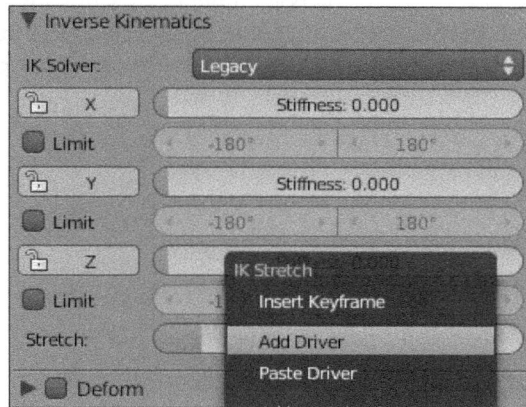

3. Go to a Graph Editor window in the Drivers mode and click on the name of the driver you've just created: IK Stretch (IK_LowerLeg.L). On the **Properties** tab (*N*), choose **Armature/LegStretch.L** in the **Ob/Bone** fields and check the **Local Space** box.

4. Finish by entering var*.1 (without quotes) in the **Expr** field. This is because a value of 1 for the stretch property is too much. The next screenshot shows the driver values:

5. To replicate the driver to the `IK_Thigh.L` bone, go to the **Bone** tab on the Properties window for the `IK_LowerLeg.L` bone, where you've created the first driver.

6. Right-click on the purple slider (the color indicates it's driven) and choose **Copy Driver**. Then select the `IK_Thigh.L` bone, right-click on the **Stretch** slider, choose **Paste**, and you're done! The file `005-Stretch-Toggle-complete.blend` has this complete setup.

## See also

*Chapter 5: Creating IK legs with a three-pivot foot*

*Chapter 1: Making an IK-FK switcher*

*Chapter 1: Customizing shapes and colors for your bones*

*Chapter 2: How to create a stretchy spine*

# Setting up the shoulders

When the animator is posing a character's arm (specially when using FK), it's often required to have two opposite features for their shoulder: with or without rotation inheritance from the torso. This is also called a "hinged" shoulder, when it doesn't inherit the rotation.

The "hinged" shoulder technique is very useful for enabling the animator to rotate the character's torso and have its arms still on the same direction. This affords similar independence to the arms from the torso as found in IK setups, while still allowing the animator to work in FK mode to have a finer control over the animation arcs.

## How to do it...

1. Open the file `005-Shoulders.blend`. It has our character model with an FK setup for his arms, ready for our work. We have custom shapes applied to the bones and a ready to use UI, with two bones (one to drive each shoulder) and an unselectable mesh in wire display mode to help us view the controller.

   As the shoulder bones are parented to the **Rib** controller in the default FK mode, if you rotate any of the torso bones they will follow the transformation, as you can see in the next screenshot:

That's fine for some situations when animating your character, but we need to give the animator the control over whether or not the shoulders should follow the body rotation.

In Blender, all bones have the properties **Inherit Rotation** and **Inherit Scale**, which are located on the **Bone** tab, under the Properties window, as we can see in the next screenshot for the Shoulder.L bone:

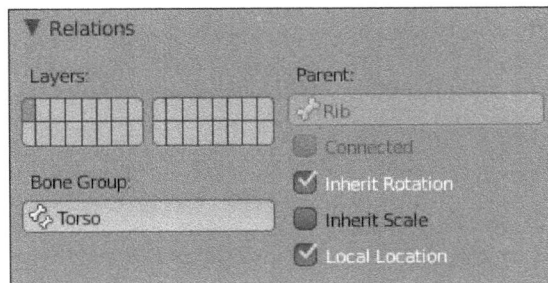

You can see that the **Inherit Scale** property is already disabled, so you can scale the character's spine without affecting the arms' size. The **Inherit Rotation** is checked but, different from the previous recipes, we don't have a slider value to drive. Is there a way to drive the on or off state of a box? Yes!

2. Select the `Shoulder.L` bone, right-click on the **Inherit Rotation** box in the Properties window and choose **Add Driver**, like you would do for a slider. The field will acquire a purple hue, which indicates that it has a driver attached to it.

3. Open a Graph Editor, selecting the Drivers mode in the window header. Click on the name of the driver that you've just created in the left panel: **Inherit Rotation (Shoulder.L)**.

4. In the Properties tab (*N*), under the **Driver** section, set the **Ob/Bone** field values as `Otto_Armature` and `Hinge-Arm.L`; leave the **X Location** channel and check the **Local Space** box. In the **Expr** field, above the **Add Variable** button, type just `var`. The next screenshot shows the panel setup:

5. Now, moving the `Hinge-Arm.L` bone on its **X** axis will drive the value, similar to a regular slider. That happens because Blender will read any driven value lower than 1 as False (thus, the disabled state), assigning True when the value is equal to 1.

Since there are only two possible (Boolean) values, the slider in our UI doesn't offer any intermediate situations: the shoulder is either "hinged" when the controller has its X position from 0 to .999, or it follows the torso rotation when the controller's X location is equal to or more than 1. The next screenshot shows our character with both shoulders in "hinged" mode:

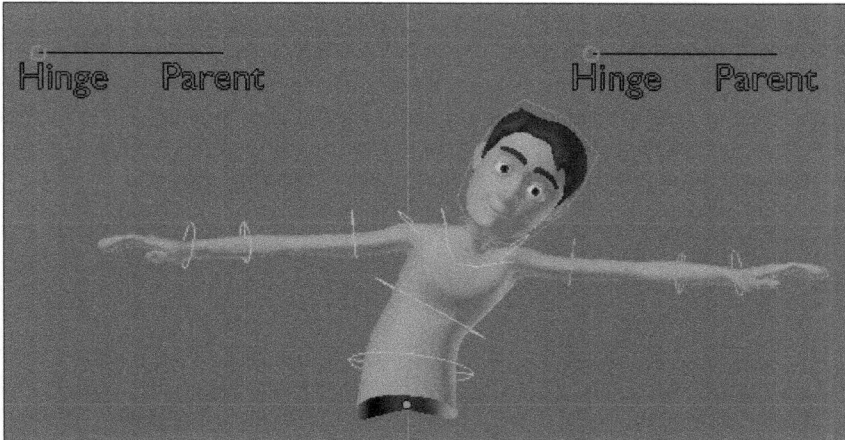

The file `005-Shoulders-complete.blend` has this finished recipe for your reference in case of any doubts.

## How it works...

By assigning a regular driver to a Boolean (True or False) field, we can control its state by having values lower than 1 interpreted as "False" and equal or higher ones as "True".

## There's more...

With this principle in mind, you can control a number of features that were impossible to animate in previous versions of Blender: from the **X-Ray** property of an armature to options inside constraint panels, you can drive everything!

## See also

*Chapter 2: Controlling the neck and head*

# Cartoon bending for arms and legs

Curves. Animators love curves. So why do we offer just those rigid limbs to our characters? Let's make them bend with a smooth curve, to help the sensation of fluidity in their movements!

## How to do it...

1. Open the file `005-Bending.blend`. It has our character model nearly completely rigged, with all the principles covered until now applied, such as IK-FK switchers and hinged shoulders. But Otto is asking for some "bendiness": that's why we also have an interface slider set up (you know, just a bone to act as a driver).

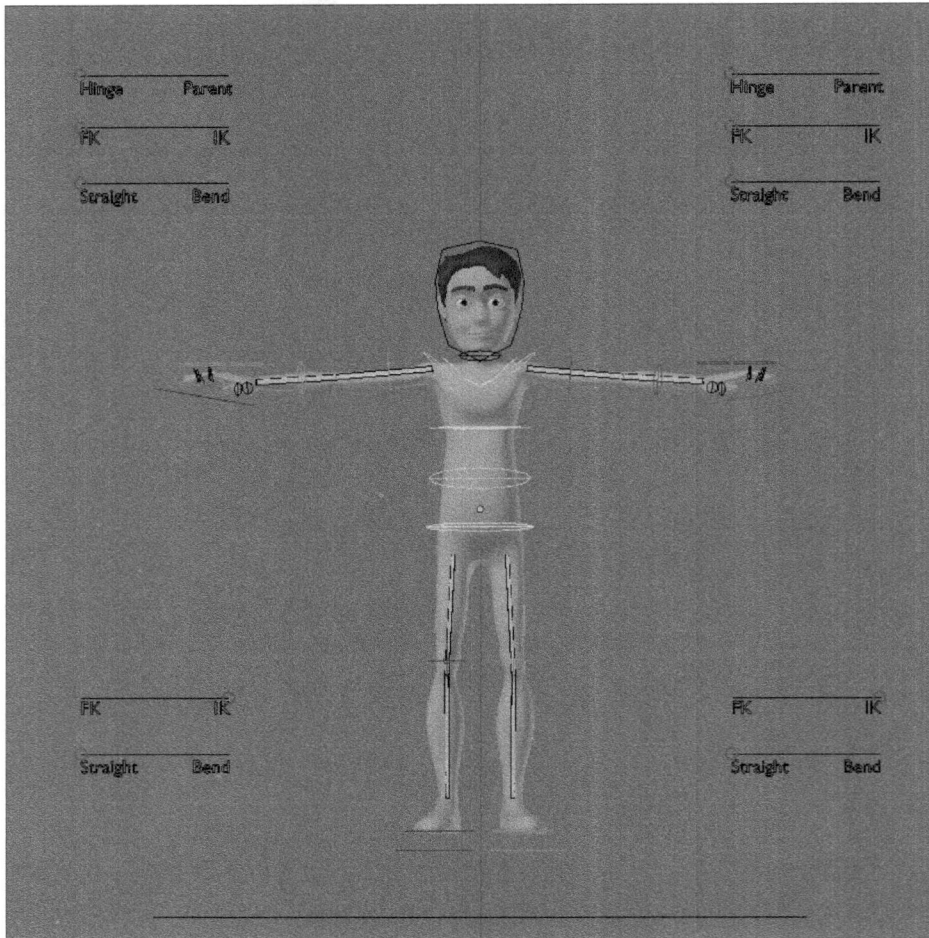

Each limb has three bone chains: one for IK, another for FK, and one for the deformation. Lets pick, for instance, the left lower arm. The three bones which compound it are `IK_LowerArm.L`, `FK_LowerArm.L`, and `D_LowerArm.L`. The deformation bones have two **Stretch To** and two **Copy Rotation** constraints each: one of each pointing to the IK bone and the others to the IK one. Their influences are driven by a bone, with opposite values: when the IK gets 1, the FK gets 0 and vice-versa.

This is good for several reasons. The obvious one is that by keeping bone chains separate we have a clear view of what each bone is doing. A less obvious benefit is that we can easily apply the bend effect without worrying about the IK and FK chains: the effect is applied to the deformation chain, so the bending occurs before the IK and FK chains.

2. Select the D_UpperArm.L bone, go the **Bone** panel in the Properties window, change its **Segments** value in the **Deform** section to 16, set its **Ease In** value to 0, right-click on the **Ease Out** value, and pick **Add Driver**. The field will get a purple hue, and the bone and its properties will look similar to the next screenshot:

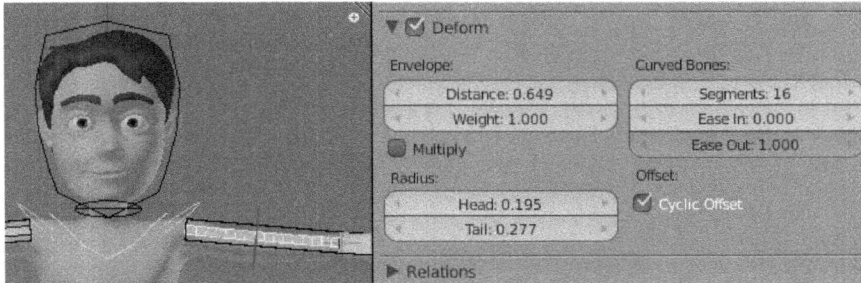

3. Now the fun part. Open a Graph Editor window, in the Drivers mode. You'll see a bunch of drivers listed on the left-hand side panel, which is normal for a nearly complete character rig. Find and click on the one called **B-Bone Ease Out (D_UpperArm.L)**.

4. At the right, on the **Drivers** sections of the Properties (*N*) panel, choose Otto_Armature and Bend_Arm.L on the **Ob/Bone** fields. Keep the **X Location** channel and enable the **Local Space** box. To finish this driver, set the value of the **Expr** field above the **Add Variable** button as var*2. The next screenshot shows the driver setup:

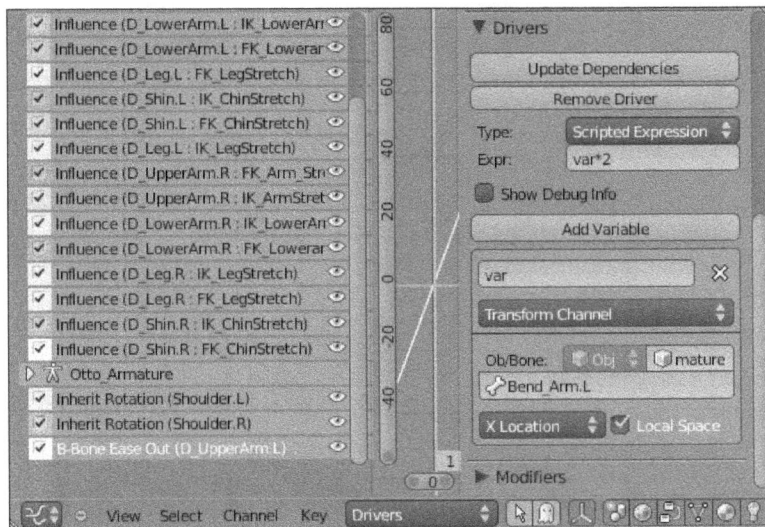

5. Back to the **Bone** panel for the `D_UpperArm.L` bone, right-click over its **Ease Out** value and pick **Copy Driver**. Select the `D_LowerArm.L` bone on the 3D View, go to the **Bone** panel, change the **Segments** field value to `16`. Now we're going to do the inverse as we did to the upper arm bone: set its **Ease Out** value to `0`, right-click on the **Ease In** field and choose **Paste Driver**.

We've inverted the settings here because we need the bend effect to occur on the elbow. The **Ease In** value controls the curve deformation on the root of the bone, while the **Ease Out** value affects the bone tip. Since the elbow is the connection between the tip of the upper arm bone and the root of the lower arm one, we need this inverted setup.

That's it! The easing values of both upper and lower arms are driven by the `Bend_Arm.L` bone. If you rotate the `FK_LowerArm.L` bone and switch the bend controller on and off, you'll get the results seen in the next screenshot in top view (*Numpad 7*):

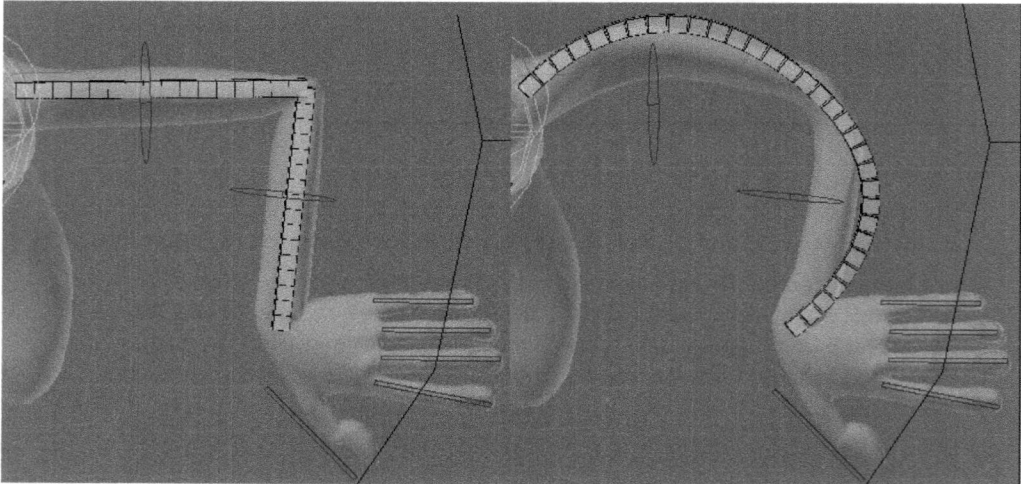

Now you can apply the same principles to the right arm and legs, binding their drivers to the `Bend_Arm.R`, `Bend_Leg.L`, and `Bend_Leg.R` bones. The file `005-Bending-complete.blend` has this setup done for all limbs, if you have any doubts. Turning off both the last armature layer, which holds the deformation bones, and the **X-Ray** property, will give you a ready-to-use setup, allowing you to achieve poses similar to the next screenshot:

## How it works...

By properly using drivers to set the **Ease In** and **Ease Out** values of bones with segments, we can easily apply the bend effect to arms or any desired bone.

## See also

*Chapter 5: Stretch those limbs!*

# Different spaces for IK hands

When using arms in Inverse Kinematics mode, the target hand controllers are disconnected from the actual chain. These controllers are often children of a "root" controller, which is the topmost level in the hierarchy of bones. This is something animators often call the "world space".

The "world space" is good for various situations, such as when the character's hands need to be held still at one point while the rest of the body moves (imagine a circus acrobat holding himself in a rope, for instance), but we often need other "spaces". For example, animators should be able to rotate the character's **Ribcage** controller and have its IK hands to follow the movement. That would be the "Ribcage space", as many others which can be required by your animation.

## How to do it...

1. Open the file 005-Spaces.blend. It has our character rig with enabled IK for both arms. Since the arms have a regular IK constraint, they are in the default "world space", with its controllers parented to the Root bone. There is a new UI slider to switch between "world" and "ribcage" spaces so that we can work on creating the controller.

2. If you go to side view (*Numpad 3*) and move the **Hips** controller to the character's front, you'll see that his hands and arms remain in place. That's okay for the legs, since we assume that they are planted on the ground, but the arms look like they are held by something. Is our character in a dungeon, with handcuffs attached to a wall?

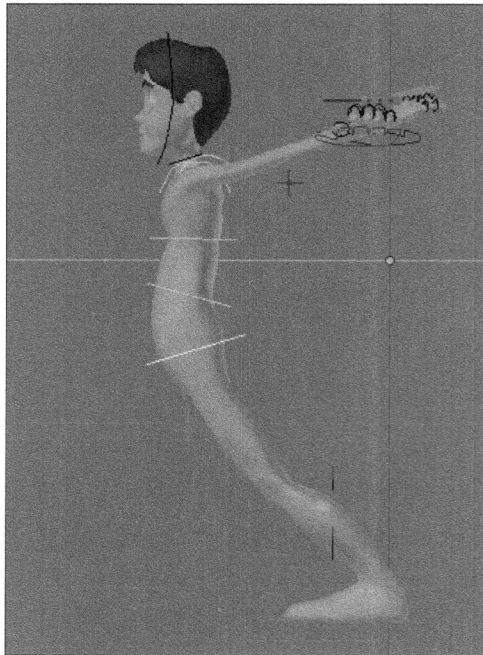

We need the arms controllers to follow the ribcage position and rotation, so the animator can make a basic pose with the character torso and then pose the arms, which will be in a more appropriate position.

3. Go back to front view (*Numpad 1*), select the **Ribcage** controller, hold *Shift* and select the Hand.L controller. Press *Ctrl + Shift + C* and pick the **Child Of** constraint. Things will look weird, but we're going to fix it now.

4. With the Hand.L bone selected, go to its **Bone Constraints** tab, under the Properties window and click on the **Set Inverse** button. Things will be back to normal. Now, right-click over the **Influence** slider and pick **Add Driver**. It will gain a purple hue.

5. Let's bind the driver to the appropriate controller now. In a Graph Editor, make sure it's in the Drivers mode, look for and click on the driver that we've just created: **Influence(Hand.L: Child Of)**.

6. In the Properties panel (*N*) on the right-hand side, under the **Drivers** section, select Otto_Armature and Space_Arm.L for the **Ob/Bone** fields. Leave the **X Location** channel untouched and check the **Local Space** option. In the **Expr** field, above the **Add Variable** button, write just var. The following screenshot shows the driver setup values:

Now, by moving the Space_Arm.L controller to the "Ribcage" position, the left hand will follow the movement of the character's torso.

You may notice that we have a hierarchy of constraints here. Since the arm is at a lower level than the shoulder controller, you may get unwanted deformations if you set its space to **Ribcage** and the **Shoulder** is in hinged mode. You should use the **Hinge** controller for the shoulders only when the IK arm is in the world space. We can fix that with a driver. First, lets see the problem.

The next screenshot shows the weird deformation when we rotate the torso with the `Hand.L` bone in the **Ribcage** space and the `Shouder.L` bone in hinged mode:

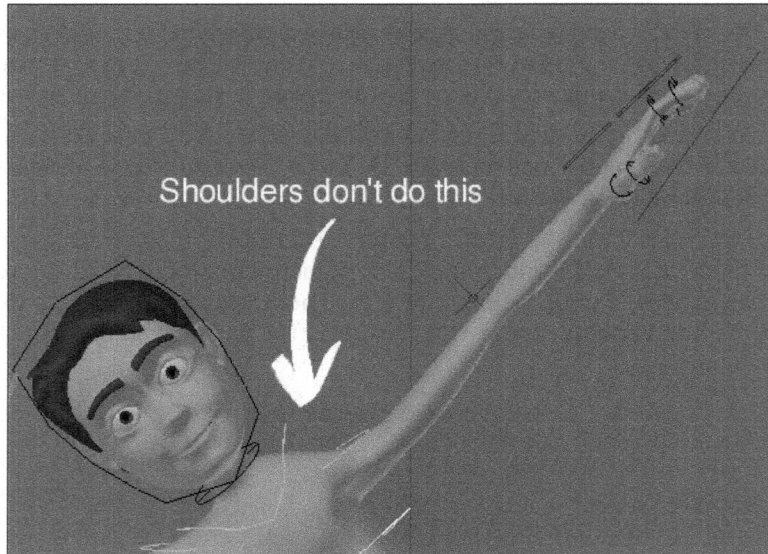

Fortunately this is very easy to do with our setup. Every controller on our UI has a **Limit Location** constraint attached to it. This constraint is to allow only the values 0 to 1 in their local **X Location**, since that is what we need for the drivers.

All we have to do is to set a driver for the **Minimum X** value in the **Hinge-Arm.L** controller. If the **Space-Arm.L** is set to 1, the **Hinge-Arm.L** must have its position locked to 1, having both **Minimum** and **Maximum X** values equal to 1. But, wait: we already have a driver set to read the **X** position of the `Space-Arm.L` bone, since it drives the **Child Of** constraint of the **Hand.L** controller. Let's copy and paste it!

7. Select the `Hand.L` bone and go to its **Bone Constraints** tab in the Properties window. Right-click on the purple **Influence** slider and select **Copy Driver**. Now select the **Hinge-Arm.L** controller, go to its **Limit Location** constraint in the Properties window, right-click on the **Minimum X** slider, and select **Paste Driver**. That's it!

Now, if you set the **Space-Arm.L** controller to **Ribcage**, you can't move the **Hinge-Arm.L** slider to the "Hinge" position. It's only allowed if you set the world space. The next screenshot shows the desired behavior with the `Hand.L` bone in the **Ribcage** space:

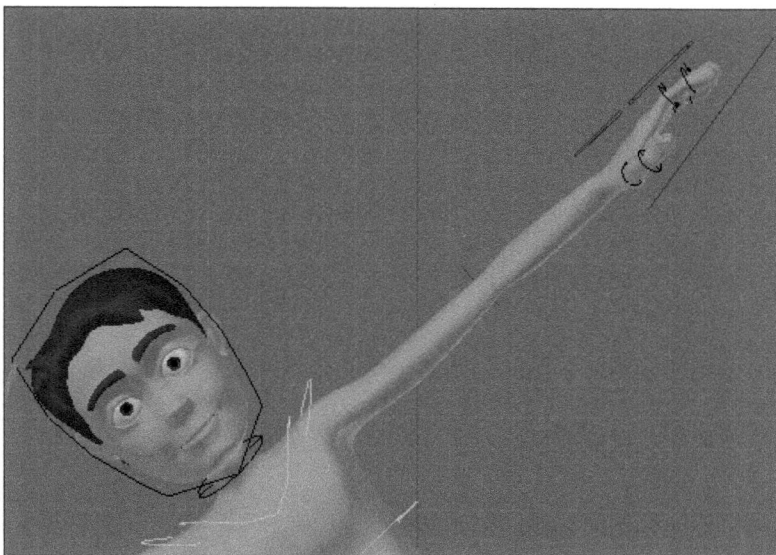

The file `005-Spaces-complete.blend` has this final setup applied to both left and right hand controllers, so you can refer to it in case of doubt.

## How it works...

By assigning a **Child Of** constraint of the IK hand controllers to the ribcage controller as target, we can change the default "space" from which the IK controllers' positions are evaluated. This gives a lot of flexibility to the animator in the way of approaching an animation scene. Because of the inherent nature of bone chains, we have to pay attention to bones between the IK controller and its target space: in this case, the shoulder controller gave us unwanted deformations when in hinged mode. A simple copy of the main driver fixes that.

## There's more...

Don't just be limited to creating a "Ribcage space"! Every animation shot is different in nature, and may require you to set various different "spaces". Imagine if your character glued its hand to its head! You should be able to move the head and affect the "glued" hand. Creating a "head" space using the principle showed in this recipe you can do that.

## See also

*Chapter 1: Making an IK-FK switcher*

*Chapter 5: Setting up the shoulders*

# 6

# Blending with the Animation Workflow

In this chapter, we will cover the following topics:

- ▶ Animating in layers
- ▶ Changing between IK and FK in a shot
- ▶ Grasping and throwing objects
- ▶ Silhouette and mirrored rendering
- ▶ Tracking animation arcs
- ▶ Using video for background reference
- ▶ Working with linked assets and characters
- ▶ Non-linear animation

## Introduction

Even the shortest piece of animation may require a lot of time to be made. For the uninitiated, producing 60 seconds of animation may sound like an easy task, but you can spend months until these few seconds are ready to hit the screen. Since animation is a very time consuming activity, having a streamlined workflow is a must.

You have to be organized in order to make things quicker and be able to fix errors easily. Imagine yourself having to throw away a week of work because things got so confusing in your scene that you found it easier to restart from scratch rather than try and fix it. That may sound acceptable if you're only making personal studies, but in a professional scenario with tight deadlines you're simply not allowed this luxury.

From this chapter on, we'll see some practices to help you stay organized, productive, and approach several kinds of animated shots. Of course, this is not a "one size fits all" set of recipes. There are various ways of bringing your characters to life, and different professionals often have unique workflows that work best for them, so be free to adapt and use what you feel its best for your productions.

# Animating in layers

If you're animating a character for the first time, you'll likely start by moving several bones and posing your character in the timeline until you're happy with the movements. That's quite similar to the "straight ahead" method in traditional 2D animation: this method is where you draw one frame after the other until you complete your animation, and it can enable you to achieve very expressive and fluid movements.

There's nothing "wrong" with that approach, but you may find yourself in trouble if you need to make changes to your scene after you have made all the poses. A good way to avoid such trouble and get a quicker feel of what your animation will look like before it's finished is working in "layers". If we keep the analogy of the traditional principles of animation, this method is more related to the "pose to pose" approach, where you define the key poses first, and then add the intermediate drawings.

> A quick intro to the **12 basic principles of animation** can be found at
> `http://en.wikipedia.org/wiki/12_basic_principles_`
> `of_animation`.

For the sake of clarity, this method will be demonstrated with a bouncing ball, but the same principles can be used with complex characters.

## How to do it...

1. Open the file `006-Layers.blend`. It has two meshes: a beach ball and one to act as our ground, with two levels of height. We're going to animate the ball roll from the left, fall and bounce until it stops. The Blender screen is divided, so you can see the scene in front view, camera view, an Action Editor and a F-Curve editor, as seen in the following screenshot:

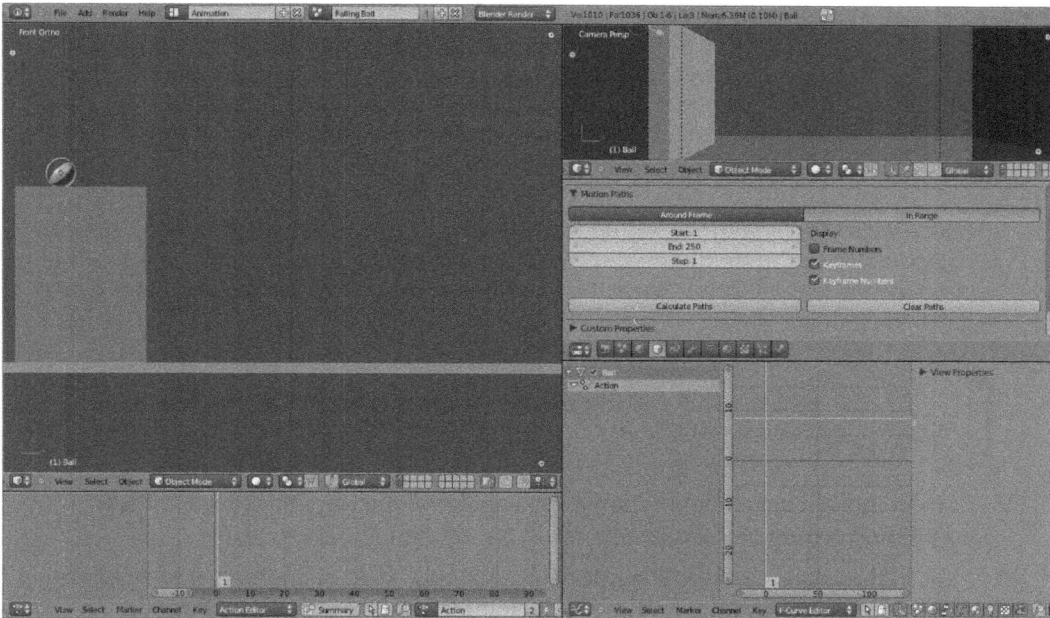

First we will define the key poses. The key poses are the most important ones in a scene, the storytelling ones. Here the "story" is: the ball rolls, falls, bounces few times on the ground and stops. Our key poses may be the first position, where the ball is still in the platform; the point where the ball leaves the platform; the first contact of the ball with the ground after falling; and the final resting position.

2. Set these four **Location** keyframes (*I*), evenly spaced by 10 frames in the timeline. We don't care about timing here, just poses. A good thing to do now is make sure all (*A*) keyframes are selected (with an orange hue) in the DopeSheet window, press *Shift + T*, and select **Constant** as the interpolation mode. This will remove any automatic interpolation that can confuse you when playing the animation with *Shift + A*. The following image shows the key poses in sequence:

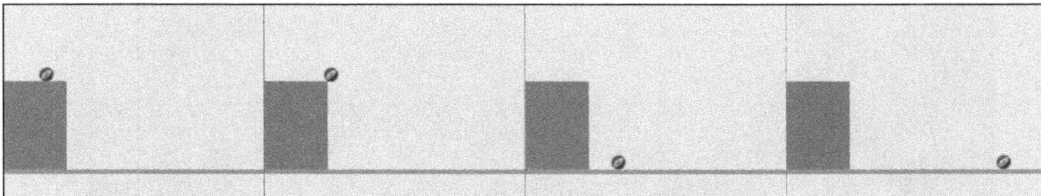

This was the first "layer", where we care only about the key positions of the scene. If we want the ball to stop further from the platform, or make the first bounce closer to it, it's easier to adjust it now. If we went on to make a fully animated ball, rolling and bouncing a few times through the floor, it would be much harder to change that.

> When working with a character rig, in this first layer you should make rough key poses, without the fine details such as fingers or facial expressions. Start by positioning the pelvic bone, which normally drives the position of the remaining FK chains, and the feet (if your character is with its legs in IK mode).

Once we're happy with the key poses, let's add another layer of refinement. Now it's time to add the "Extreme" poses. These are, essentially, the positions where a change in direction occurs. In our case, the Extremes are every contact position of the ball with the ground on each kick.

> The key poses in a scene are normally also Extremes, but the inverse is not necessarily true.

3.  Select the last column of keyframes you saved on the DopeSheet window with a right-click on one of the saved points in the column and pressing *K*.

4.  Still in the DopeSheet window, move (*G*) that column to the right, to frame 90, so we can save the Extremes between the third and fourth key poses. Position the ball at the places you find ideal for the bounces and set new keyframes (*I*) through the timeline. Six bounces between the key poses is a reasonable number. Remember that the spaces between each bounce get shorter until the ball stops: look at the next screenshot to see the marked points and frames where the poses have been set:

You can see that our timeline is very organized and easy to adjust, with keyframes set in a visually easy to understand manner.

The next step is to create the **Breakdown** positions, which are in essence the intermediate poses between two Extremes. In our case, the Breakdowns can be the peaks between each bounce.

5. We can visually distinguish the Extremes, Breakdowns, and regular keyframes on the DopeSheet by applying different colors for them. Select the keyframes you want to mark on the DopeSheet and press *R*. A menu will appear with the option to mark them as Extremes (pink), Breakdowns (blue), regular keyframes (white), or "Jitter" (green), a special type for marking any other saved positions you wish to tell apart from the rest. Position the ball (*G*) and insert new keyframes (*I*) between each saved Extreme, and remember that in each bounce the ball goes up lower than the previous one. The next screenshot shows our Breakdowns set:

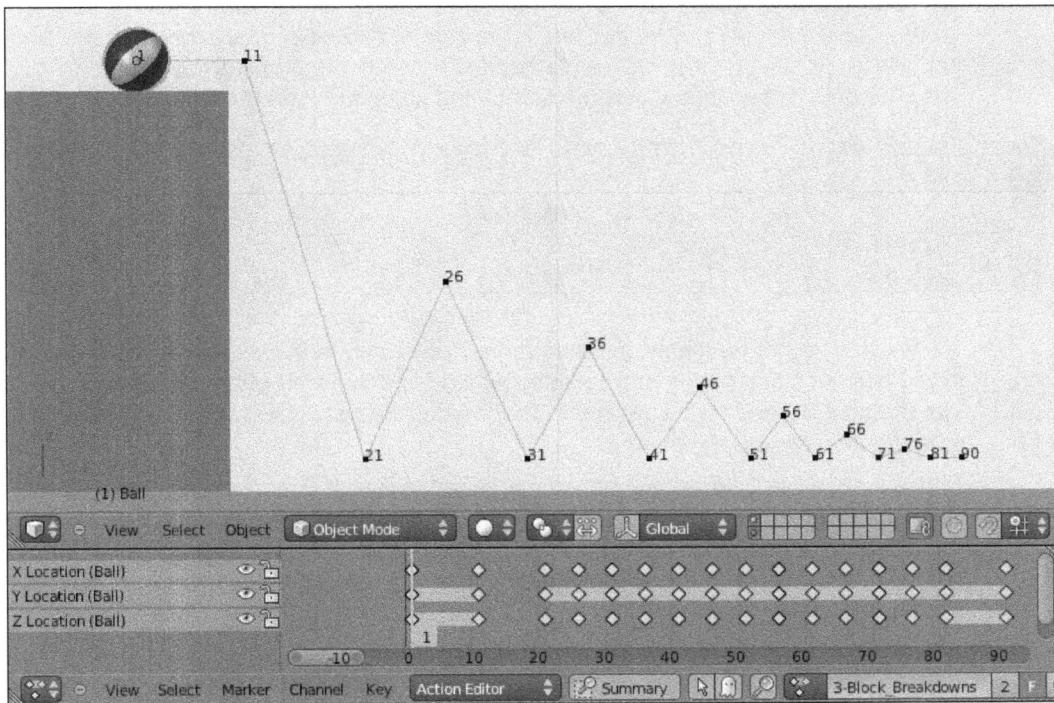

Until now we have just worried about spacing, which is about "where" our action occurs. Now we're going to set the timing, which - as you've probably guessed - is about "when" an action happens.

6. Since we're working with just one thing at a time in an organized way, it's easy to adjust the timing after we're happy with the positioning. It's just a matter of selecting the columns (*K*) on the DopeSheet window and moving (*G*) them to the sides. Press *Alt* + *A* to check the timing.

> The technique of creating key poses, Extremes (and sometimes the Breakdowns), along with rough Timing adjustment is called **Blocking**. It's a widely used technique in professional environments, allowing the animator to have a preview of the timing and placement of the characters and objects in a scene. Usually, there's no interpolation between poses (the Constant interpolation mode that we've been using up until here) so the animator can see the action without unwanted automatic interpolation.

7. Until now the keyframes have no interpolation between them. Select all keyframes on the DopeSheet (*A*) and press *Shift* + *T* to select the Bezier interpolation mode. You can always press *Alt* + *A* to view a playback of the animation to see if the timing is fine. The next screenshot shows the first timing adjustment on the DopeSheet:

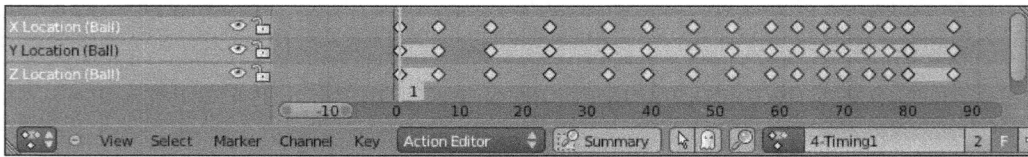

You will notice that until now our animations don't really look like a bouncing ball. The saved positions and timing may be fine, but we need to have better control over the interpolation between the keyframes. That's when we need the Graph Editor window to add another layer of refinement.

Take a look at the **Z Location** channel curve at the Graph Editor window. Since the **Z Location** represents the up or down movement of the ball, it's easier for us to relate the curve to the actual animation. When a ball bounces, it spends little time on the ground and more time in the air. We need to change the automatic curves generated by Blender.

8. Right-click on the handles and move (G) them until you have shorter times on the Extremes and longer on the Breakdowns. The next screenshot shows the **Z Location** curve before (above) and after (below) our changes, where the timing was also adjusted a little:

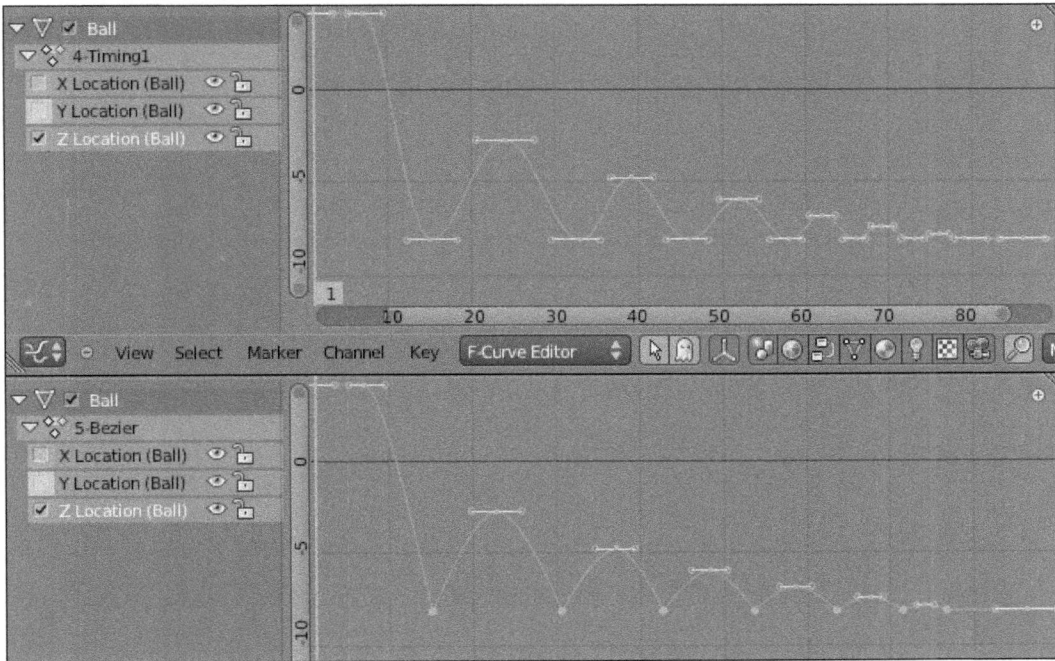

Now if you look to the **X Location** curve on the Graph Editor you'll see a big ascending and irregular curve. This curve drives the horizontal movement of our ball, and this irregularity can cause some unwanted results. Since we want our ball to make a regular translation, decreasing its speed until it stops, it's a good idea to remove the unnecessary keyframes.

The following screenshot shows this curve before (above) and after (below) we remove the extra keyframes to achieve a smoother movement:

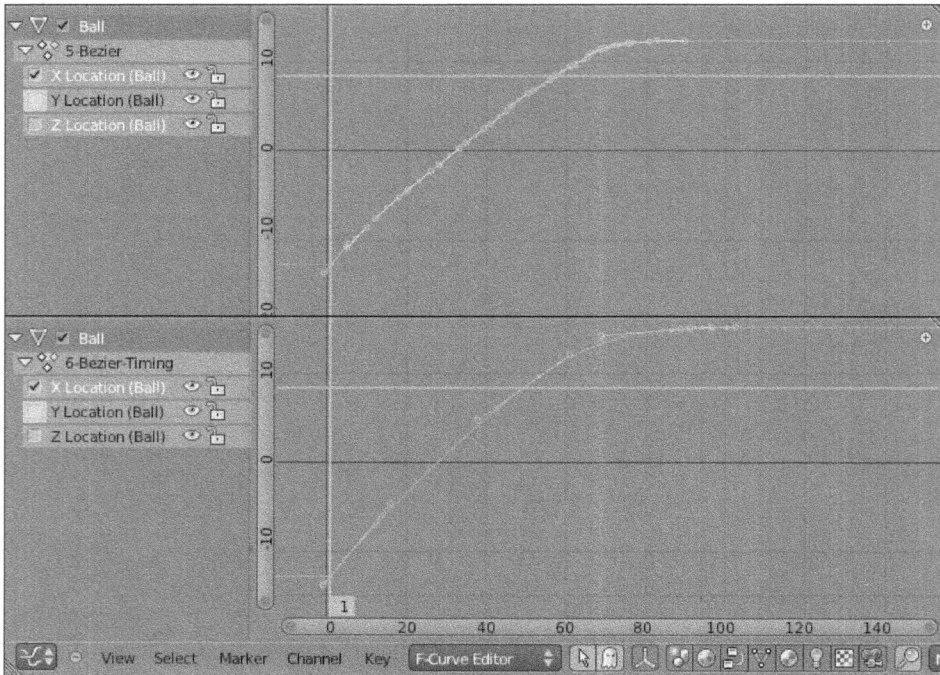

After you're happy with the main ball movement, it's time to add the secondary transformations. One of them is the ball rotation. Now that you can see where the ball starts and ends its movement, along with its velocity, it's easier to guess how many rotations the ball should make.

9. Go to the first frame of the animation and set a rotation keyframe by pressing *I* and choosing **Rotation**. Go to the last one, press *R*, and make it spin a few times and add another **Rotation** keyframe. After that, adjust the **X Euler Rotation** curve in the Graph Editor until you're happy with the results.

Other secondary movements can include very small bounces just before the ball stops and a subtle movement backwards after the ball stops. These new movements will add more keyframes on top of the ones you're already happy with.

When animating characters, these layers of details range from the basic blocking of the torso and limbs to the subtleties of facial expressions, eyes, and fingers. You can save each layer as a separate **Action** in the DopeSheet window: when you finish one layer, make sure that you're in the Action Editor mode and click on the plus (**+**) sign next to the action name. This will duplicate the current action so that you can work on it without modifying the original. Our example file was created this way.

The file `006-Layers-complete.blend` has the final animation of the bouncing ball, and you can see all layered steps mentioned in this recipe in the DopeSheet window, by selecting the appropriate Actions.

## How it works...

Using an organized approach of adding layers of refinement, you can achieve animations that are quicker and easier to manage. You should start from the basic poses, from Keys, Extremes, Breakdowns, and then adjust the channel curves to achieve smooth movements. Only after you have a solid foundation should you go to the next level of detail.

## See also

*Appendix*: *Extremes, Breakdowns, Inbetweens, ones and twos*

*Chapter 6*: *Non-linear animation*

*Chapter 7*: *Easy to Say, Hard to Do: Mastering the Basics*

# Changing between FK and IK in a shot

*Inverse or Forward Kinematics?* This is a question that haunts most animators. Some only use IK, while others claim that IK arms make the characters look like puppets pulled by strings. Both have pros and cons, and it's a good idea to take advantage of what they are best at.

Normally legs are in IK mode by default. That's because their main point of control is where the feet touch the ground, and IK allows the feet to remain fixed while the rest of the body moves. Making a walk cycle with FK legs would be something very difficult. Arms, by contrast, are normally an appendage of the torso and are held by the shoulders, rotating around them.

This setup with IK legs and FK arms usually works fine in most situations, but there are cases in which you need to change modes. Imagine a scene where your character is walking, slips on a banana peel and falls to the ground, using the hands to absorb the impact. During the impact, the arms stay fixed on the ground while the torso is falling, so we need to change their mode to IK.

Normally, during the planning phase of your shot, you already know what modes are needed based on what will happen. That's when you can decide for going only IK, only FK or using a mix of both on the same shot.

## How to do it...

1. Open the file `006-IK-FK.blend`. It has a very basic animation of our character Otto walking and slipping on a banana peel. His arms are on FK mode, because they are only moving for his balance on the walk and don't hold onto anything. At frame 11, the character starts his contact with the ground after the slip, and must use his hands to absorb the impact. The next screenshot shows three frames from this animation:

2. As you can see, in the last frame of the animation both arms cross the ground line, following their parent bones as you'd expect from a FK chain. Press *Alt + A* to play the animation and see the slipping action and the arms passing through the ground.

   We need to, at some point in the animation, set the arms in IK mode so we can position the hands touching the ground and have the arms to be properly positioned.

3. Go to frame 9 and, in front view (*Numpad 1*), select four controller bones on the rig UI: `IK-FK_Arm.L`, `IK-FK_Arm.R`, `Space_Arm.L`, and `Space_Arm.R`. Insert a location keyframe (*I*) for all of them in their default positions, as seen in the next screenshot:

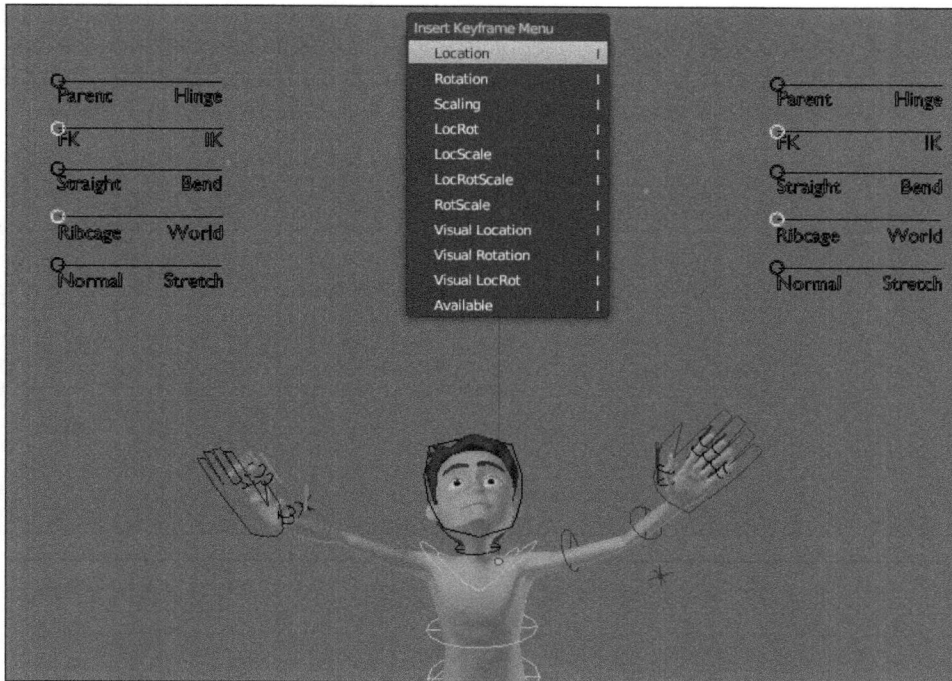

4. Still in frame 9, select both hand bones and set a **LocRot** keyframe (*I*) for them. Now go up one frame (*Right arrow*), with the hands still selected, press *I* one more time and select **Visual LocRot** in the menu.

5. Next, select again the four IK/FK and Space controllers that we set a keyframe for earlier and move them (*G*) to the right to enable the IK and World modes for the arms. Press *I* and choose **Location** to set a keyframe for them.

   Now both arms are in IK mode, with the hands on the same position where they were in FK mode, because we set the **Visual LocRot** keyframe just before we changed the sliders. If we didn't do that in this exact order, the hand controllers would go back to the rest position and we would have trouble positioning them back.

> We set the IK arms to the World space because the default mode on this rig is to have both IK hands to follow the ribcage controller. Since we need the hands to be independent from the torso in this scene, this is the right choice for us. Otherwise we would have the same trouble positioning the arms as we would have with FK arms.

6. Now we can move, rotate, and set keyframes to the hands and elbow controllers to pose the arms in IK mode, so that our character can protect himself from the fall. Frame 11 is a good one to insert a keyframe of both hands touching the ground. The next screenshot shows a sequence of the animation with the arms in IK mode:

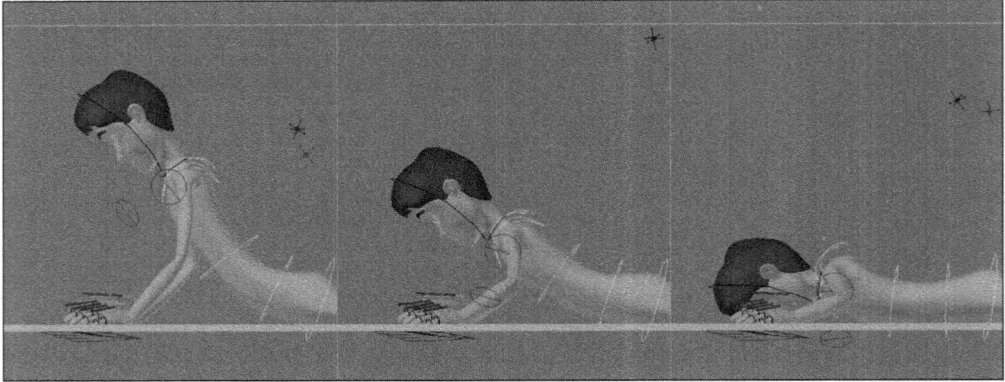

You can see the final exercise in the file `006-IK-FK_complete.blend` for your reference in case of any doubts.

## How it works...

Using a rig with controllers to switch between IK and FK modes, you should carefully set keyframes in order to make a seamless transition between each mode. By setting a **Visual LocRot** keyframe, you can position the controller properly to create a one-frame seamless transition between FK and IK.

This workflow is for use with this rig, and may be a bit different in other setups. The important thing to know is that you must be careful with posing both IK and FK chains before and after the switch in order to achieve a seamless transition.

## See also

Chapter 1: *Making an IK-FK switcher*

Chapter 5: *Hands down! The limbs controllers*

# Grasping and throwing objects

When animating a scene, you will often have to animate a character interacting with props, such as grasping a cup of tea, a sword, a gun, or a flower bouquet. These props are not part of the main rig, but you need a way to control them easily.

Let's imagine a scene where our character finds a giant diamond and picks it up with his left hand.

## How to do it...

1. Open the file `006-Props.blend`. It has our character Otto in front of a stand with a big diamond on top. The character has a very basic animation with three Extreme positions defined to pick the diamond with his left hand. The next screenshot shows the first keyframe:

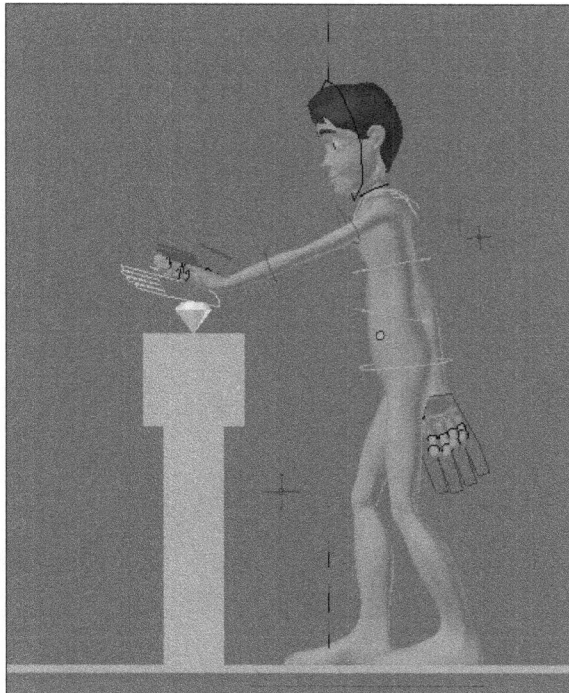

2. Press *Alt + A* to see the animation. The character reaches out for the diamond with his left hand and tries to take it from the stand, but there's something wrong: the diamond remains still. That's because we need to tell Blender to make the diamond follow the character's hand at a certain point in the animation, and we're going to do this with a constraint.

3. Go to frame 8, where the character reaches the diamond and closes his hand over it. This is the moment where the "holding" happens, and the diamond needs to start following the hand. This frame is also where we need to set the constraint.

4. Select the `Hand.L` bone, hold *Shift*, and select the **Diamond** mesh. Blender automatically changes to Object Mode, since you're selecting two objects of different types. Now, press *Ctrl + Shift + C* and choose the **Child Of** constraint, as seem in the next screenshot:

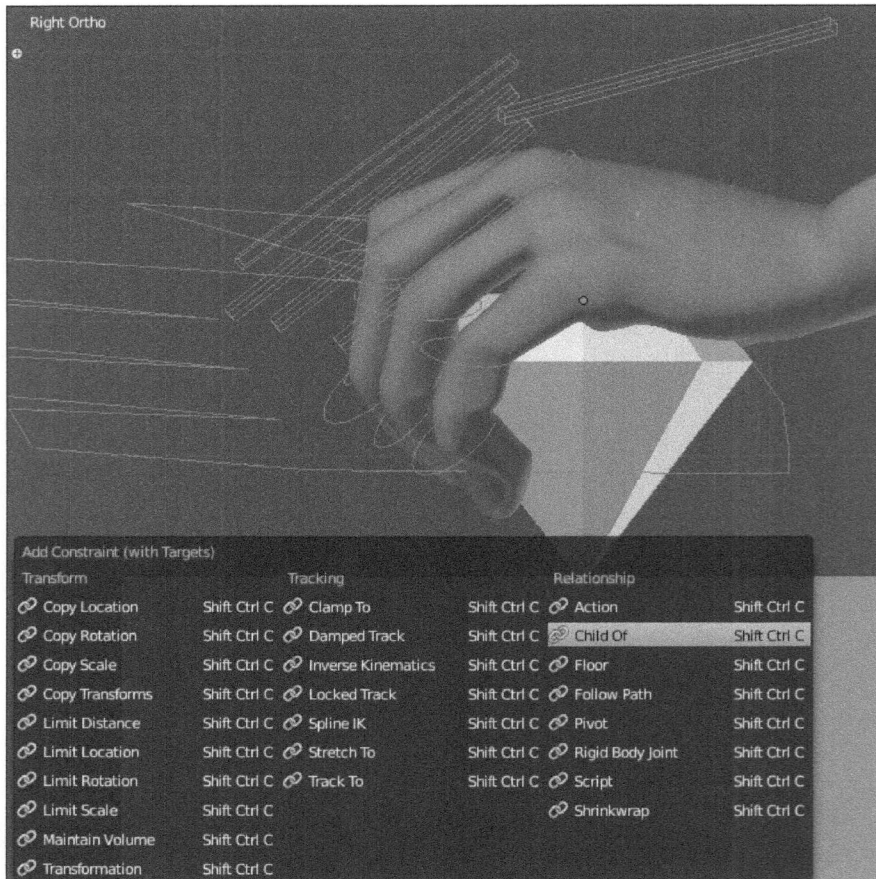

5. With the **Diamond** mesh selected, go to the **Object Constraints** tab in the Properties window and find the constraint you've just added. In the **Bone** field, select `Hand.L`. You'll see that the diamond changes its position, so click on the **Set Inverse** button to make it go back to its original place. That's why we need to set the constraint on the frame where the holding action begins: this is the position Blender has to take into account when evaluating the constraint, and the reason why we clicked on the **Set Inverse** button.

Now, if you play the animation again, you'll see that the diamond is attached to the hand even before the hold action happens, which is not what we want. We need to animate the influence of the constraint.

6. Go to frame 8, where the holding happens, and navigate to the **Object Constraints** tab in the Properties window for the `Diamond` object. Right-click over the **Influence** slider and select the **Insert Keyframe** option.

7. Now go back one frame (*Left Arrow*), set the **Influence** slider to 0, right-click over it again, and set a new keyframe. If you play the animation again, you'll see that everything works as expected, and our character successfully takes the giant diamond. The file `006-Props.blend` has the complete example, and the next screenshot shows the three keyframes of this animation:

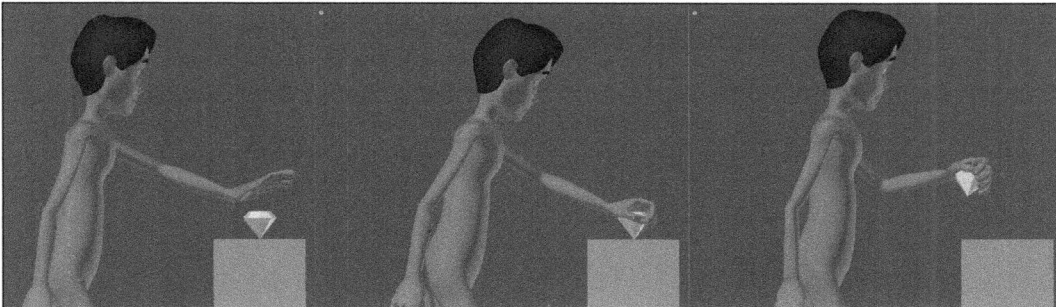

## How it works...

You can use a **Child Of** constraint for an object to make it follow a character's bone. By carefully defining the constraint in the frame where the contact takes place and animating its influence on the timeline, you can make your character interact with props.

## There's more...

You can use the same principle to throw an object away. You should set a constraint and animate its influence in the opposite way, from 1 to 0 on the frame where the object should be thrown. From that point, you should animate the object independently.

## See also

*Chapter 8: Animating a Tennis Serve*

# Silhouette and mirrored rendering

Rendered frames of a 3D animation can be thought of as individual drawings of traditional 2D animation. Similar to animating with pencil and paper, we must check our digital 3D drawings to see if everything looks proper on the screen.

Two often used techniques to check the quality of a pose for animation are viewing it as a silhouette and with a mirror. When we stare at our work for great amounts of time—and that is particularly true for animators—it becomes difficult to spot imperfections.

When you have a silhouette version of your drawing, all fine details such as textures and shading are removed, and you can focus only on the main shape of your pose. If your pose can be "read" by the audience in silhouette form and communicates what your character feels, you can be sure it will work in the full, shaded version.

Traditional animators also often use mirrors to check their drawings. After being so long in front of a picture, our eyes get used to that shape and we can't see all of the imperfections. A mirror "creates" another shape, one that we're not accustomed to and that we can look at to spot mistakes.

## How to do it...

1.  Open the file `006-Silhouette-and-mirror.blend`. It has our character Otto with a basic pose as if he is running. Looking at it for a long time, moving and rotating bones can deceive our eyes, causing us to lose focus, making us unable to pay proper attention to some bad shapes. Lets try to spot them.

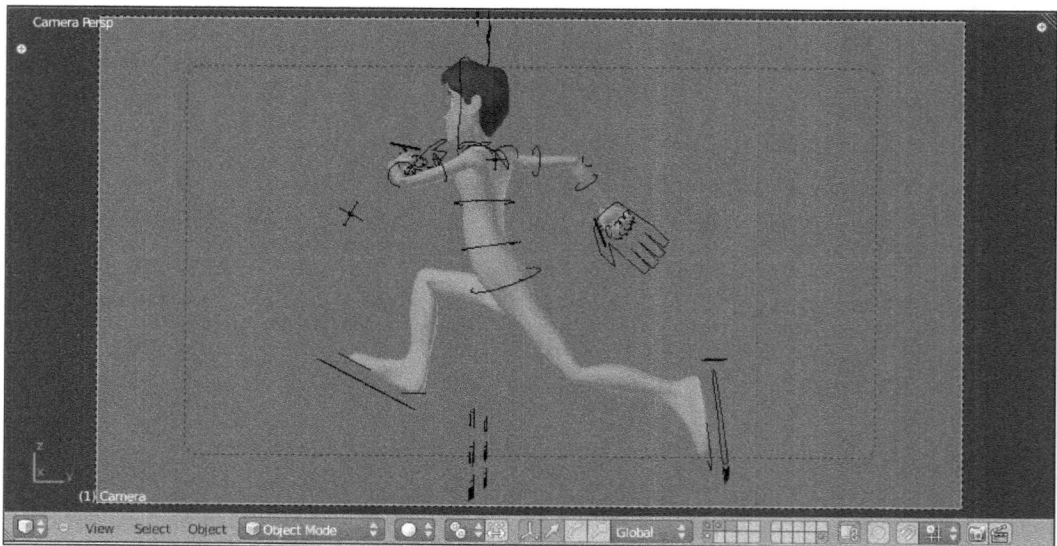

2. Open a Node Editor window and select the **Compositing Nodes** type on the window header. Select the **Use Nodes** and **Backdrop** options. The latter shows the result of the composite in the background of the nodes window, while the former makes the scene nodes actually used by Blender.

3. Hit *F12* to render this frame, pressing *Esc* when it's done to return to the previous screen. This step is necessary so that you can actually use the scene information for the composite. If you need more space, keep the mouse cursor over the Node Editor window and press *Ctrl + Up Arrow* to maximize it.

> To create the silhouette view, all the information that we need to use in this scene is held by the Alpha channel, since there are no concurrent meshes in front of or behind our character, such as props or walls. In more complex scenes, make sure you only have the meshes you want to check in the silhouette visible. You can move the extra meshes to a disabled layer for this purpose.

4. Lets add a **ColorRamp** node. Press *Shift + A* and select **Convertor | ColorRamp** on the menu, as seen in the next screenshot:

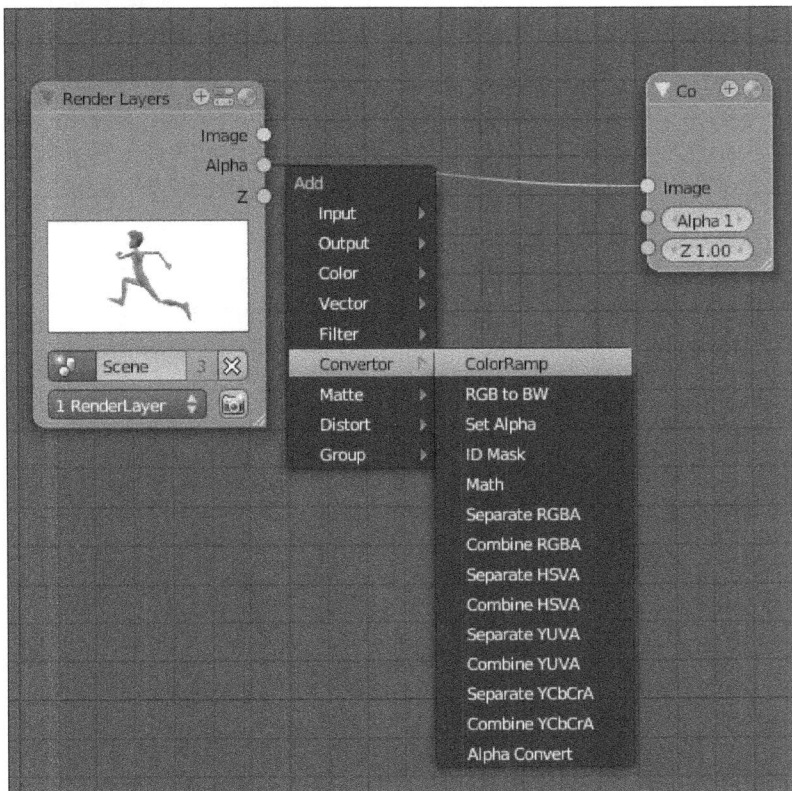

5. Now, click on the **Alpha** grey circle on the **Render Layers** node and drag its output to the grey input circle at the left-hand side of the ColorRamp node, connecting them. To see the result on the backdrop, select the **ColorRamp** node by clicking over it, press *Shift + A*, and select **Output | Viewer**. This will create a **Viewer** node connected to the output of the **ColorRamp** and show the resulting image on the backdrop, as seen in the following screenshot:

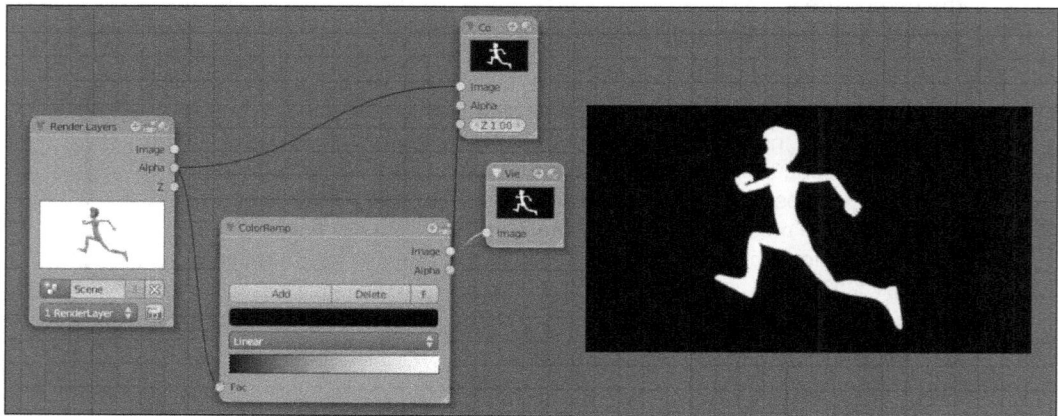

> To move the nodes around, just click on them and press *G*, as you do with objects in the 3D View. To move the backdrop, hold *Alt*, right-click over the image and drag it around. You can make the backdrop bigger with *V* and smaller with *Alt + V*.

This would make our silhouette view of the scene, but we can enhance it further by making the character black over a white background (or the color that you like best). First, take a look at the gradient box on the **ColorRamp** node: there is a dotted line on the left border and a black and white one on the right. The dotted one indicates that it's the active point, and you can drag it over the ramp. You can also click on the other point to make it the active one.

6. Select the first point on the ramp and change its color from black to white on the color selector just below the **Add**, **Delete**, and **F** buttons. Do the same to the second point, changing its color to black, as seen in the following screenshot:

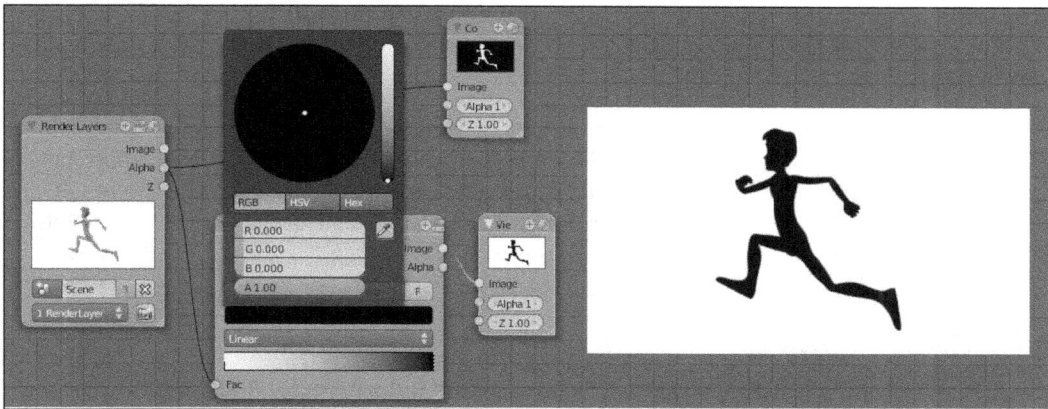

This will finish our silhouette setup. Now you can check for problems on the overall shape to correct the pose.

7. To make further observations on the shape, we're going to create the mirrored setup on top of this one. With the **ColorRamp** node selected, press *Shift + A* and select **Distort | Flip** to add the **Flip** node already connected to the ramp node. With the **Flip** node selected, press *Shift + A* and pick **Output | Viewer** to create a second viewer node already connected to it. Now, by clicking on each of the viewer nodes you can switch the backdrop image to check for imperfections in your pose, as seen in the next screenshot:

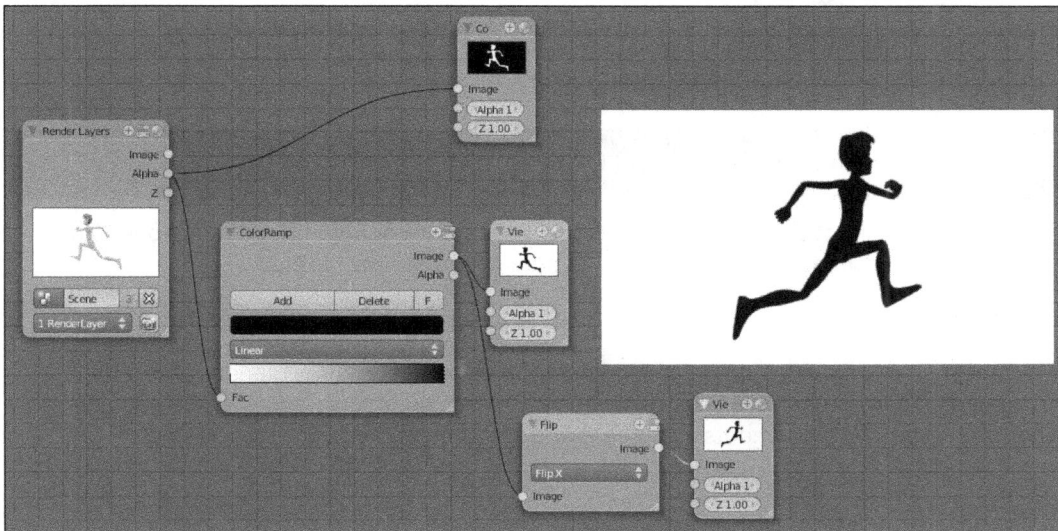

Now, while creating your poses, you can use this setup to check them quickly by viewing them in silhouette and mirrored modes. Just remember to render the scene again after you make the changes.

Since our goal here is just a quick view of our poses, we don't need to enable the compositing nodes on our **Render** panel in the Properties window, but you can render an animation this way if you wish (specially if you want to render the full scene in silhouette to see the result in motion). The file `006-Silhouette-and-mirror-complete.blend` has this complete example, waiting for you to press *F12*.

## How it works...

Using the Alpha information of a scene, you can use the **ColorRamp** and **Flip** nodes to check your character's poses in silhouette and mirrored modes, to look for imperfections that are harder to spot on detailed images.

## There's more...

To speed up this already quick rendering process, make sure that you disable all options on the **Shading** panel in the **Render** settings of your scene. You can also move all the lamps in your scene to a disabled layer, since we're only making use of the Alpha channel and discarding everything else. Just remember to enable these options back to make the final renders of your scene.

## See also

Chapter 7: *Easy to Say, Hard to Do: Mastering the Basics*

# Tracking animation arcs

*Arcs.* Animators are obsessed with arcs. This is because most organic actions happen along an arched path, giving fluidity and realism to human and animal motions.

Mechanical movements, on the other hand, usually happen along straight paths.

Whether you are animating an organic being or a mechanical device, Blender allows the tracking of motion paths. This is extremely helpful when animating, and can give you answers when you watch the movements you create and feel that "something isn't quite right".

## How to do it...

1. Open the file `005-Tracking.blend`. It has our character Otto with some very basic and unfinished animation of a jump. Let's track the arcs so we can make our animation better.

2. First, let's track the path made by the `Hips` bone, since it's the center of gravity for our character. Select it, make sure you're on side view (*Numpad 3*), go to the Properties window, on the **Object Data** tab, and find the **Motion Paths** panel. Make sure the options **Frame Numbers**, **Keyframes**, and **Keyframe Numbers** are selected and click on **Calculate Paths**. You'll see a result similar to the next screenshot:

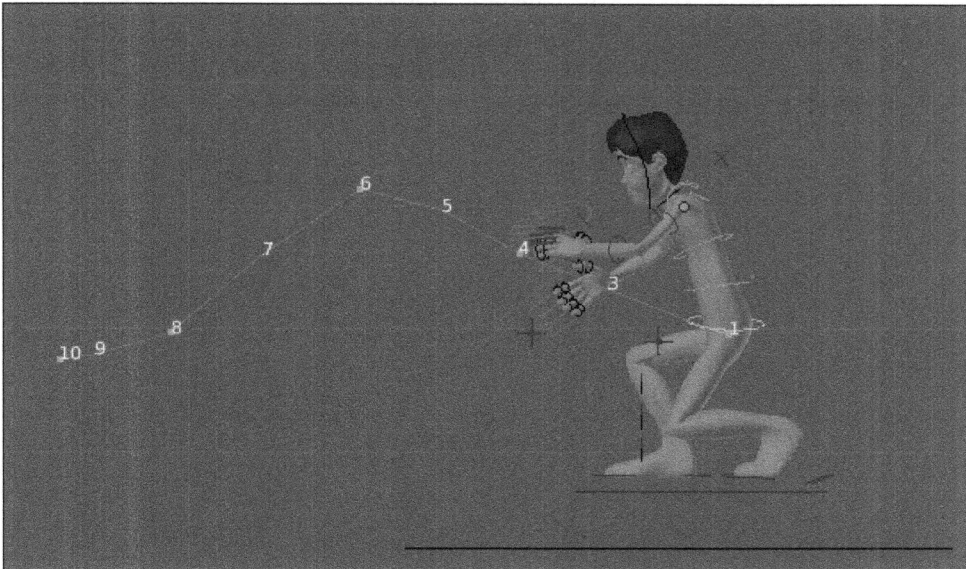

Blender has tracked the path of the `Hips` bone in the 3D View with highlights on the frames, marking the keyframes with squares and the interpolated frames with dots. The frame numbers also have a different hue where the keyframes are set. It's very helpful to really see the path and keyframes in 3D, so we can spot any imperfections in the motion. Let's enhance it.

If you scroll the timeline, the path remains in place and the current frame is highlighted. First, let's try to adjust our current keyframes.

3. In frame 1, move the `Hips` bone a bit below its current position and replace its **LocRot** keyframe (*I*). At frame 4, drag it up a little and replace its keyframe.

4. You'll notice that the path hasn't changed despite your updates. You need to click on **Calculate Paths** again to see the updated arc of motion. The change may be subtle, but isn't that what animation is about?

5. Let's continue tweaking the keyframes. On a Graph Editor window, make the **Y Location** the only channel visible for the `Hips` bone. This channel controls the up or down movement. Edit its handles until you get a softer curve. You can change the way the handles behave by selecting the desired mode in the *V* menu. The next screenshot shows it before and after the editing:

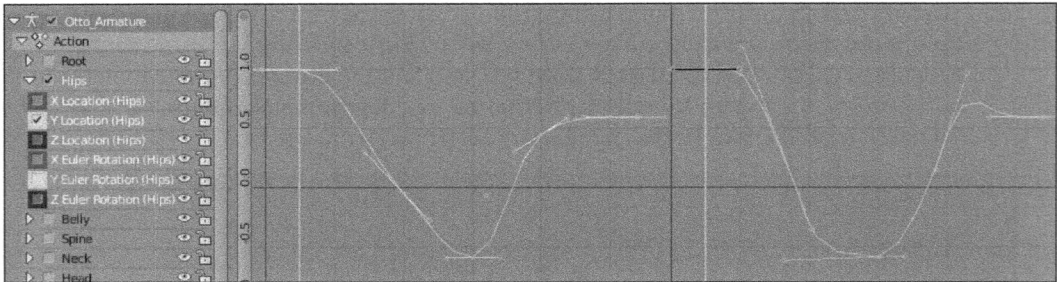

6. If you click on the **Calculate Paths** button again, you'll see that the motion curve for the `Hips` bone has improved significantly. The following screenshot shows the new and improved path:

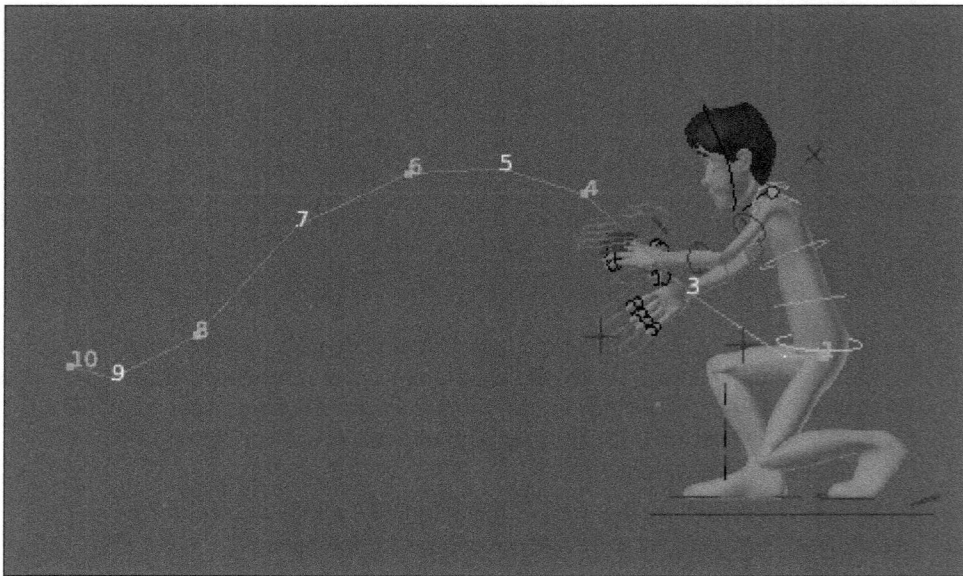

7. When you're happy with the `Hips` path, click on the **Clear Paths** button on the **Motion Paths** panel. It's time to check the paths for other interesting bones. After the hips controller, you can check the head, arms, and feet, since they are commonly the center of attention in this kind of broad movement.

Just be sure to remember the bone hierarchy when correcting paths: when you change the position of a parent bone, such as the `Hips`, the paths of its children (FK arms, head, and so on) will also change. That's why we should begin with top level bones on the rig hierarchy. The file `006-Tracking-complete.blend` has this recipe with the `Hips` path corrected.

## How it works...

Blender has a nice feature for calculating the **Motion Paths** for bones and other animated objects in the 3D View. These traced paths allow the animator to easily see what problems occur in the motion path and what frames should be corrected. By carefully tweaking the bones which are higher on the rig hierarchy first, the animator can quickly build good animation arcs.

## There's more...

Along with the **Motion Paths** feature, Blender has a similar feature called **Ghost**. This feature is also called "Onion Skin" in other animation software, and allows the animator to see a translucent copy of the selected bone or object for different positions on the timeline.

This feature is located on the same **Object Data** tab as the **Motion Paths**, and can be configured to display the translucent copies in various ways. One advantage of it over the **Motion Paths** is that the copies are automatically updated on the 3D View when you change a keyframe. The **Ghost** feature can be used alone or together with the **Motion Paths**, giving very good visual aids to the animator.

## See also

*Chapter 7: Easy to Say, Hard to Do: Mastering the Basics*

# Using video for background reference

Some animators say using video reference is cheating. Don't be fooled by that. Since the days of the *Nine Old Men*—the core pioneer animators of Walt Disney Productions who created classics such as *Snow White* and *Pinocchio*, which helped define the art of animation as we know it—animators have studied and used video reference. The main difference is that today it's much easier and more accessible for us to do that.

Reference is something extremely important for animators to get inspiration from and understand the essence, physics, and motivation behind movements. From video reference you can get good visual ideas to apply to your animations, especially for acting subtleties, secondary actions and timing.

Blender allows us to easily insert videos or image sequences on the 3D View background to use as reference, and we're going to see how to do it. For this recipe, an excerpt video is used from a public domain movie called **WILLIAM BENDIX IN RILEY, SAVINGS BONDS SALESMAN**; maintained by the **National Archives and Records Administration**. It's available at `http://www.archive.org/details/gov.archives.arc.11866`.

You can also visit a group page on the **Vimeo** website, which is maintained by animators and allows you to watch hundreds of live action video footage for reference at `http://vimeo.com/groups/aniref/videos`.

## How to do it...

1. Open the file `006-VideoReference.blend`. It has our character Otto in his resting position. In the support files there is a file called `006-VideoReference.mp4`, which is an excerpt from a public domain video encoded with a MPEG-4 codec and a frame rate of 30 frames per second. We'll use it for help posing our character.

> Most common video containers and codecs are supported by Blender to be used as background. Movies in `.mov`, `.avi`, `.mp4`, or `.flv` can usually be loaded without any hassles.

> Knowing the frame rate of the video is essential, because our Blender file has to match it. You can discover the video's frame rate using the free and cross-platform multimedia player **VLC** (available at `http://www.videolan.org/vlc/`), by opening the video with this player and pressing *Ctrl + I* to see the media information. The frame rate of the video is shown in the Codec Details tab.

2. Go to the Properties window, on the **Render** tab, and find the **Dimensions** sections. Change the **FPS** field to `30`.

3. Go back to the 3D Window, and open the **Properties** panel (*N*). Scroll it down until you see the **Background Images** section. Enable that option, click on the triangle on the left-hand side and click on **Add Image** to access the background settings, as seen in the next screenshot:

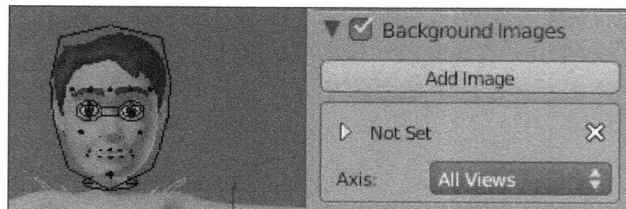

After clicking on the **Add Image** button, a new slot is created so you can select a background image or movie.

4. To select the file, click on the triangle next to **Not Set**. A new set of buttons will appear on the bottom, where you can select an existing file within Blender or select an external one. Click on the **Open** button to look for our video file. The window will turn into a file selector, and you'll be able to see thumbnails of the video and image files to find what you want easily.

5. Click on our video file and then on **Open** to load it into our scene. Blender will automatically set the first frame of the movie as the background, and our panel will change to accommodate more settings, as you can see in the following screenshot:

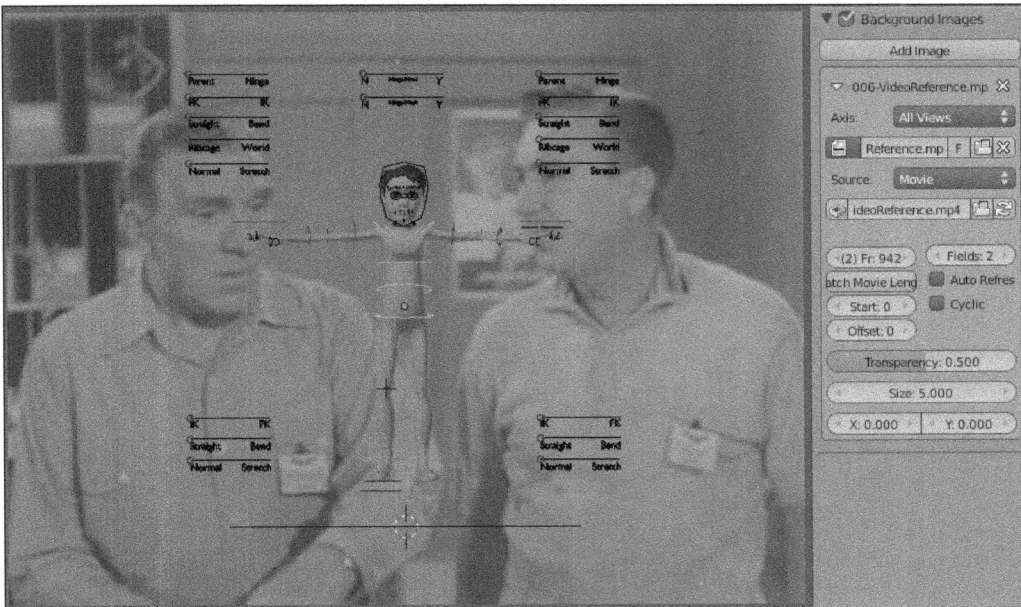

Among these settings, it's important to enable the **Auto Refresh** option, which will update the viewport when you change the current frame in the timeline. There are also two similar options: **Start**, which tells Blender to start the background playback on a specific frame, useful for when you want to use the reference on a later part of your animation; and **Offset**, useful if you want the first frame of your timeline to be synchronized to a later part of the reference movie. There are also quite easy to understand settings such as **Size**, **Transparency**, **X** and **Y**, to control size, opacity, and position.

Since the video reference uses a real world perspective, using it in orthographic views doesn't make much sense, as these views are only mathematical representations of a real perspective. We can tell Blender to use the background video only in the Camera view, with a matching perspective.

6. Select the **Camera** option in the **Axis** field in the video reference slot. Now, you'll see the movie as a background only when in Camera view (*Numpad 0*). A good use for this setup is with the Quad View *Ctrl + Alt + Q*, which is new in Blender 2.5 and divides your 3D window in four views: Top Ortho, Camera Persp, Front Ortho, and Right Ortho. After enabling it, you'll be able to pose your character nicely within the views and have your background video set only in Camera view, as seen in the next screenshot:

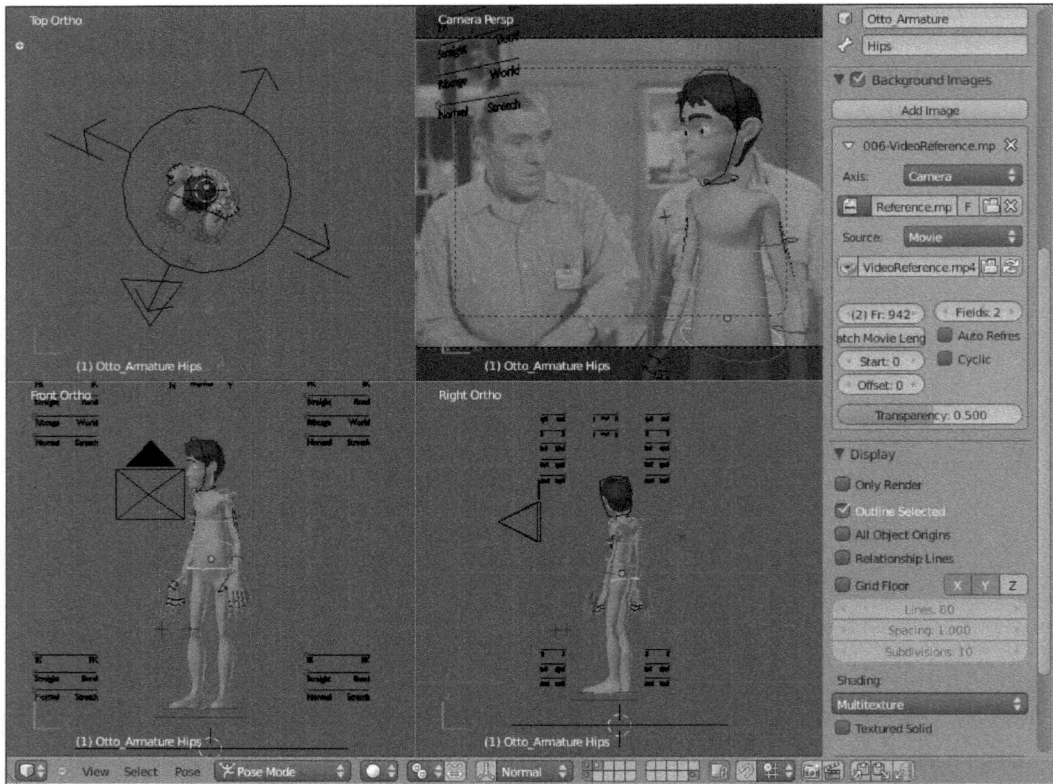

Another nice thing about using background videos and images in Blender is that you can use more than one at a time.

7. Click one more time on the **Add Image** button in the Properties panel to create another image slot. Repeat the same you did for the movie file, but now select the image called 006-VideoReference.png in the same folder and set it to be shown only in **Camera** view. It's a grid with the Rule of Thirds to help you set up your camera and achieve a better visual composition. Set its **Transparency** value to 0, so it's fully visible on top of the video reference, as seen in the next screenshot:

The file `006-VideoReference.blend` has this complete example, so you can refer to it and compare your results.

## How it works...

Using video reference is very important for animators, and Blender allows the use of both images and video as a background on the 3D view. By stacking video and compositing guides, along with taking care of the frame rate of the scene and video reference, it's a nice feature on the animator's toolbox.

## See also

Chapter 7: Easy to Say, Hard to Do: Mastering the Basics

# Working with linked assets and characters

When working in a production environment, in a studio with other professionals or even as a freelance artist, it's important to work with linked assets. Having separate Blender files for characters, environments and props is crucial for an organized and sane workflow, avoiding redundancy and making the update process easier.

Imagine if, at a later stage of your animation, you have to make changes in the shape or materials of your main character. If, in order to do that, you have to reopen and alter all your already finished shots, your workflow is far from optimized. If using linked libraries, all you have to do is change the main source file and automatically all scenes making reference to it will be updated.

The use of linked libraries also allows different professionals to work on different aspects of a production at the same time. While the animator is posing the character, another professional can work on refining its mesh or materials, for example.

## How to do it...

1. Open the file `006-Libraries.blend`. It has an empty scene with only a camera and some lamps. Lets add our character to this scene. On the top header, in the Info window, go to the **File** menu and choose the **Link** option, as seen in the next screenshot:

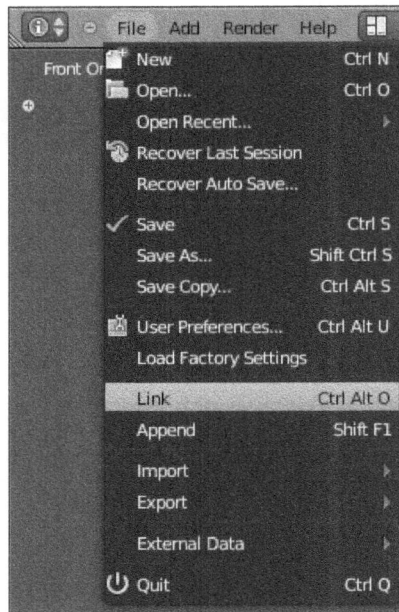

The **Link** option is to create a reference to an external library, while the **Append** one is for creating a local (and independent) copy of it.

2. The Blender window will open a file browser, through which you should find and click on the file `006-Libraries-Otto.blend`. When you click on it the file browser interprets it as a regular folder, which has sub-folders to represent the various kinds of data in a Blender file, as you can see in the next screenshot:

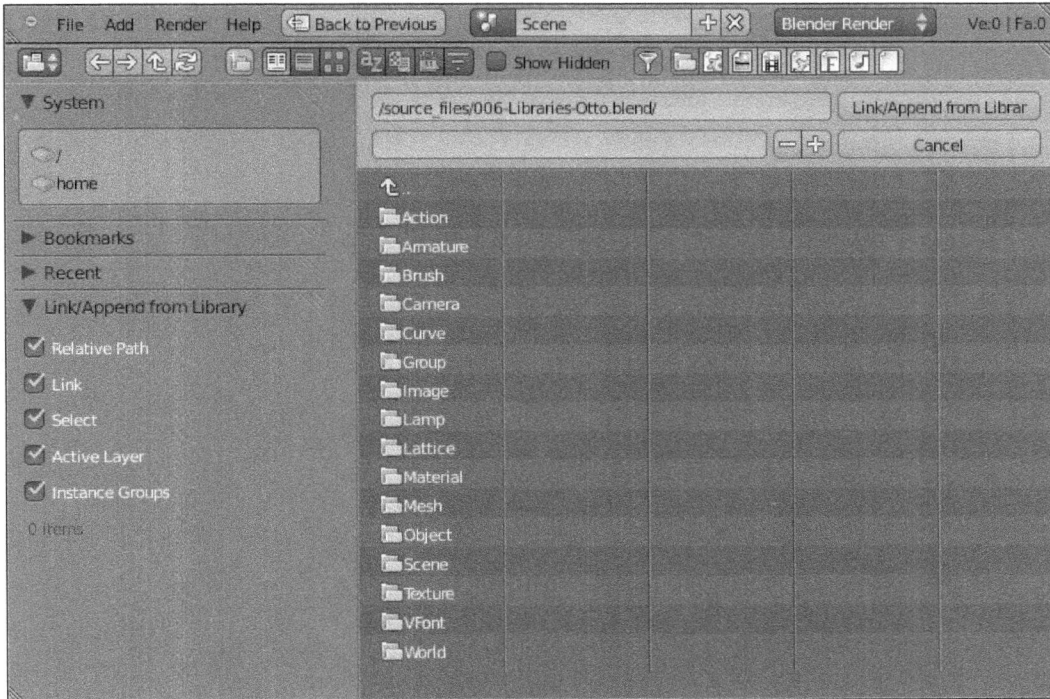

3. Make sure all options under the **Link/Append from Library** panel are enabled, navigate to the `Group` folder, select the `Otto` group, and click on the **Link/Append from Library** button to bring it to our scene.

> It's important to have an established file hierarchy on your system. If you keep renaming or moving the library file to another location, all scenes with links to it will be broken!

You'll see our character positioned at the center of our scene, already selected. Since we've linked our character as a linked group, you cannot select individual items such as the mesh or armature. You also cannot enter in Edit Mode, because all structural changes must be made in the original library file.

4. To be able to pose and animate the character, we need to create a proxy instance of the armature. A proxy acts like a linked and limited copy that enables you to work on to add keyframes. With the group already selected on the 3D view, press *Ctrl + Alt + P* and select **Otto_Armature** from the list, as seen in the next screenshot:

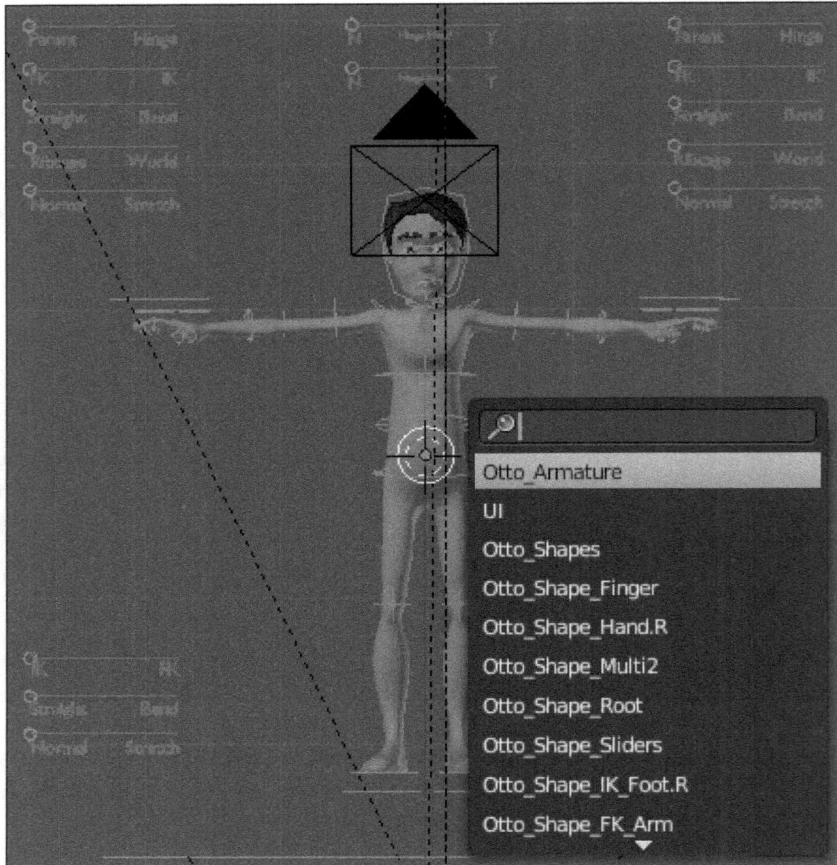

This would create a proxy instance of our armature, making it the selected object in the 3D View. Now you can press *Ctrl + Tab* to enter in Pose Mode and animate our character. If you try to enter in the armature's Edit Mode with *Tab*, nothing happens because of the limited nature of the proxy object.

5. Save this file and open the original library file, `006-Libraries-Otto.blend`. Try changing something on its mesh or materials and reopen the scene file. Everything you changed will be automatically updated on the linked instance.

   This method of linking a group is very useful for its simplicity: when linking an external library, only the group should be selected. On the other hand, you should be very careful when creating the group. You must make sure that **every** object needed for the rig is on the group.

6. Open the library file, `006-Libraries-Otto.blend`, again. In an Outliner window, select the **Groups** display mode. You'll see the only group on that file, Otto, as the root of a hierarchy of several objects, including the character meshes, armature, and helper objects, such as empties, shapes for bones and lattices. Notice that even hidden objects are included. The next screenshot shows the group with all included objects:

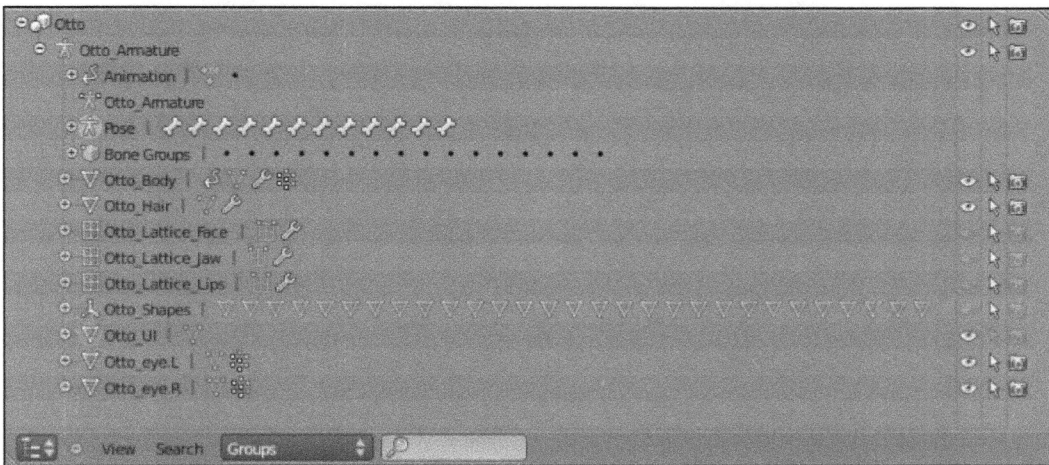

It's far easier to pick only a group of objects instead of linking each one separately. This linked group, for instance, has 41 different objects. Another advantage is that you can add or remove objects from the group on the library and all linked instances are updated.

7. Let's add another object to this Otto group. Add a sphere in the 3D View through *Shift + A* | **Mesh** | **UV Sphere**. Move (*G*) and rotate (*R*) it as you wish, then go to the **Object** tab on the Properties window, under the **Groups** section. Click on the **Add to Group** button and select **Otto**. Save the file and open the file `006-Libraries.blend` again. You'll see the new object automatically added on the scene, as you can see in the following screenshot:

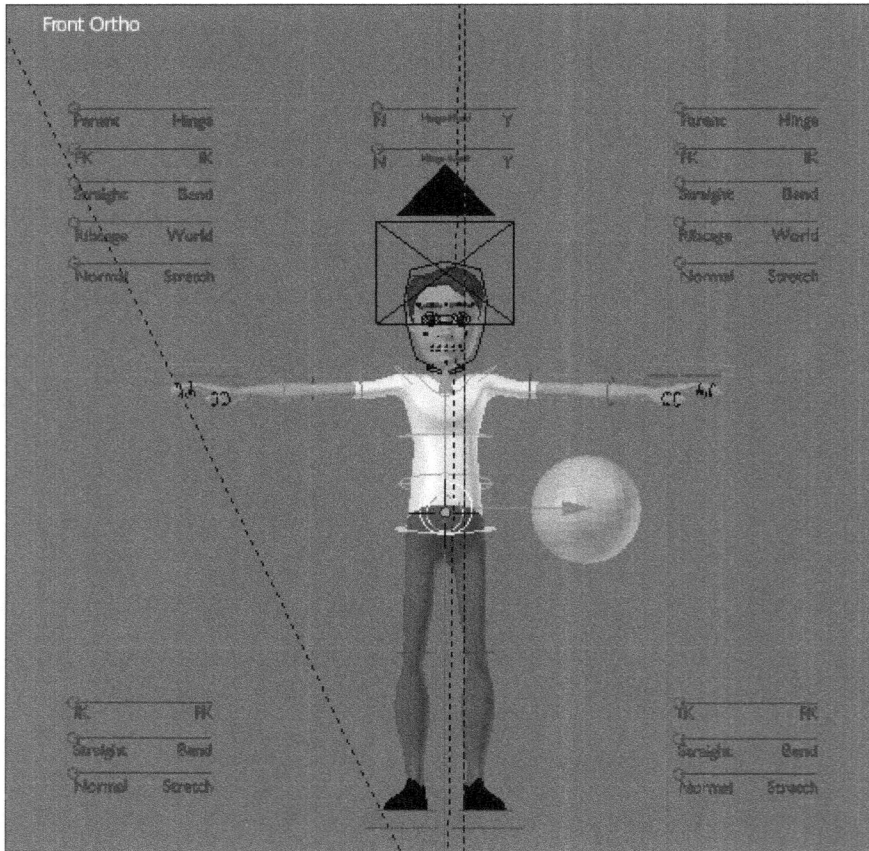

The file `006-Libraries-complete.blend` has this completed example, with the only difference that it has a linked group from the file `006-Libraries-Otto-final.blend`.

## How it works...

Working with linked assets makes your workflow organized, easier to manage and without unnecessary redundancies. For characters, it's a good idea to create a group with all necessary objects, including shapes used for the rig. Linking a group is a good practice, since you can add or remove objects to a rig without breaking existent scenes.

*Appendix*: *Naming conventions*

# Non-linear animation

Along with the more "traditional" way of animating characters, Blender offers the **Non-linear Animation** (**NLA**) Editor, where you can mix different actions to produce new movements. This editor allows a lot of flexibility, with the ability of stacking simple movements to create a more complex animation. Tasks such as repeating and reversing an animation, which demands time and care to do in the DopeSheet, are very simple to do on the NLA.

## How to do it...

1.  Open the file `006-NLA.blend`. It has our character Otto with a basic animation of a jumping jack exercise. You'll notice that the arms movement is missing. Let's do them using the NLA Editor. The following screenshot shows our starting point, with the first pose in the 3D View and its keyframes set in a DopeSheet window:

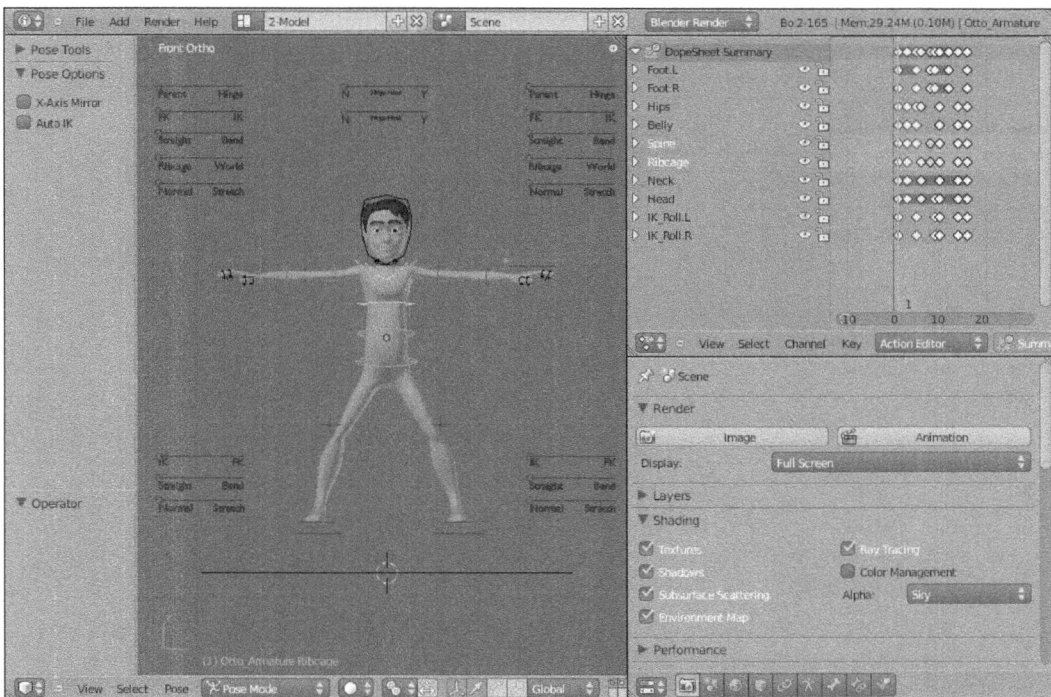

2. Press *Alt + A* to playback the animation. You'll see that, along with the missing arm movements, there is only one jump. We need this action to be repeated for a number of times so we have a real jumping jack exercise.

3. Change the Properties window below the DopeSheet into a NLA Editor using the window header. You'll notice a red line with some keyframes. This is our jumping action defined on the DopeSheet. Let's turn it into an Action Strip, so it can be treated independently as a layer of animation. Click on the "snowflake" icon right next to the action name to turn it into a strip, as shown in the next screenshot:

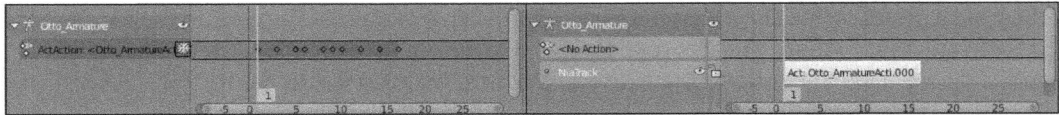

You'll notice that all keyframes set on the DopeSheet window are gone. They are now grouped inside the yellow action strip you see in the NLA Editor. To edit the keyframes of this action, select it on the NLA Editor and press *Tab*, just like you do to enter Edit Mode for objects. Once you finish editing, press *Tab* again.

4. Now let's create the arms action. The first frame has the legs spread wide, so the hands need to be touching overhead. Move and rotate the arms, hands and shoulders on frame 1, setting a new keyframe (*I*) when you're happy with the results. When you set the first keyframe, you'll see that a new **Action** is automatically created on the NLA Editor above the saved strip, as you can see in the following screenshot:

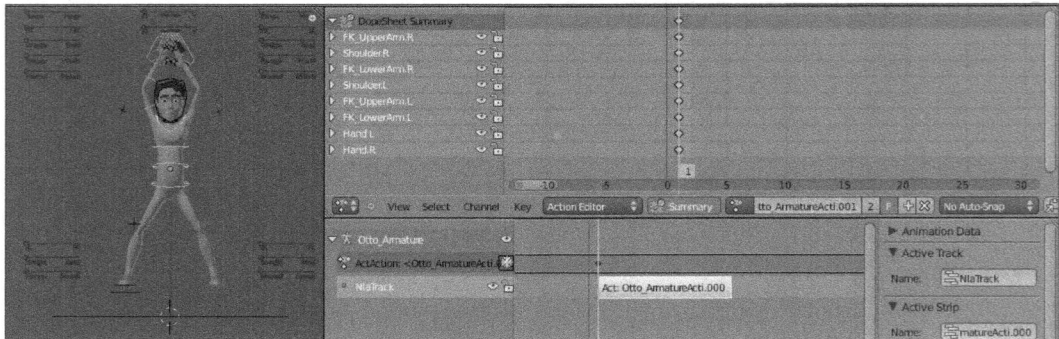

The first action of the legs and torso has 16 frames, and we want our arms action to be the same length to a perfect match. Since it's a repeating action, the first frame should be identical to the last.

5. Select all keyframes set on the first frame by holding *Alt* and right-clicking over one of the yellow keyframes; press *Shift + D* to create a copy and move them to frame 16.

6. Frame 9 is where the feet stay together and the torso is straight, so the arms and hands need to be down. Create another extreme keyframe there. Continue adding more keyframes to create good breakdown positions and in-betweens until you have a nice movement of the arms. Once you finish, go to the NLA Editor window and click on the "snowflake" icon for this new action to create another strip.

7. You may rename the strips and tracks on the Properties panel (*N*) at the right-hand side.

8. Now, for the repetition. This is very easy to do in the NLA Editor. In the DopeSheet you'd have to manually duplicate the keyframes, causing an undesirable redundancy. In the NLA however, it's just a matter of selecting the desired strip and changing the **Repeat** value in the **Action Clip** section of the Properties panel, as seen in the next screenshot, where the strip is set to repeat five times:

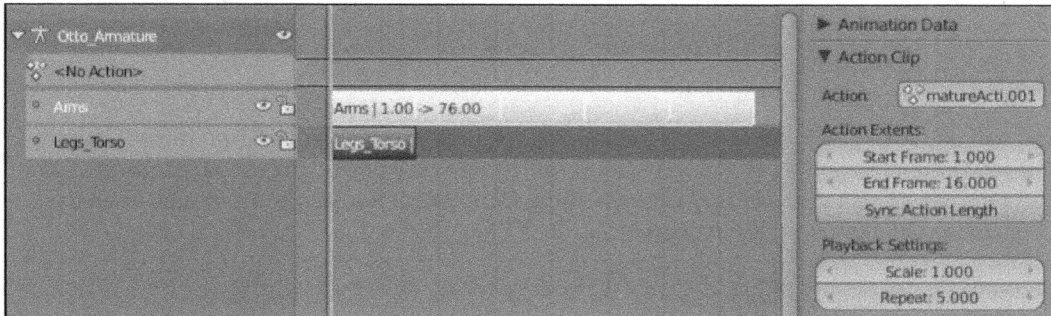

9. Select the bottom strip and change its **Repeat** value to 5 also, so both strips have a matching length. In the NLA you can drag strips around to change their sync, so you can easily offset motions to increase the sense of overlapping actions. If you play the animation with *Alt + A,* you'll see the animation repeating seamlessly for five times.

> Using the Properties panel in the NLA Editor you can also change the overall timing of a strip by changing its **Scale** value. Reversing a strip is just a matter of enabling the **Reversed** option. Strips can also receive modifiers, so you can add a random noise to movements or simulate the feel of a stop-motion video by using a stepped interpolation.

10. Make a quick OpenGL rendering of the active 3D viewport by clicking on the clapperboard button on the 3D view header. After finishing, play the results by pressing *Ctrl + F11.* You may feel this animation is too quick, so it's a good idea to slow it down a bit.

In the "traditional" way, using the DopeSheet, we would have to move keyframes around to adjust the timing, but on the NLA Editor you can just change the **Scale** value on the Properties panel to 1.5 for both strips. Blender will automatically resize the strips and calculate the new timing for them. That's very useful when you need to adjust the timing for an entire action.

The file 006-NLA-complete.blend has this finished recipe, and you can refer to it if in doubt or to compare your results.

## How it works...

The Non-linear Animation (NLA) Editor in Blender allows us to logically separate and stack pieces of animation, making it easy to combine different movements, and make repetitions and timing adjustments. The pieces, or strips, are seen by Blender just like film strips in a non-linear video editor, where you can move around and mix layers of different actions.

## There's more...

You can use the NLA Editor to apply the layered refinement approach that we talked about on the recipe *Animating in layers*. Each step of refinement (key poses, Extremes, Breakdowns) can be a separate action visually layered on the NLA Editor. This way you can also keep the steps separate in a non-destructive way.

## See also

*Chapter 6: Animating in layers*

*Chapter 7: Adjusting and tracking the timing*

*Chapter 9: It's time for secondary actions*

# 7
# Easy to Say, Hard to Do: Mastering the Basics

In this chapter, we will cover the following topics:

- ▶ Adjusting and tracking the timing
- ▶ Spacing: favoring and easing poses
- ▶ Anticipating an action
- ▶ Using squash and stretch
- ▶ Breaking the symmetry

## Introduction

The most difficult thing in animation is, quite ironically, mastering the basics. Young animators often have an urge to do "complicated" things such as complex dialogues and action scenes, but fail to understand aspects such as timing, spacing, asymmetry, or squash and stretch.

Following the principle of working in layers of refinement, covered in the previous chapter we must take care to make the basic underlying layers first, and make them well. Before attempting the fancy stuff, we need to make sure we have a good foundation. This foundation must work on its own: you should be able to communicate the actions and its motivations without all the polish.

# Adjusting and tracking the timing

Timing, by itself, is a subject that goes well beyond the scope of a simple recipe. It is, in fact, the main subject of a number of animation-related books. Strictly speaking, **Timing** in animation is how long it takes (in frames or seconds) between two Extreme poses.

You can have your character in great poses, but if the timing between them is not right, your shot may be ruined. Maybe it is a difficult thing to master because there are no definite rules for it: everyone is born with a particular sense of timing. Despite that, it's enormously important to look at video and real life references to understand the timing for different actions.

Imagine a tennis ball falling to the ground and bouncing. Think of the time between its first and second contact with the ground. Now replace it with a bowling ball and think of the time required for this bounce. You know, from your life experience, that the tennis ball bounces slower than the bowling ball. The timing between these two balls is different. The timing here (along with spacing, subject of the next recipe) is the main factor that makes us perceive the different nature and weight of each ball.

The "rules" of timing can also be broken for comedic effect: something that purposely moves faster or slower than usual may get a laugh from the audience. We're going to see how different timings can change how we perceive a shot with the same poses.

## How to do it...

1. Open the file `007-Timing.blend`. It has our character Otto with three poses, making him look from one side to the other:

2.  Press *Alt + A* to play the animation. You may think the timing is acceptable for this head turn, but this method of checking the timing is **not** ideal. When you tell Blender to play the animation through *Alt + A*, you're relying in your computer's power to process all the information of your scene in real time. You'd probably end up seeing something slower than what you'll actually get after rendering the frames.

> When playing the animation inside the 3D view, you can see the actual playback frame rate on the top left corner of the window. If it's slower than the scene frame rate (in this case, 24 fps), it means that the rendered animation will be faster than what you're seeing.

When adjusting the timing, we must be sure of the exact results of every keyframe set. Even a one-frame change can make a huge impact on the scene, but rendering a complex scene just to test the timing is out of the question, because it just takes too long to see the results. We need a quick way to check the timing precisely.

Fortunately, Blender allows us to make a quick "render" of our 3D view, with only the OpenGL information. This is also called "playblast", and is exactly what we need. Take a look at the header of our 3D view and find the button with a clapperboard icon, as seen in the next screenshot:

> OpenGL stands for **Open Graphics Library**, and is a free cross-platform specification and API for writing 2D and 3D computer graphics. Not only are the objects inside Blender's 3D view made using this library, but also the user interface with all its buttons, icons, and text are drawn on the screen with OpenGL. From OpenGL version 2.0 it's possible to use GLSL, a high level shading language heavily used to create games and supported by Blender to enhance the way objects are displayed on the screen in real time. From Blender 2.5, GLSL is the default real time rendering method when the user selects the Textured viewport shading mode, but that option has to be supported by your graphics card.

3. Click on that clapperboard button, and the active 3D view will be used for a quick OpenGL render of your scene. This preview rendering shares the **Render** panel settings in the Properties window, so the picture size, frame rate, output folder, file format, duration, and stamp will be the same. If you can't see the button in your 3D View header (it is available only in the header) it may be an issue of lack of space; you can click with the middle button (or the scroll wheel) of your mouse over the header and drag it to the sides to find it.

4. After the OpenGL rendering is complete, press *Esc* to go back to your scene and press *Ctrl + F11* to preview the animation with the correct frame rate to check the timing.

> Starting with the Blender 2.5 series, there's no built-in player in the program, so you have to specify one in the User Preferences window (*Ctrl + Alt + U*), on the File tab. This player can even be a previous version of Blender in the 2.4 series or any player you wish, such as DJV (`http://djv.sourceforge.net/`) or Mplayer (`http://www.mplayerhq.hu`). With any of these options you must tell Blender the file path where the player is installed.

Now that you can watch the animation with the correct frame rate, you'll notice that the head turns quite fast, since it only takes five frames to complete. This fast timing makes our action seem to happen after the character listens to an abrupt and loud noise coming from his left, so he has to turn his head quickly and look to see what happened.

Let's suppose our character is watching a tennis match in Wimbledon, and his seat is in line with the net, at the middle of the court (yep, lucky guy). Watching the ball from the serve until it reaches the other side of the court should take longer than what we have just set up, so let's adjust our keyframes now.

5. In the **DopeSheet** window, leave the first keyframe at frame 1. Select the last column of keyframes by holding *Alt* and right-clicking on any keyframe set at frame 5. Move (G) the column to frame 15 (hold *Ctrl* for snapping to the frames), so our action takes three times longer than the original.

> Another way of selecting a column of keyframes is through the **DopeSheet Summary** option on the window header. It creates an extra line above all channels. If you select the diamond on this line, all keyframes on that column will be selected. You can even collapse all channels and use only the **DopeSheet Summary** to move the keys along the timeline to make timing adjustments easily.

6. Now, the Breakdown, or intermediate position between two Extreme poses. It doesn't have to be at the exact middle of our action. Actually, it's good to avoid symmetry not only in our models and poses, but in our motions too. Move (G) the Breakdown to frame 6, and you'll have something similar to the next screenshot:

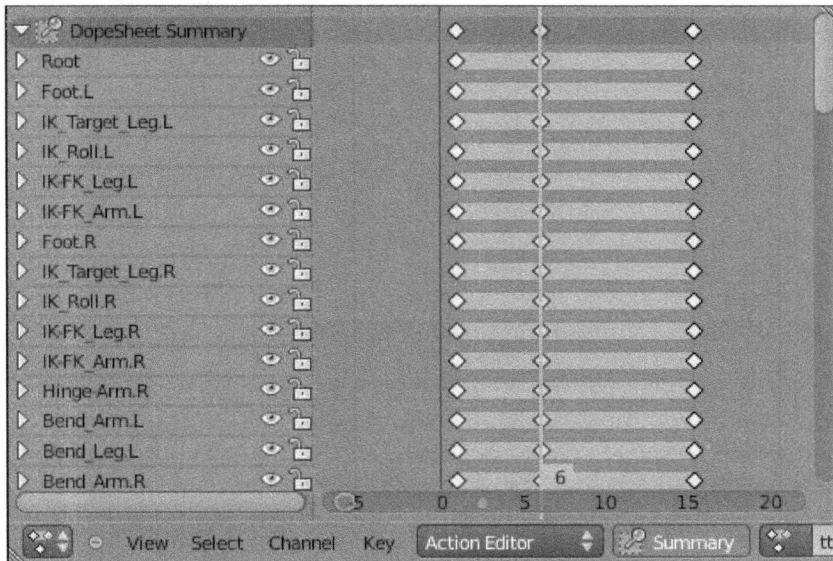

Now you can make another OpenGL render to preview the action with the new timing. You can choose to disable the layer where the armature is located, the second, by holding *Shift* and clicking over it, so you don't have the bones on the preview. Of course this is far from a finished shot: it's a good idea to make the character blink during the head turn, add some moving holds, animate the eyeballs, add some facial expressions, and so on. This rough example is only to show how drastically the timing can change the feel of an action. If you set the timing between the positions even higher, our character may seem like he's looking at something slower (someone on a bike, maybe?) moving in front of him.

## How it works...

Along with good posing, the timing is crucial to make our actions vivid, believable, and with a sense of weight. The timing also is very important to help your audience understand what is happening in the scene, so it must be carefully adjusted. To have a precise view of how the timing is working in an action within Blender, it's best to use the OpenGL preview mode, since the usual *Alt + A* shortcut to preview the animation inside the 3D View can be misleading.

## There's more...

Depending on the complexity of your scene, you can achieve the correct frame rate within the 3D view with *Alt + A*. You can disable the visibility of irrelevant objects or some modifiers to help speed up this real time processing, like lowering (or disabling) the Subdivision Surface modifier and hiding the armature and background layers.

## See also

*Appendix: Extremes, Breakdowns, Inbetweens, ones and twos*

*Chapter 6: Non-linear animation*

*Chapter 7: Spacing: favoring and easing poses*

# Spacing: favoring and easing poses

The previous recipe shows us how to adjust the timing of our character's actions, which is something extremely important to make our audience not only understand what is happening on the screen, but also know the weight and forces involved in the motion. Since timing is closely related to spacing, there is often confusion between the two concepts.

**Timing** in animation is the number of frames between two Extreme poses. **Spacing** is how the animated subject moves and shows variations of speed along these frames. Actions with the same timing and different spacing are perceived differently by the audience, and these principles combined are responsible for the feeling of weight of our actions.

We're going to see how the spacing works and how we can create eases and favoring poses to enhance movements.

## How to do it...

1. Open the file `007-Spacing.blend`. It has our character Otto turning his head from right to left, just like in the timing recipe. We don't have a Breakdown position defined yet, and this action has a timing set to 15 frames.

   First, let's understand the most elementary type of spacing: linear, or even spacing. This is when the calculated intermediate positions between two keyframes have the same distance among them, without any kind of acceleration. This isn't something we're used to seeing in nature, thus it's not the default interpolation mode in Blender.

2. To use it, select the desired keyframes in a DopeSheet or a Graph Editor window, press *Shift + T*, and choose the **Linear** interpolation mode. The curves between the keyframes will turn into straight lines, as you can see in the next screenshot showing the channels for the `Head` bone.

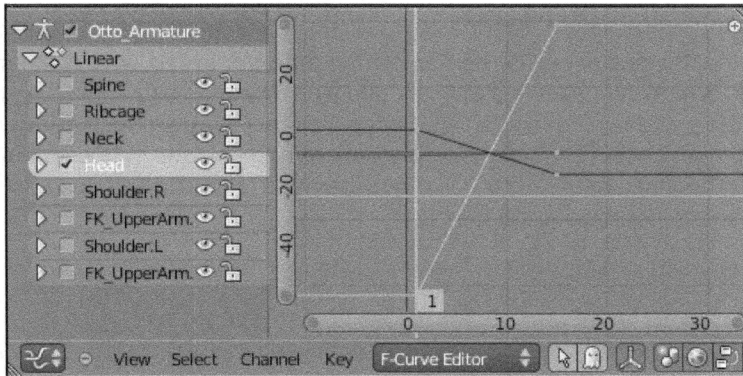

If you preview the animation with *Alt + A*, you'll see that the movement is very mechanical and unappealing, something we don't see in nature. That's why this interpolation mode isn't the default one.

Movements in nature all have some variation in speed, going from a resting state, accelerating to a peak velocity, then slowing down until another resting state. These variations of speed are called **eases**, and are represented with curved lines on the Graph Editor. When there is an increase in speed we have an **ease out**. When the movement slows down to a resting state, we have an **ease in**.

3. This variation in speed is the default interpolation method in Blender, and you can enable it by selecting the desired keyframes in a DopeSheet or Graph Editor window, press *Shift + T* and select the Bezier interpolation mode. The next screenshot shows the same keyframes with easing:

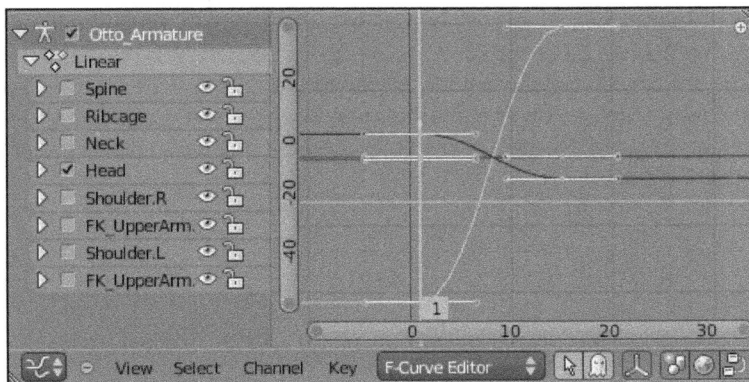

When we adjust the curve handles on the Graph Editor, we're actually defining the eases of that movement. When you insert keyframes in Blender, it automatically creates both eases: out and in (with same speeds). Since not all movements have the same variation of speed at their beginning and end, it's a good idea to change the handles on the Graph Editor. This difference of speed between the start and end keyframes is called **favoring**.

When the Spacing between two poses have different eases, we say the movement "favors" one of the poses, notably the one which has the bigger ease. In the next screenshot, the curves for the Head bone were adjusted so the movement favors the second pose. Note that there is a softer curve near the second pose, while the first has sharper lines near it. This will make the head leave the first pose very quick and slowly settle into the second one.

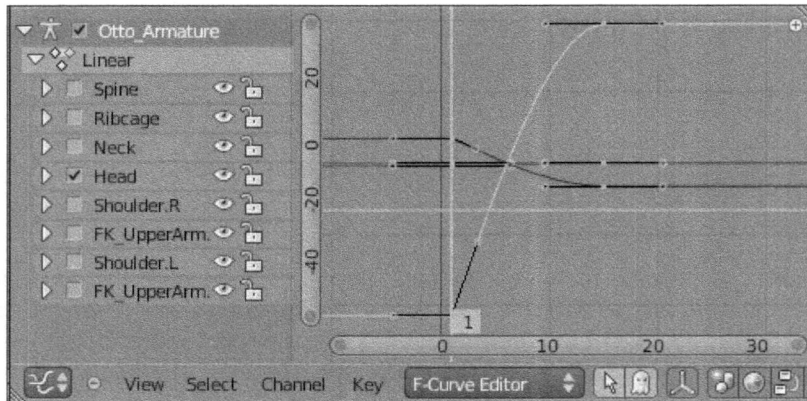

In order to create sharp angles with the handles in the Graph Editor window, you need to select the desired curve channels, press *V* and choose the **Free** handle type.

4. Open the video file 007-Spacing.mov in a video player, which enables navigating through the frames (such as DJV—http://djv.sourceforge.net), to watch the three actions at the same time. Although the timing of the action is unchanged, you can clearly notice how the interpolation changes the motion. In the next screenshot, you can see that at frame 8, the Favoring version has the face closer to the second pose:

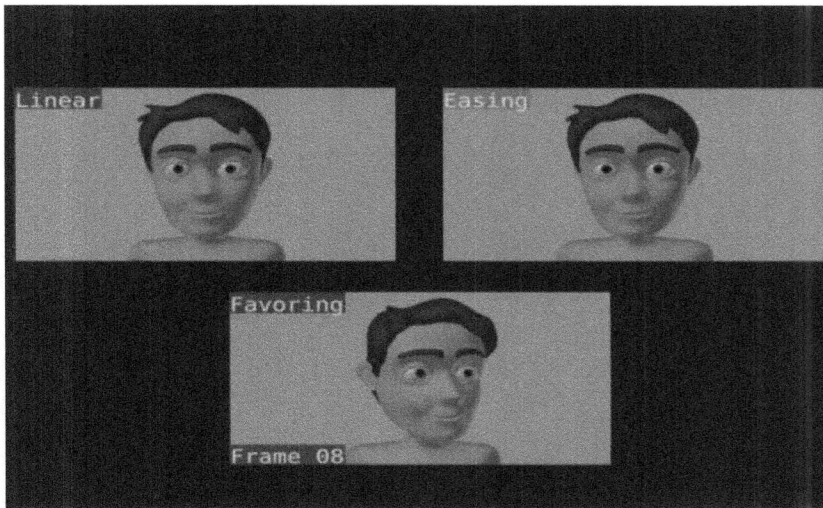

Now that you understand what spacing is, know the difference between the interpolation types, and can use eases to favor poses, let's add a Breakdown position. This action is pretty boring, since the head turn happens without any arcs. It's a good idea to tilt the head down a little during the turn, making an imaginary arc with the eyes.

Especially during quick head turns, it's a good idea to make your character blink during the turn. Unless your character is following something with the eyes—such as in a tennis court in our example—a quick blink is useful to make a "scene cut" in our minds from one subject to the other.

5. On the DopeSheet window, in the Action Editor, select the **Favoring** action. Go to frame 6, where the character looks to the camera. Select and rotate (*R*) the `Head` and `Neck` bones to front on their local X axis, as seen in the next screenshot, and insert a keyframe (*I*) for its rotation:

Since Blender automatically creates symmetrical eases on each new keyframe, it's time to adjust our spacing for the `Head` and `Neck` bones on the Graph Editor window. If you play the animation with *Alt + A*, you'll notice that the motion goes very weird because of that automatic ease. The F-Curves on the X axis of each bone for this motion are not soft. Ideally, since this is a Breakdown position, the curves between it and its surrounding Extreme poses should be smooth, regardless of the favoring.

6. Select the curve handles on frames 1 and 6, and move (*G*) them in order to soften the curve peak in that Breakdown position. The next screenshot shows the curves before and after editing. Notice how the peak curves at the Breakdown in the middle get smoother after editing:

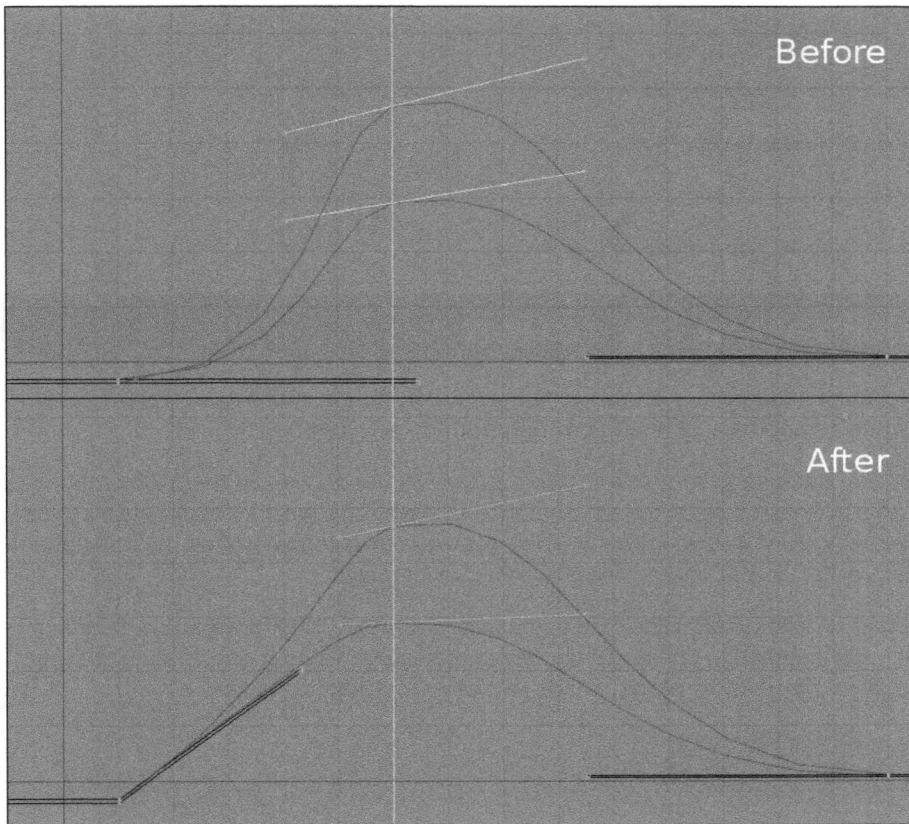

Before

After

Now the action looks more natural, with a nice Breakdown and favoring created using the F-Curves. The file `007-Spacing-complete.blend` has this finished example for your reference, in which you can play the animation with *Alt + A* to see the results.

## How it works...

By understanding the principle of Spacing, you can create eases and favoring in order to create snappy and interesting motions. Just like visible shapes, the pace of motion in nature is often asymmetrical. To make your motions not only more interesting, but also more believable and with accents to reinforce the purpose behind the movements, you should master Spacing. Be sure to check out the interpolation curves in your animations: interesting movements normally have different eases between two Extreme positions.

## See also

*Appendix*: Extremes, Breakdowns, Inbetweens, ones and twos

*Chapter 6*: Non-linear animation

*Chapter 6*: Tracking animation arcs

*Chapter 7*: Adjusting and tracking the timing

# Anticipating an action

In nature, most actions have a preceding movement. Be it a subtle eye or eyebrow movements to anticipate a head turn, or a full-body preparation for a jump.

Giving proper premise to your characters' actions will not only make them look more natural, but will also give visual clues to your audience so they know what's happening on the screen and where to look next. If you think of it like that, you may conclude that the anticipation principle is a storytelling resource in the animator's tool set.

As any other animation principle, you can use it (or remove it) for dramatic or comedic purposes. For instance, a character may leave the screen without anticipation, leaving only dust in its place and a proper sound to make the audience laugh.

## How to do it...

1.  Open the file `007-Anticipation.blend`. It has our character Otto with some basic poses for a jump. From right to left in the next screenshot: he is standing before the jump; the start of the jump; the moment where he finishes the jump, with his left foot touching the ground. We have a very important missing position here, the anticipation pose where he takes impulse for the jump. This pose must be between the first and second positions.

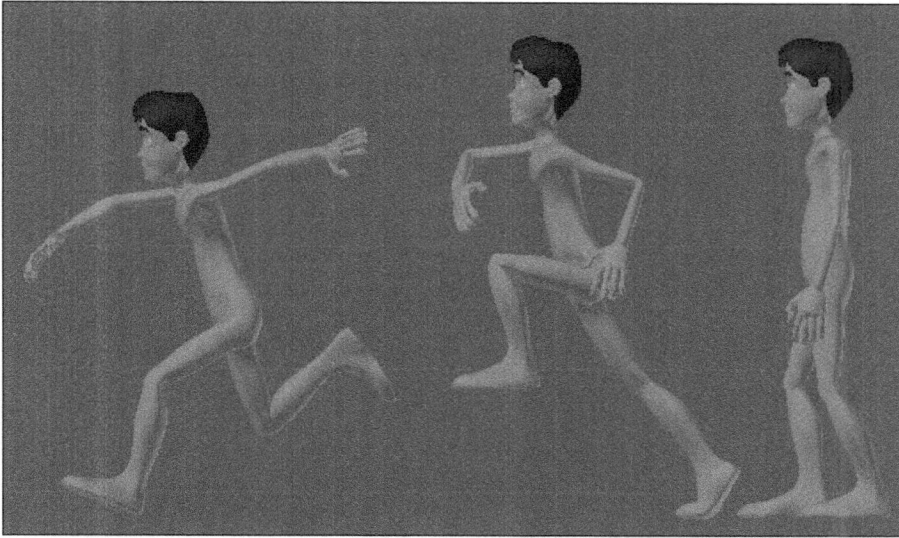

If you play the animation using *Alt + A* or render a playblast, you'll see that our character needs an impulse to accomplish the jump in a natural way. The timing is also something that we need to adjust, since we have only basic poses equally distributed on the timeline.

2. On a DopeSheet window, leave our first keyframe at frame 1. Move (*G*), the second column of keyframes to frame 17, the third to frame 19, the fourth to frame 22, and the last to frame 26. You'll notice a big empty space between the first and second keyframes, as shown in the next screenshot. We're going to fill it with an anticipation pose.

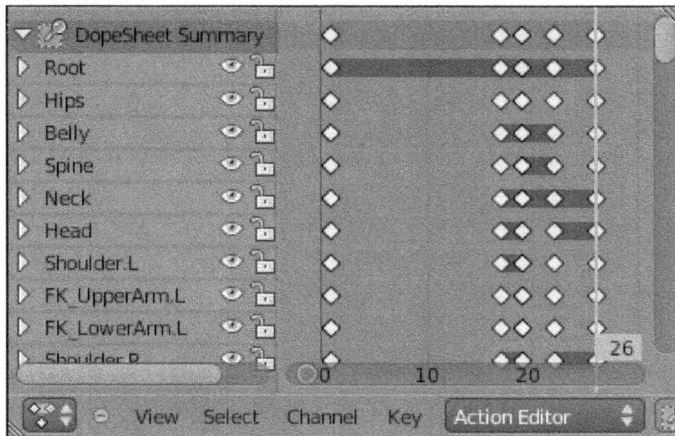

3. Go to frame 11 and adjust the pose so our character bends his torso and both knees in order to prepare for the jump. Rotate (*R*) the **IK_Roll.R** controller to make the left leg stand over the ball of the foot, and also the finger controllers to close them a bit.

4. You'll notice the right foot in the next keyframe is a bit forward to help the impulse. You can select the diamond related to the `Foot.R` bone on frame 17, duplicate (*Shift + D*) it, and bring the copy to frame 11. Refer to the next screenshot to base your pose on:

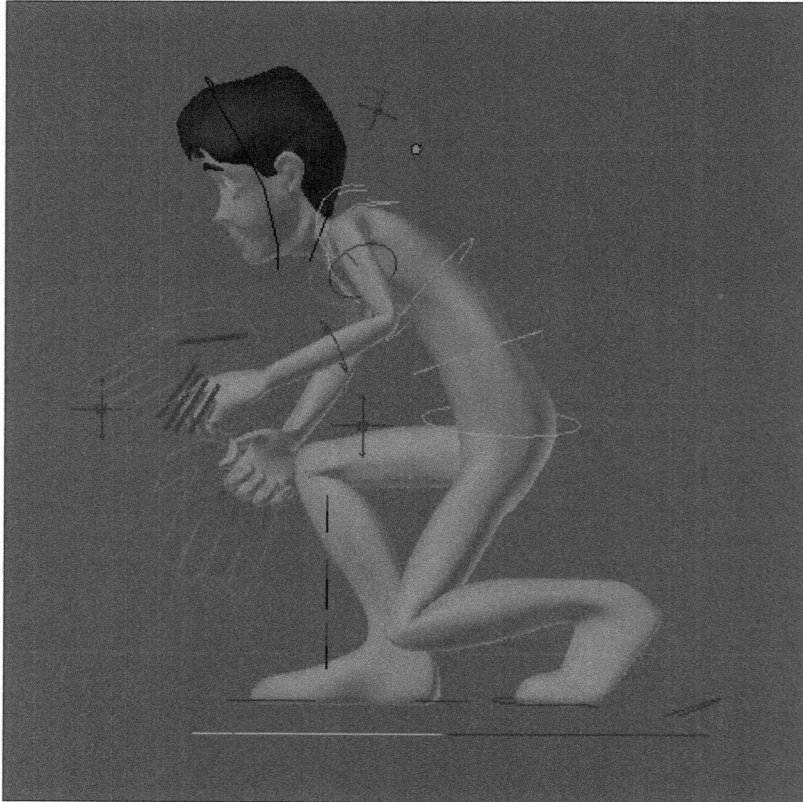

Now, with our basic poses ready and with a proper anticipation to the jump, it's just a matter of adding more subtleties and fixes to our motion. Since the computer is a "dumb" inbetweener, we need to add more positions before and after our Extremes and Breakdowns in order to achieve good arcs (refer to the Tracking animation arcs recipe, in the previous chapter).

The file `007-Anticipation-complete.blend` has this complete exercise with some more positions added, so you can refer to it and compare your own results.

## How it works...

By understanding the principles behind motion, you'll be able to add proper anticipation to your character's actions. Along with more physical examples similar to those in this recipe, you should think of this principle as a storytelling device with subtleties, such as making your character look at an object before picking it up, or looking to one side prior to a head turn.

## See also

*Appendix*: *Extremes, Breakdowns, Inbetweens, ones and twos*

*Chapter 6*: *Tracking animation arcs*

*Chapter 7*: *Using squash and stretch*

# Using squash and stretch

The animators at Disney, notably Frank Thomas and Ollie Johnston, stated that the animation principles were discovered instead of defined. Among those discoveries, arguably the most important is the fact that organic bodies squash and stretch its shapes during movement.

Most people associate this principle only with cartoony and exaggerated animation, but small amounts of squash and stretch are very welcome to "realistic" types of motion to help emphasize extreme poses. That's why it's a good idea to have a squash and stretch enabled character rig.

## How to do it...

1.  Open the file `007-Stretch.blend`. It has our character Otto making a jump, just like the result of our previous recipe on anticipation. To enhance the feeling of impulse and help lead the eyes of our audience, we're going to add a little squash and stretch to the torso and legs.

    First, the torso. Our rig enables us to stretch the torso region by simply scaling the desired controllers. In our scene, the character gets into its crouching position at frame 11. We need a soft squashing here to enhance the feeling of weight after the body stops the down movement.

2.  At frame 11 the torso shouldn't have squashed yet, so go to this frame, select the `Belly` and `Spine` bones, and insert a keyframe (*I*) for their resting sizes.

3. Our character starts its ascending movement and makes the jump at frame 17. Go to this frame and insert another keyframe to the resting size of the bones. Up until now nothing has changed: we have just defined when the squashing action will start and end.

4. Now go to frame 13. Scale (S) down these bones slightly so you have a nice squashing action in the middle of the crouching action, as seen in the next screenshot:

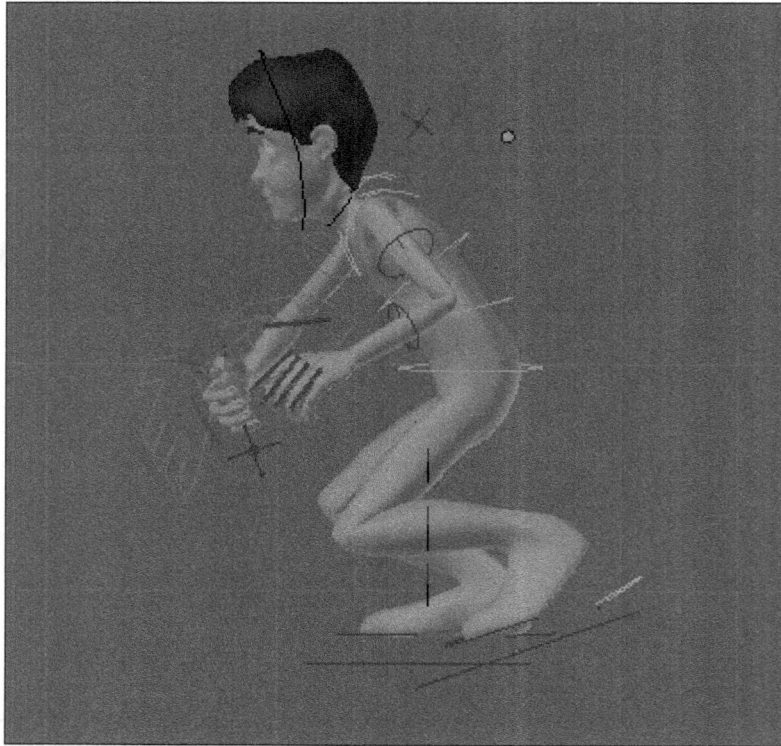

This will create a subtle squashing action. Besides being subtle, it enhances the pose and the feeling of weight behind the action.

5. Now we're going to do the same for the peak of the jump, when the torso should be fully stretched. Go to frame 19 and scale (S) the two bones up, inserting another size keyframe (*I*) for them, as you can see in the next screenshot:

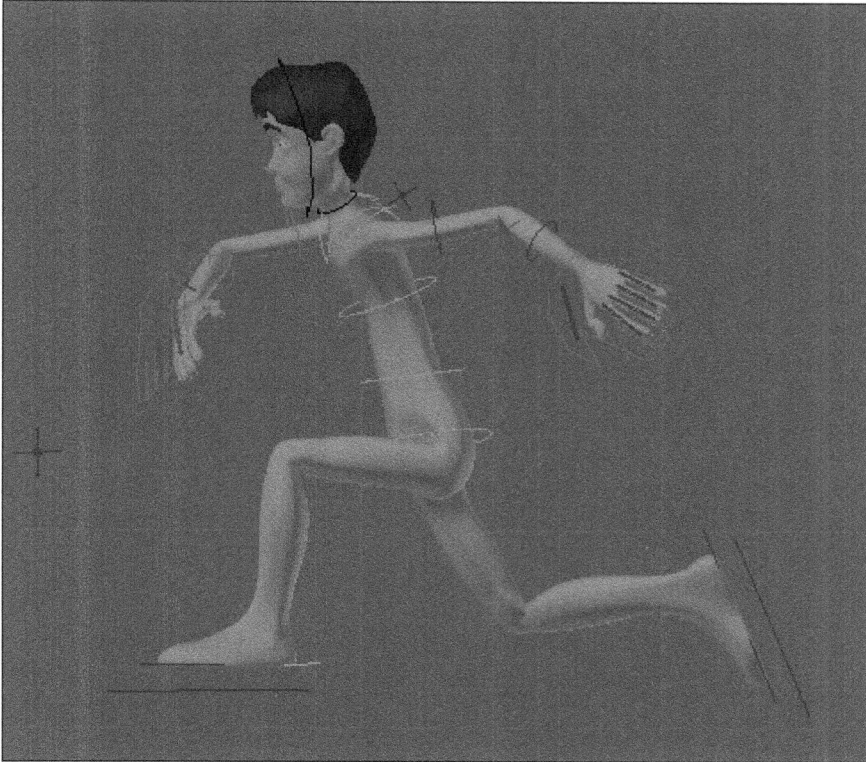

6. Go to frame 23 and, since this is where the impact happens, scale down the controllers to achieve another squashing. Finally, go to the last frame of the action (23), return the size of both controllers to their default (*Alt* + S) and save another scale keyframe for them. This will create a nice and subtle variation of squashing and stretching during the action, reinforcing the feeling of weight and forces involved.

If you expand the channels for the Belly and Spine controllers on the DopeSheet window you'll see that the number of rotation and location keyframes is higher than the number of scaling ones, which are responsible for this "layer" of squashing and stretching, as you can see in the next screenshot:

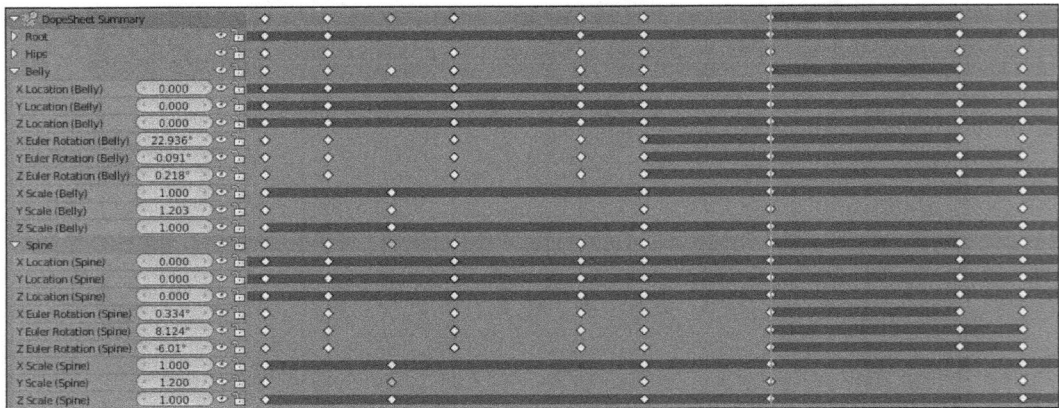

7. Now, the legs. Since they're in IK mode, we need to enable the stretching feature in our rig. Go to front view (*Numpad 1*) at the first frame of the animation, select and move (*G*) both stretch controllers for the legs to the right, and insert a location keyframe (*I*) for them, as seen in the following screenshot:

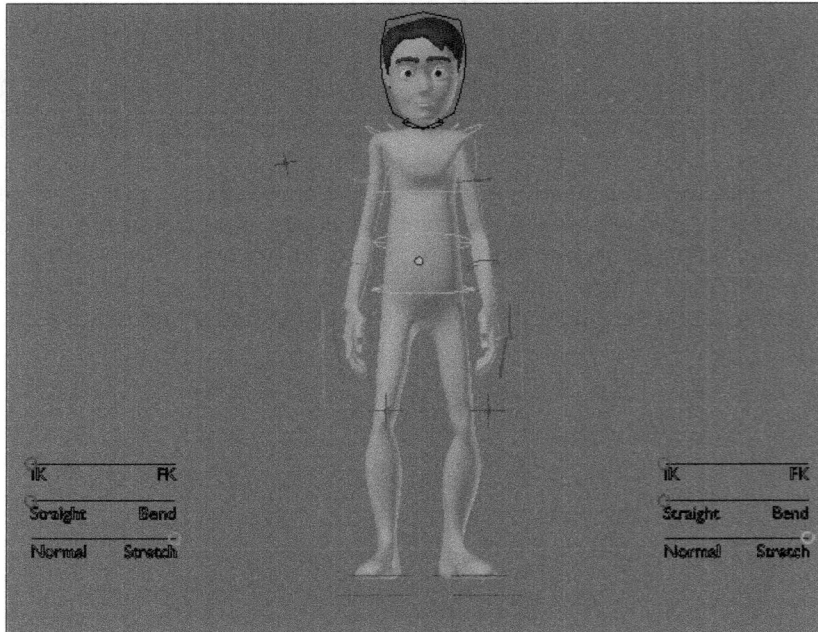

8. Now go back to side view and adjust the **Foot.L** and **Foor.R** controllers to slightly stretch the legs where applicable. When you move the controller beyond the regular extension of each leg, they'll stretch to follow it. It's a good idea to add a little stretching to the right leg at frame 18 in order to enhance the feeling of impulse, and the left leg at frame 21 to enhance the foot contact to the ground. The next screenshot shows the two legs stretching at their frames:

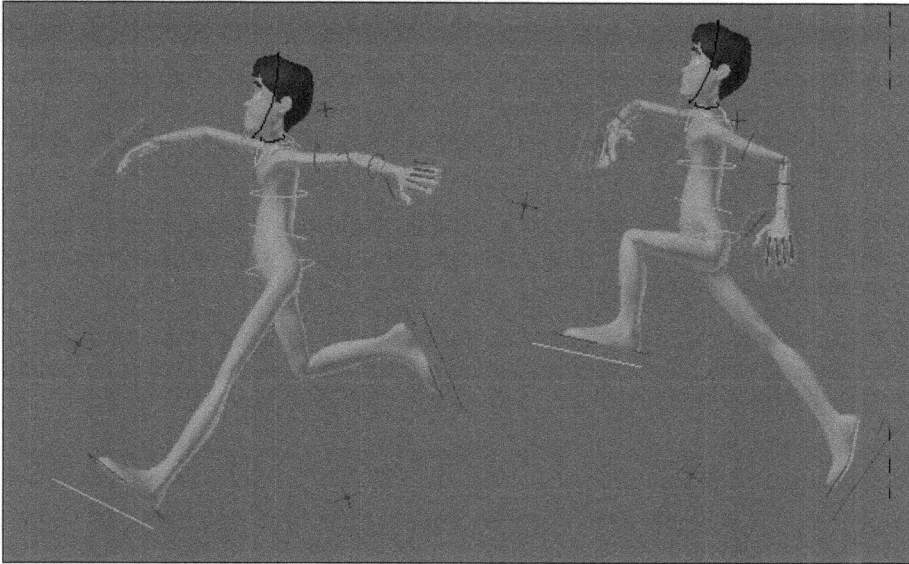

Those stretching actions on the torso and legs last for a couple of frames, look weird when viewed alone, but they do add some charm and help the action when watched in continuous motion. Now it's just a matter of rendering an OpenGL playblast (the clapperboard icon on the 3D window header) and watching the animation on its correct timing.

The file `007-Stretch-complete.blend` has this completed example for your reference.

## How it works...

In nature, all organic structures are somewhat flexible, achieving levels of squashing and stretching while in motion. The squash-and-stretch principle can enhance the feeling of weight and forces involved in motion, and should be used not only in cartoon animations, but also as a layer of improvement.

## See also

Chapter 6: *Animating in layers*

Chapter 7: *Anticipating an action*

# Breaking the symmetry

Among the 12 basic principles stated by the animation legends Frank Thomas and Ollie Johnston, there is one called **Solid Drawing**. Even if you can't draw anything else other than a stick figure, this principle remains as important for those who use the computer as is does for classical 2D animators.

Think of the computer and its software as a highly sophisticated and expensive kind of pencil. A pencil doesn't make a masterpiece for itself, nor the computer. It's the person behind the tool who makes the difference.

When posing your character on the screen you're creating a "drawing", even if there's no pencil and paper involved. Thus, you have to take control of the shapes presented on the screen to make this drawing more appealing to the audience and tell a story.

Images rendered in a 3D application tend to look **too** perfect and symmetrical, and that does not feel natural. A big part of the work of artists involved in the processes of modeling, texturing, and lighting is to add "imperfections" to their work in order to make the images look more natural, believable, and interesting. The work of an animator shouldn't be different.

## How to do it...

1. Open the file `007-Symmetry.blend`. It has our character with four basic poses applied to it in an action of falling to the ground. We are not worried about the timing just yet, because we need to finish our poses first. You will notice that his poses are absolutely symmetrical, as the next screenshot shows it in front and side views:

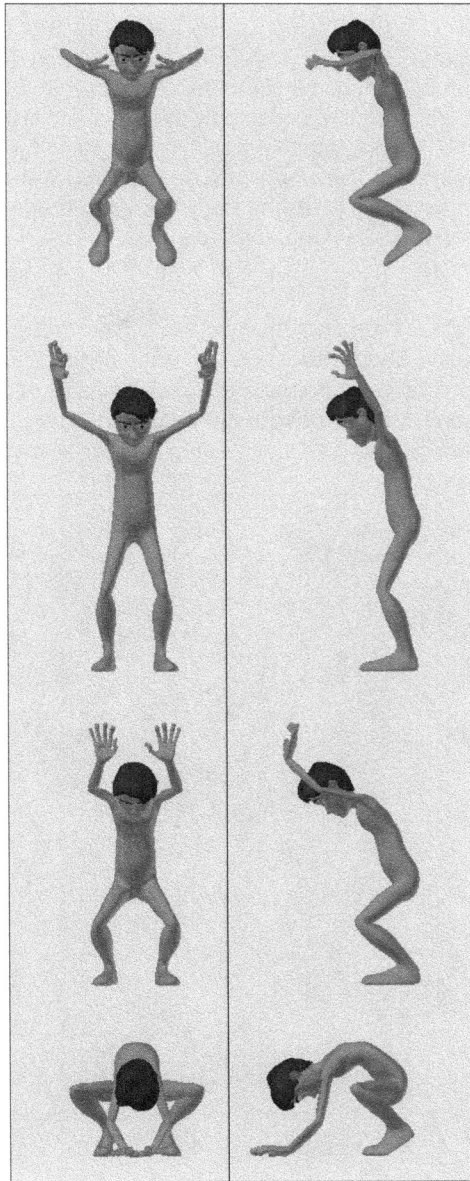

Nobody falls like that! In the side view, we can't even tell whether he has more than one arm or leg, since they are at the exact same position. We need to bring a bit of asymmetry to these poses to make the fall appear more natural.

> Although a symmetrical pose isn't something desirable for a natural motion, it can be useful to use this symmetry as a starting point. In this case, I've posed only the torso and left limbs and copied the flipped pose to the right limbs. Since the bones have the .L and .R suffixes, you can use the **X-Axis Mirror** option on the Toolshelf panel (*T*) or the **Copy Pose** and **Paste Flipped Pose** buttons on the 3D Window header.

2. Go to frame 1 and start breaking this symmetry. Rotate (*R*) and move (*G*) the bones to have a more relaxed and natural pose on each of the four "drawings" we have on the timeline. Don't forget to replace the keyframes (*I*) of each bone that you've changed. It's also useful to check your changes in all views at the same time with the quad-view split option toggle (*Ctrl + Alt + Q*). The next screenshot shows our first pose with a more natural shape:

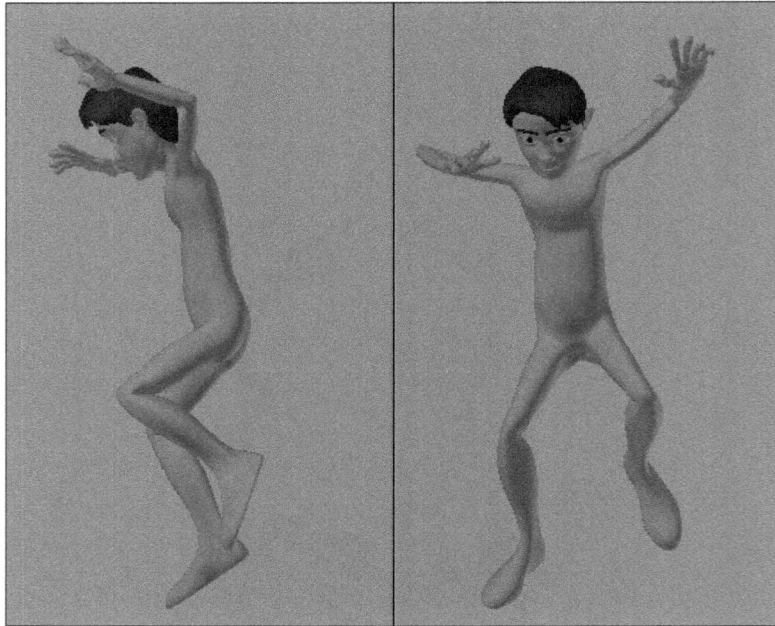

3. This is looking much better. Once you feel happy with the resulting first pose, go change the next ones. Remember to make the adjustments in a coherent way; for instance, if the right leg is closer to the ground prior to the impact, it will most likely touch the ground first.

That leads us to another way of thinking about the asymmetry: not only the shapes on the screen shouldn't be symmetrical, but also the motion. The animation principle of the Overlapping Action tells us that different parts of an organic body move at different speeds. Taking this into consideration, both our character's hands and feet shouldn't touch the ground at the same time, for instance.

Another implication of it is that we'll need more positions set in our timeline than what we already have to address this overlapping actions. That shouldn't be an issue, since we're actually going to add more positions anyway: the computer is a "dumb" inbetweener and obligates us to add more keyframes than the regular Extreme and Breakdown positions.

The following screenshot shows our adjusted poses, and the file `007-Symmetry.blend` has our complete recipe with the correction applied to the poses for your reference. To finish this action we need to add some extra keyframes and adjust the timing and spacing, but that is out of the scope of this recipe. Check our recipes covering timing, spacing, and arcs to learn more about this.

## How it works...

Most organic (or non-mechanical) creatures move in a non-symmetrical way. Despite having some sort of physiological symmetry, such as the bilateral symmetry on humans, there are some "imperfections" that our eyes are very used to perceive. The lack of these imperfections both in shape and motion is something we notice very quickly, breaking the "illusion of life" that we want to create as animators. Adding a fair amount of asymmetry helps our animations to be more believable, looking more natural and fluid.

## See also

*Appendix*: Extremes, Breakdowns, Inbetweens, ones and twos

*Chapter 6*: Non-linear animation

*Chapter 6*: Silhouette and mirrored rendering

# 8
# Shake That Body: The Mechanics of Body Movement

In this chapter, we will cover the following topics:

- ▶ Animating a tennis serve
- ▶ Heavy metal (weight lifting)
- ▶ Glory for your team: kicking the ball
- ▶ Run, Forrest! (in cycles)

## Introduction

The previous chapter was about some basic aspects of character animation, things you should learn and know by heart. With practice you'll notice that these principles will become second nature to you when you animate.

In fact, the next few recipes don't require much more than what we've already learned in the previous chapter: we're going to use what we've learned, and more than one principle at a time. We're going to apply what we know about timing, spacing, anticipation, asymmetric posing, squash-and-stretch, and a few new things that we'll see along the way.

Since we're going to deal with scenes are a bit more complete, it's strongly recommended that you read the *Creating thumbnails with Grease Pencil* article in the Appendix of this book. Planning is an often overlooked step when animating, but it's hard to stress enough how important planning is to help you make better animated shots. Along with planning, it's also crucial to look at moving references (record yourself, your friends, search YouTube, rent a movie, watch people on the street, and so on; whatever works for you) to figure out the mechanics behind the particular movement you need to create.

# Animating a tennis serve

One of the nice things about being an animator is the chance to bring the illusion of life to different characters. These characters often don't have similarities with your own personality, but you have to study them and create appropriate movements in order to tell a story and make the audience believe what they see on the screen.

You don't need (although it may help if you are) to be a skilled martial artist to create a fight scene, or be a tennis player in order to animate a character playing tennis. What you really need is to look for good references and study the movements you need to create.

In this recipe we're going to animate our character making a tennis serve. Nowadays it's just a matter of browsing through a website to see lots of good references on almost every subject imaginable, so a quick search for "tennis serve lesson" on YouTube offers you a long list of detailed video lessons intended to teach you how to perform a tennis serve with your own body. The difference is just that you'll transpose the principles behind that lesson to your character's body. Pick the video lesson you like best and pay attention to the timing, weight, anticipation, position of hands, feet, and torso.

A bonus of using this kind of reference is that you'll not only be able to animate your character, but you'll also know what to do when you're in a tennis court with a racket and a yellow ball in your hands!

## How to do it...

1. Open the file `008-Tennis.blend`. It has our character Otto properly dressed in a tennis court with a ball and racket near his hands, as seen in the next screenshot:

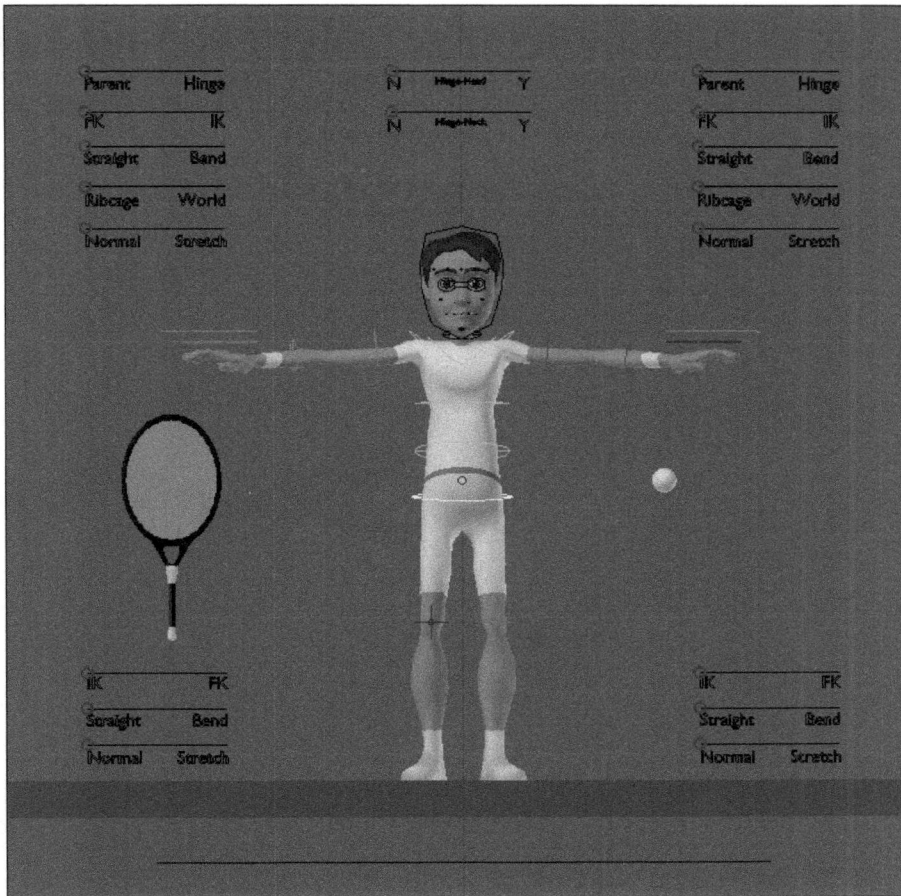

2. The first thing you should do after the planning phase and studying visual references is to place the racket and the ball in his hands. The racket will be attached to the hand for the complete duration of the shot, while the ball will be thrown in the air for the serve. Both situations can be solved with a **Child Of** constraint, with the difference that only the ball will have an **Influence** value for the constraint animated. *Chapter 6, Blending With the Animation Workflow* has a recipe called *Grasping and throwing objects*, which talks about this kind of situation.

3. With our character rig still at its resting position, select, move (*G*), and rotate (*R*) the `Tennis_Racket` and `Tennis_Ball` objects so they stand near the palm of the right and left hands of the character, respectively.

4. After you're happy with these objects' positioning, select and rotate the fingers' controllers so that the hands look like they're holding the racket and ball. Make sure you're at frame 1, insert a rotation keyframe (*I*) for the fingers' controllers, and add a **Child Of** constraint so they follow the hands' controllers. The next screenshot shows both the racket and ball being held after these steps:

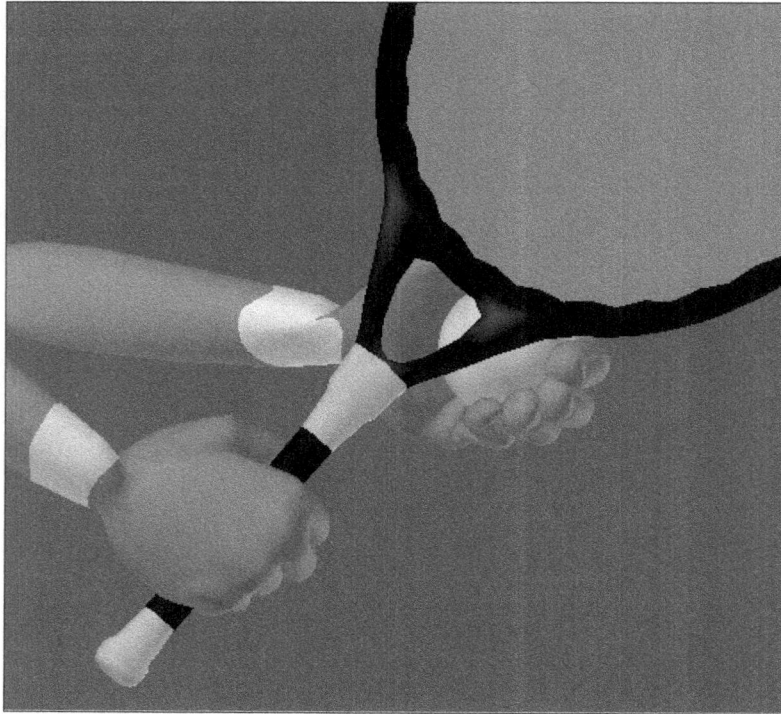

With the objects in place, we're going to the blocking phase. By watching the references we'll define the Extreme positions over which we're building our animation. Don't worry about timing yet, just make sure you have Extreme poses that tell the visual story of this action.

When making these Extreme positions, set only the **Location** and **Rotation** keyframes (*I* **| LocRot**) for the head, torso, and limb bones for now. The squash-and-stretch effect should be added later. In our case, we can define the following Extreme positions:

- ❏ The character starts leaning forward and looks to the other side of the court.
- ❏ The body swings back, with his weight over the right leg, while the left leg is totally straight.
- ❏ He swings towards the front, while both arms go down and behind his torso.

❏ The character throws the ball up, having the left arm totally straight up and forming an imaginary straight line with his torso; the right arm holds the racket behind his head to a strong serve and both legs bend in anticipation to the jump.

❏ He jumps towards the front with the body to hit the falling ball.

❏ After the serve, his body touches the ground with the left foot in a follow through action. The right arm with the racket goes down in front of the torso, while the left arm goes back to give balance. This pose is a good example of the *Follow Through* animation principle in action.

❏ His body goes again to a straight up position, getting ready to attack the ball again (if the opponent succeeds in his defense).

5. After you're happy with the Extreme poses, make a basic timing adjustment in the **DopeSheet** window. Make sure you have the **DopeSheet Summary** enabled to make it easier to adjust the saved positions, as you can see in the next screenshot:

The following screenshot shows the Extremes along with the frame number where they were set for your reference:

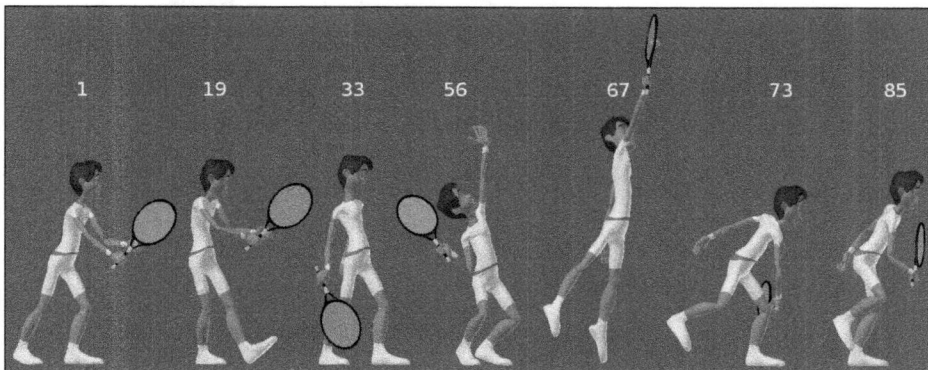

> Remember that these frames are just for guiding you, and you may find that a different timing gives a more pleasing result for your eyes. Another thing is that these poses presented here are in side view only for clarity's sake.

The most important view for your blocking process is the Camera view (*Numpad 0*). That is the only one your audience will actually see, and this is where you must focus your efforts. You should use all orthographic views to help you build your poses, but the poses **must only look good in Camera View**. For example, it's OK to have a pose that doesn't look perfect in Side view if it looks good in the Camera view. The next screenshot shows how the pose at frame 33 looks very different in the Side and Camera views:

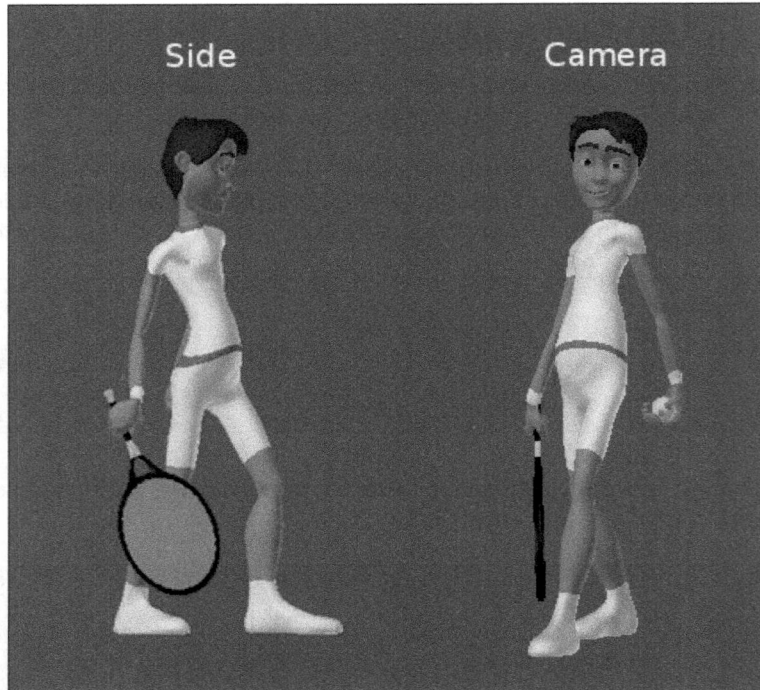

6. Once you're happy with the Extreme poses and the timing, make the remaining Breakdown positions and set keyframes wherever you need to achieve better arcs and overlapping action.

> To make it easier to distinguish Extremes, Breakdowns, and extra keyframes in the DopeSheet window, you can use the shortcut (*R*); this will make the selected saved positions in a different color (pink for Extremes, blue for Breakdowns, and white for other keyframes).

[ *Chapter 7, Easy to Say, Hard to Do: Mastering the Basics* has a recipe on *Breaking the symmetry*, which is about creating uneven and natural poses and overlapping action. The principle of overlapping action says that different parts of an organic body move at different speeds. ]

7.  After you make these adjustments and are pleased with the overall movement, it's time to animate the tennis ball. Since it has a **Child Of** constraint, you should animate this constraint's influence along with the position of the ball in the 3D space. First, go to the last frame where the ball is still held by the left hand, open the constraints tab on the Properties window, locate the **Child Of** constraint, right-click on the **Influence** slider at value of 1, and choose **Insert Keyframe**.

8.  Go up one frame, change the slider value to 0 and add another keyframe. Position the ball a bit over the hand, as if it had been just released and then add another keyframe for its location. Then you animate it over the next few frames to make it go up, fall, and be hit by the racket.

9.  After animating the ball and making any necessary timing adjustments on the character, it's time to clean up the animation curves and tweak the Eases. As most things in animation, this takes some time to do. The next screenshot shows an adjusted curve where **(1)** an unnecessary control point was removed to achieve a softer curve and **(2)** the easing was changed:

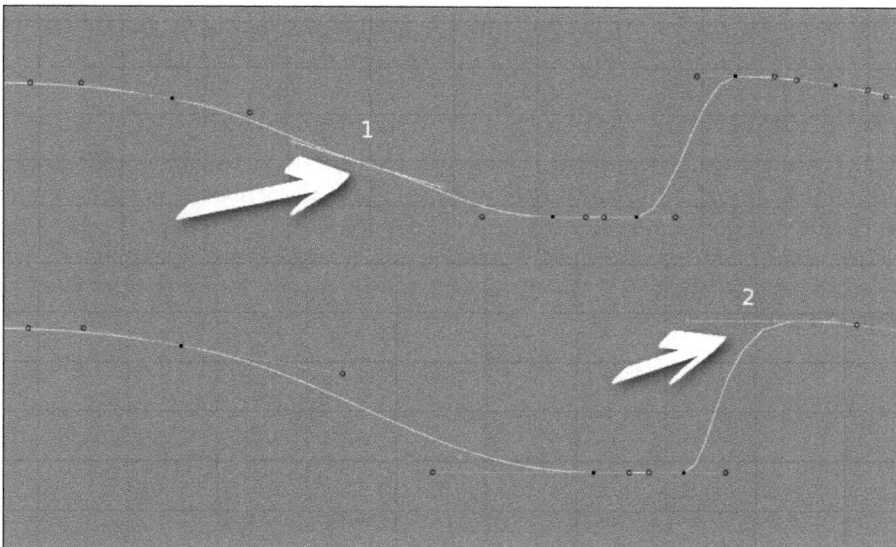

After you're done with the curve editing, it's time to work on facial expressions and details such as fingers and squash and stretch. Since this shot is a Full Shot, where we can see our entire character and its surroundings, the audience cannot see much detail in the eyes and facial expressions. Also, this is a physical action, with no dialogue. Although the audience tends to look at the face of our characters most of the time, this scene focuses on the body movement. Nevertheless, we need to create some expressions in order to make our action more believable:

- ❏ Before the serve, make the character look to the other side of the court as if he is deciding where the ball should go.
- ❏ While throwing the ball up, he must follow it with his eyes to know the time and place to hit it. Eyebrows should go up, and the mouth is possibly opened.
- ❏ During the hit, make his facial expression exhibit the physical strength needed to make the serve. Possibly a blink just after the hit, so the eyes change their focus from the sky to the other side of the court.
- ❏ After the serve, you can choose what his face should look like; happy after making an "ace", sad after missing the field, or worried because the other player successfully hit the ball back to his court.

[ 💡 Always remember to go back and forth to Camera view and check that everything looks as expected. If it does, call it Final! ]

The file `008-Tennis-complete.blend` has an example of this shot for your reference.

## How it works...

By watching the video reference closely, using an organized workflow, and understanding the principles of movement and animation, you can create physical actions such as a tennis serve. While animating, you may face the issue of dealing with objects such as the racket and ball. This is solved by using animated constraints. You should also remember to make the Extreme poses first, adjust the timing, add Breakdown poses, and then start working on refinement and details.

Another point to focus on is that your poses need to look good **only** in camera view. That is the only thing your audience will see. If your pose looks great in all angles, this is great, but not strictly necessary. If your planning phase was properly finished, you should already know where your camera is. Use it to ensure your poses and animation really tell the story for the camera.

## See also

*Appendix*: *Extremes, Breakdowns, Inbetweens, ones and twos*

*Chapter 6*: *Grasping and throwing objects*

*Chapter 6*: *Animating in layers*

*Chapter 7*: *Easy to Say, Hard to Do: Mastering the Basics*

# Heavy metal

The feeling of weight is something extremely important to your animations, making them look believable. When looking at shapes on a screen (be they realistic, cartoon, or abstract), the way they move frame to frame is what makes the audience perceive their mass.

The weight lifting exercise is one of the most repeated in animation schools worldwide. This is where animation students can test and learn the body mechanics necessary to express the feeling of weight with animated shapes. In this recipe, our character is dressed as a thief and will try to take a safe full of money with him.

It's a good idea to act it out yourself (maybe recording it, if you have a webcam or better equipment) to figure out the body mechanics involved. As with in any animation shot, you should plan what you want to accomplish with rough sketches or using Blender's Grease Pencil function.

## How to do it...

1. Open the file `008-Weight.blend`. It has our character properly dressed as a thief and a safe in front of him. By the size and nature of the safe you see in the next screenshot, we can tell this is not going to be easy for him:

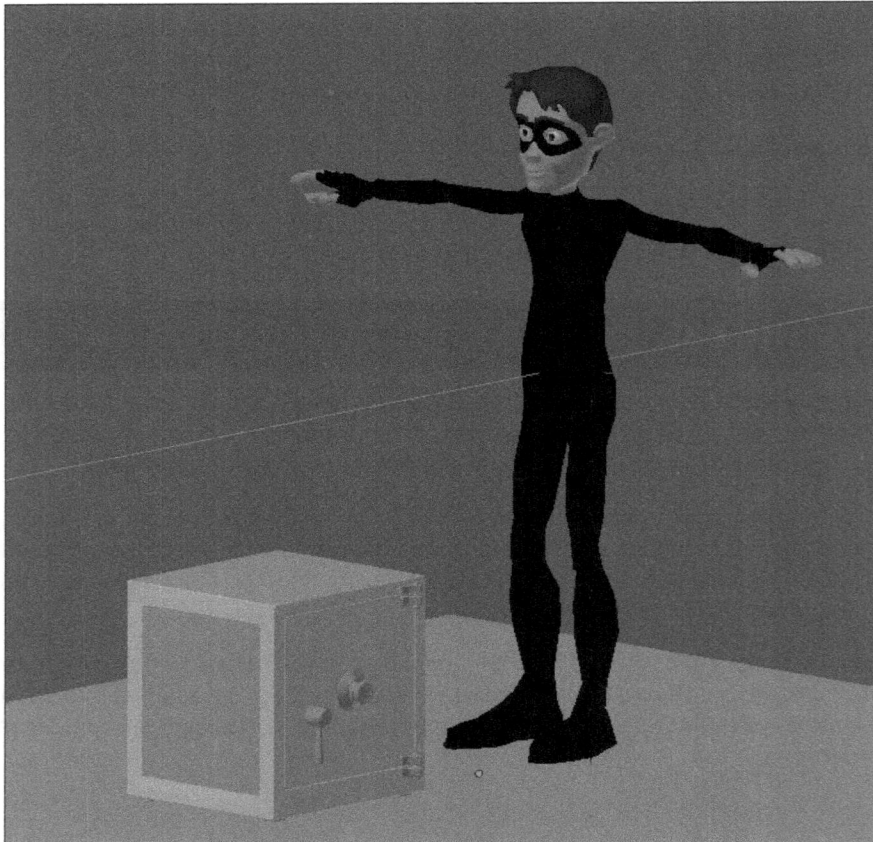

> Here we're going to focus only on the strict act of lifting the safe. In a complete scene, it could be interesting to add a little preparation before the attempt at lifting. When planning for the shot, maybe you can make the character look at a good place to hold it, try using devices or tools to break in, and so on. For learning and brevity's sake, only the mechanics involved in the actual lifting will be covered. The acting required to make this shot more interesting is beyond our scope here.

2. Since our character's hands will be fixed holding the safe, this is a perfect case for using IK in both arms. Trying to match the position of the arms, hands, and the safe in FK would be too difficult, and it would affect the overall quality of your animation. So, make sure you're at frame 1, move (G) both IK-FK sliders for left and right arms to put them in the IK position, and insert a location keyframe (I) for them, as seen in the next screenshot:

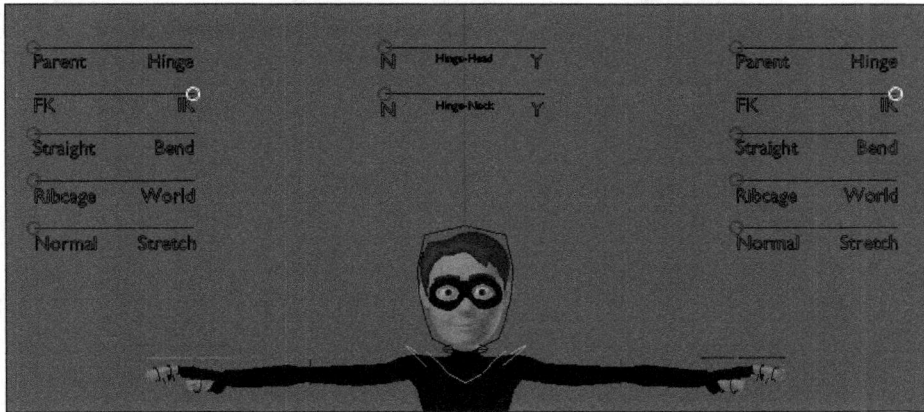

3. Another thing that you should consider changing is the "space" evaluation for both IK hands from "Ribcage" to "World". In the "Ribcage" mode, the hands controllers will follow every transformation made to the torso. Here we need to make the hands stick to the safe while being able to move the character's torso freely to enhance the feeling of weight involved. Move the two hand "space" controllers (**Space_Arm.R** and **Space_Arm.L**) to the World position and also insert a location keyframe for them.

Now you have the rig set up to start the blocking phase. It's important to have this configuration defined prior to the blocking stage because it can be harder to fix the poses if you change the settings after creating them.

> You may also enable the stretching of arms to enhance the poses. This can make the safe look heavier, along with helping the fluidity and comic feeling of this animation.

4. In the planning phase we define the basic Extreme poses needed for this action. Here, the first Extreme is when the character holds the safe to start the lifting. You should use the Quad View (*Ctrl + Alt + Q*) to have a better notion of what your pose looks like from all angles, as seen in the following screenshot:

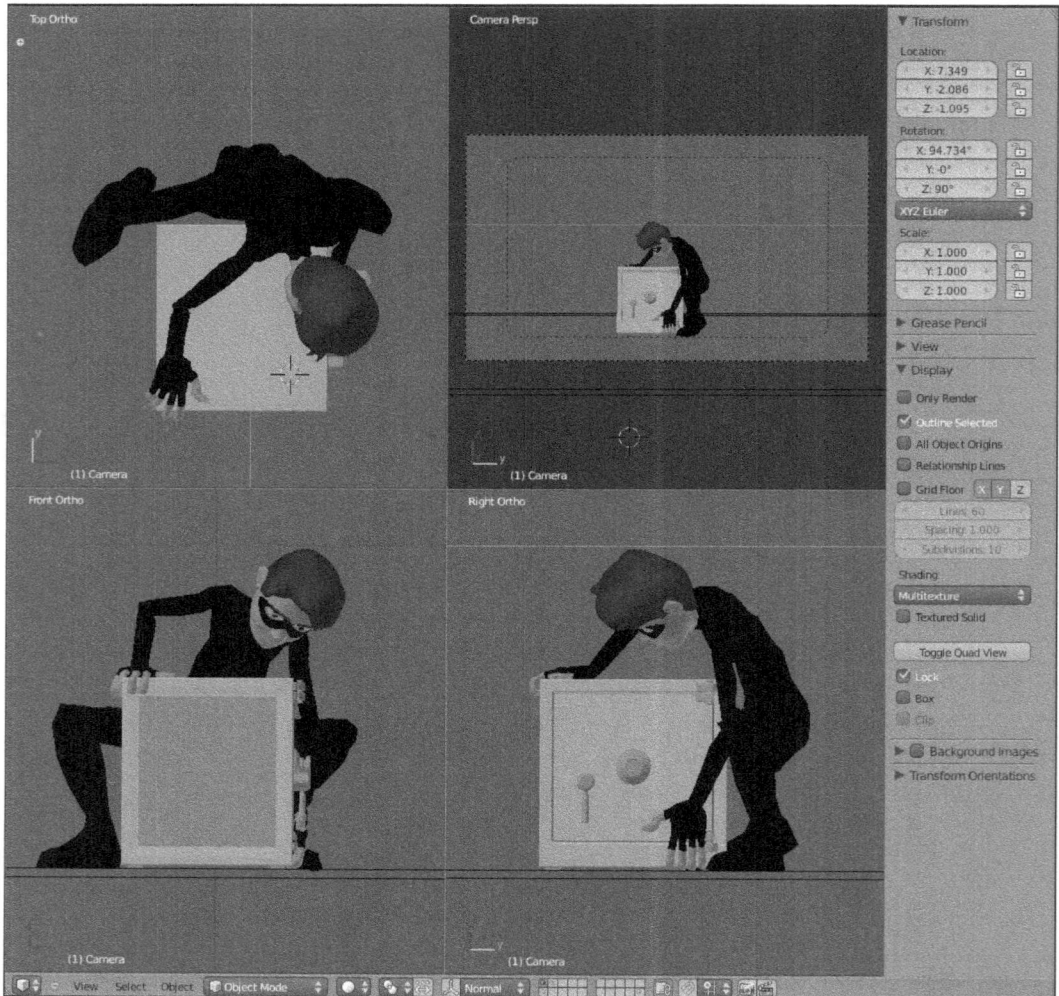

5. Now that you have the first contact between the character and the safe set in the Extreme pose, you need to create a **Child Of** constraint for the safe object. This is the same situation described in *Chapter 6, Blending With the Animation Workflow*, in the recipe *Grasping and throwing objects*.

6.  Since both hands are holding the safe, it would be good to move them together so they remain fixed on the safe's surface while moving it around. This is just a matter of adding another **Child Of** constraint to one of the hands just like we did with the safe object. In our case, make Hand.R the child of Hand.L. When moving the Hand.L bone, both the safe and the Hand.R bone will follow nicely. You can move the right hand and add keyframes to it at anytime, if you wish.

    A different challenge is when you need to rotate the safe in a pivot point different from the bone that is a "parent" of the safe and the other hand. The pivot point of the hand is in its wrist, but we need it to rotate around the safe's edge.

7.  To achieve this, place the 3D cursor at the position where you want this pivoted rotation to happen either with a left-click on the 3D View on the desired location; or selecting an object located exactly at the place where the pivoting should happen, press *Shift* + S and choose **Cursor to Selected**. Then you should select both hands controllers, press . (the period key), and rotate them nicely. The . shortcut tells Blender to rotate the selected objects around the cursor instead of the objects' centers. You can also choose how the pivot point should be evaluated on the selector placed at the 3D View header, as seen in the following screenshot:

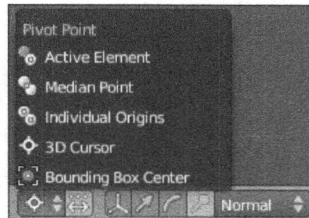

The following screenshot shows our pivot in action. Here the 3D cursor is placed near the edge of the safe, as if the safe edge is in contact with the ground. If we didn't use a pivot in this case, the safe would rotate around the root of the Hand.L bone, which is located above the ground. The arrows indicate both the pivot point and the rotation that happens with this method:

8. Now start making the next Extreme poses without thinking about the Timing between them. Just make sure your poses look good and can be clearly "read" in Camera View (*Numpad 0*) for now. The Extreme poses here are crucial to give the feeling of weight: since the safe is very heavy, it shouldn't move much despite our character's huge efforts. The timing, which we'll adjust later, will work along with the spacing to make the safe look very heavy.

[ *Chapter 7, Easy to Say, Hard to Do: Mastering the Basics* has more information on Timing and Spacing, if you need a clearer understanding on those concepts. ]

In order to move the safe out of the frame, our character needs to make an enormous effort. In this case, that means we need a good amount of Extreme positions to reflect all of his pulling and pushing to take the safe with him. In the complete example, there are 18 Extreme positions to reflect all of his effort to move the safe. For brevity's sake, the next screenshot shows just some of them:

9. After you're happy with your Extreme poses, let's make the timing adjustment. In the **DopeSheet** window, select all saved Extremes, press *R*, and select **Extremes** to shade them in a pink hue and make it easier to distinguish them from Breakdowns and regular keyframes later. Make sure the **Summary** option is enabled in the window header and start dragging the Extremes on the timeline until you're happy with the timing.

10. With the Extremes carefully created and with its Timing adjusted, you now may create the Breakdowns and additional keyframes to make the animation more fluid, with overlapping actions and follow through. Don't forget to use the tools in Blender to track the arcs made by the bones as demonstrated in *Chapter 6, Blending With the Animation Workflow*.

11. Once the main body movement looks good, move on to add details such as fingers, eyes, and facial expressions. It's a must to work from the lesser to the higher levels of detail to ensure a workflow where it's easier to make adjustments and fixes. Having the saved positions colored in different hues to distinguish Extremes, Breakdowns, and regular keyframes is also very important. The facial controllers are located on the first bone layer of the armature, as indicated in the next screenshot:

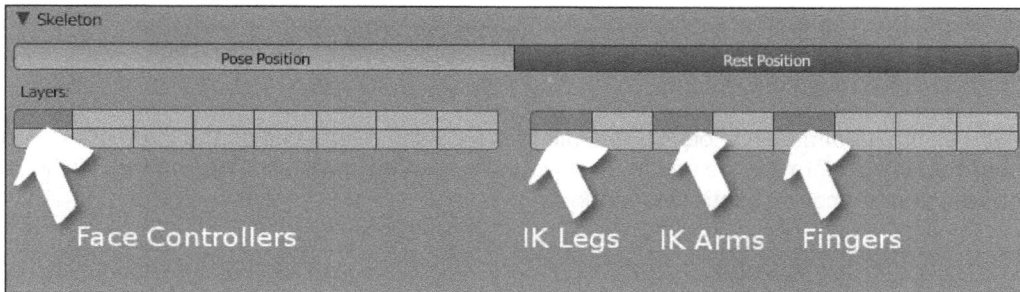

12. When you finish setting all those positions, it's time to work on the F-Curves, adjusting the eases and creating favors as explained in *Chapter 7, Easy to Say, Hard to Do: Mastering the Basics*.

The file `008-Weight-complete.blend` has this finished example which you can explore for reference, although it's strongly suggested that you to come up with your own touch for this scene.

## How it works...

By combining the concepts and principles of motion such as easing, timing, spacing, anticipation, and use of the **Child Of** constraints, you can create a scene where your character lifts a heavy object. A proper planning phase and reference analysis allow you to know what features of the rig should be used, while understanding how Blender works with different pivot points helps you to be more efficient and create convincing actions.

## See also

*Appendix*: *Extremes, Breakdowns, Inbetweens, ones and twos*

*Chapter 6*: *Grasping and throwing objects*

*Chapter 6*: *Animating in layers*

*Chapter 7*: *Easy to Say, Hard to Do: Mastering the Basics*

# Glory for your team: kicking the ball

Another common animation exercise to understand body mechanics involves your character kicking a soccer ball. It includes anticipating the action, the actual kick, and the follow-through movements.

As with all other animation shots, you should look for video references on the Internet or even record yourself performing the action. Then you should make quick sketches on the best ideas for poses prior to moving controllers around.

## How to do it...

1.  Open the file `008-BallKick.blend`. It has our character Otto properly dressed as a soccer player with a ball in front of him. It also has a camera set for this action, from which we see the objects in 3D view as default, as pictured in the following screenshot:

During the research and planning phase, you should notice some peculiarities to this action. Let's assume that the character kicks the ball with his right leg:

❑ The soccer player runs towards the ball looking firmly towards it.

❑ His torso remains a bit curved to the front, reinforcing his attention towards the ball.

❑ Just before the kick, he takes a bigger step to position the left foot on the ground next to the ball while moving the right foot up and behind his body in order to make a strong hit.

❑ Just after the kick, his body gets twisted in the follow-through: the right leg is up and pointing towards the left, the torso gets more curved towards the front and twisted to the right, and the left arm follows it and points towards the right, while the right arm points to his back.

❑ During the whole action, his arms swing in opposite directions to his legs, to balance his body.

2. Keeping these points in mind, it's time to make sure that our rig is properly set up before we start making the Extreme poses. Since the hands will not hold anything, we're going to leave the arms in the default FK mode. Our first observation tells us that the character looks firmly towards the ball while running at it, so it's a good idea to enable the **Hinge** property for the **Neck**, as seen in the next front view screenshot. The neck and head will rotate independently of the ribcage, and it would be easier to make the character look at a fixed point.

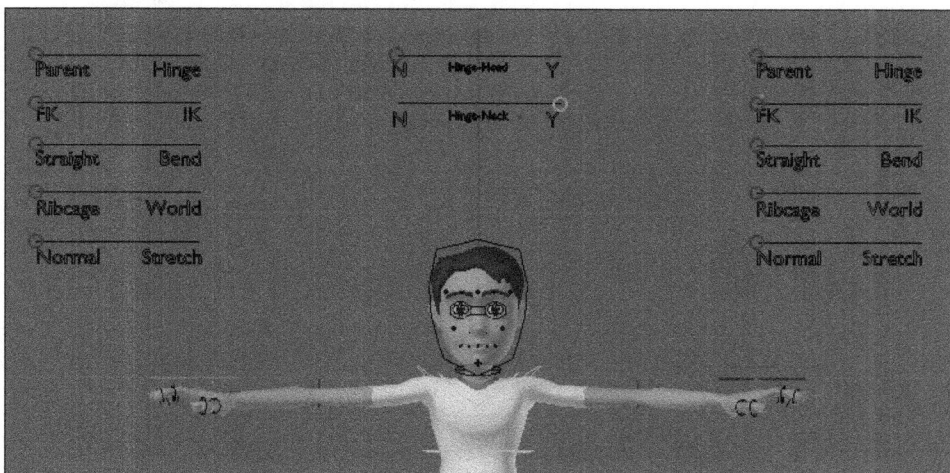

3. Now you should start with the Extreme poses, using the sketches, annotations, and references you've made so far. Use the Quad View Toggle (*Ctrl + Alt + Q*) to see the poses from more angles to help you create the Extremes.

   At this stage you shouldn't worry about timing yet. Just make sure you have a good set of Extreme poses defined on the **DopeSheet** to adjust them later. When creating the Extremes, it would be good to think of the overlapping action on the hands: creating this sense of "drag" on the Extreme poses will save you a good time, since you don't need to make lots of changes on your Extremes later.

4. Once you have all Extreme poses set, it's a good idea to have them marked as such in the **DopeSheet** window to tell them apart from the Breakdowns and other keyframes. With all Extreme poses selected on the **DopeSheet** window (*A*), press (*R*) and choose Extreme to give the diamonds a pinkish hue.

   The following screenshot shows four Extreme poses for this action as reference:

5. After you're happy with your Extreme poses, move on to the timing adjustment. Make sure the **DopeSheet Summary** option is enabled on the **DopeSheet** window and move (*G*) the Extreme poses on the timeline. You may find your poses need a bit of adjustment when you navigate through the timeline, and it's now the perfect time to do that. The following screenshot shows the Extreme positions with the timing adjustment on the **DopeSheet** window:

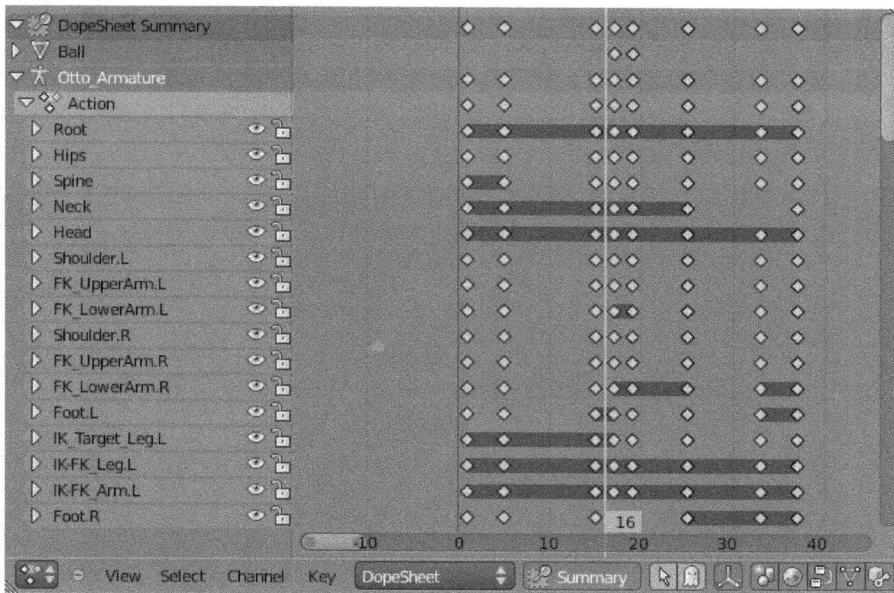

6.  After the timing adjustment, start adding the Breakdown positions and additional keyframes. Make sure you get good arcs described by the character's limbs. This is also good to ensure the overlapping action, especially in the arms and hands, looks good.

> You can tweak your pose by using some built in tools in Blender. With the armature in Pose Mode, the Toolshelf panel (*T*) shows three buttons: **Push**, used to exaggerate a pose; **Relax**, which does the opposite, making it look closer to the surrounding ones; and **Breakdowner**, which tries to figure out how the Breakdown position should be. Be wary to use them only as helpers, not the main pose builders.

7.  When you're happy with the new poses and—eventually—further adjustments on the timing, start focusing on the details such as fingers, facial expressions, and moving holds for when the character goes to a resting pose. You can even add a little squash and stretch to enhance the feeling of the strength involved in the kick, although it's not required.

8.  As a final touch, animate a slight rotation of the camera from right to left, following our character performing the kick for the glory of the team. The file `009-BallKick-complete.blend` has this finished example for your reference, along with a background to make this shot more interesting, as you can see in the next screenshot:

## How it works...

With both planning and study of video references, you can make a convincing action of a ball kick. By setting up a hinged neck, the character keeps the head still and looking at his target while running. The workflow of creating Extreme poses, adjusting the Timing, adding the remaining Breakdown and regular keyframes and refinement keeps your timeline organized, easy to understand and to adjust.

## See also

*Appendix*: *Extremes, Breakdowns, Inbetweens, ones and twos*

*Chapter 6*: *Animating in layers*

*Chapter 7*: *Easy to Say, Hard to Do: Mastering the Basics*

# Run, Forrest! (in cycles)

Whether you're animating for a game or film, you're likely to face the need to create cycled animations, and that is especially true for the former.

Run and walk cycles are normally created in two ways: the character may stay in a fixed position, while his feet "slide" on the ground with its positioning set at a later stage; or the character really makes two steps forward, while Blender takes care of appending the beginning of the next cycle where the first ended—making the character really move forward in a straight line. The latter is what we'll cover here.

## How to do it...

1. Open the file `008-RunCycle.blend`. It has our character Otto in its resting pose, ready for our work. We're going to create a funny jog run cycle. When the term "cycle" is used in animation, it means the last position of the action must be equal to its first one. This ensures that it can be repeated indefinitely in a seamless manner.

2. First let's create the Extreme positions of this run cycle. We can set them as frames where the character's body is on one foot, with the supporting leg flexed a bit in order to transition to the next step. This way, we'll have two different Extreme positions here: one for the right leg and one for the left. The third Extreme should be where our second cycle begins, so the difference between this and the first is only the position on the Y axis. For this funny run cycle, an animated sequence by the renowned animator Richard Williams was used as reference. The next screenshot shows our Extreme positions set:

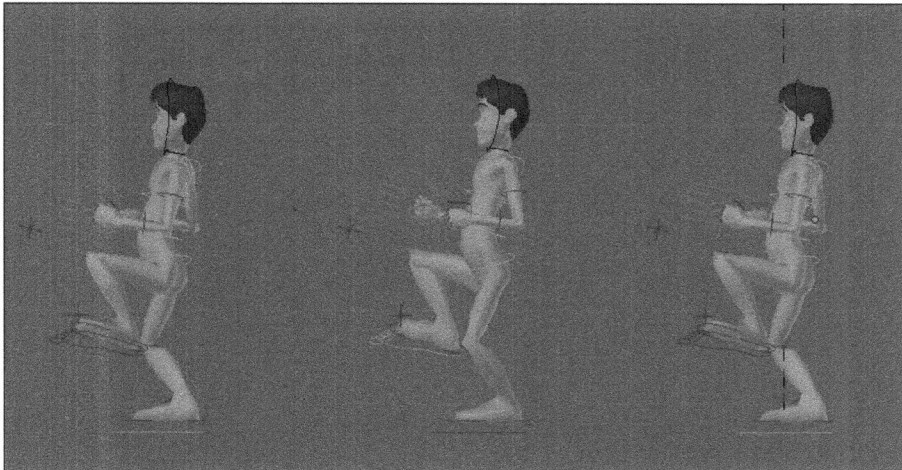

3.  In order to create the second Extreme position, you can use the mirrored first pose as the base. To do that, go to the frame where you've set the first Extreme, select all the bones from the character's body (not the switcher ones, such as IK-FK, nor the `Root` bone), press *Ctrl + C*, go up 10 frames (*Up arrow*), and press *Ctrl + Shift + C*. This will copy the first pose and paste it mirrored on the selected frame in the timeline.

> For the cycle action, you shouldn't add keyframes for the `Root` bone. We're going to use it to make the cycle move forward later, so it shouldn't have any keyframes set or we could end up with unexpected results.

4.  You'll notice that the character remains on its Y axis position, so you need to select the bones `Foot.R`, `Foot.L`, and `Hips`, and then move (G) them to the front until you think it's is a good distance for the second step. With all bones selected, insert a new keyframe (*I*) to save this position.

> Since nobody walks on mirrored steps, use this mirrored pose only as a base for your work. Make it slightly different so the character's motion looks natural.

5.  The third Extreme needs to be an exact copy of the first, so you can go to the first pose, select all the character's bones and copy the pose with *Ctrl + C*. Then you go up 20 frames (since the second step is at frame 11) and paste the pose with *Ctrl + V*. Now you just need to move the character on the Y axis, using the same three bones we used to create the second Extreme, and insert a new keyframe for this pose.

6.  After you're satisfied with your Extreme poses, mark them as such on the **DopeSheet** window by selecting them all (*A*), pressing (*R*), and selecting **Extreme** on the pop-up menu.

7.  On the **DopeSheet** window, make sure the **Summary** is enabled and make a quick Timing adjustment by moving the summary diamonds on the timeline (hold *Ctrl* to snap them to the exact frames). Press *Alt + A* to watch it or make a playblast using the OpenGL render preview.

    When you're happy with the timing, start creating the Breakdown positions. In this jog run action, the Breakdown happens when both feet are off the ground, in the middle of the step.

8.  Move the character's torso up, leaving the supporting foot from the first Extreme behind his body on the air and the other foot up in front, in preparation for the next step. The second Breakdown can be created by using a mirrored copy from the first Breakdown as a starting point, just as you did with the Extreme positions. The next screenshot shows the five positions (three Extremes and two Breakdowns superimposed):

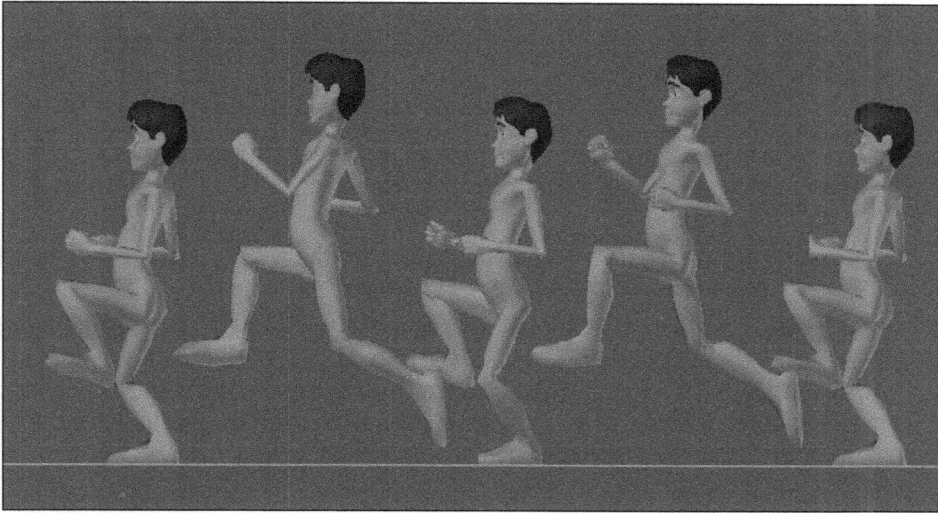

9. After adding the Breakdowns, add the remaining poses: notably the one where the foot loses contact with the ground and the one where it touches it again with the heel. The next screenshot shows all poses from this cycle superimposed:

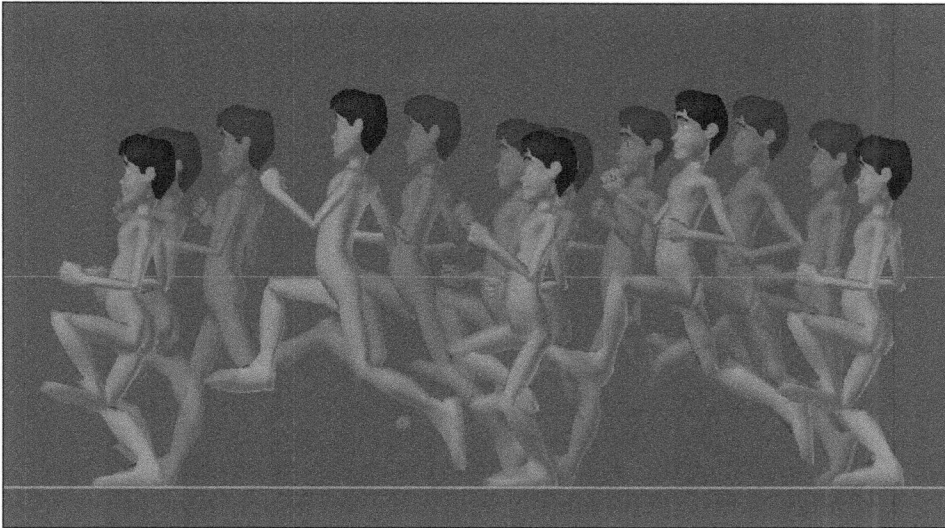

Now our first part is done. We have defined the cycle, but how can we make it really loop while going forward? This is where we're going to use the Root bone and the NLA Editor.

10. Still in the **DopeSheet** window, change the window mode to **Action Editor** and define the name of this action as **Cycle**. Make sure the Root bone doesn't have any keyframes set on this action.

> The Root bone is the parent of all bone chains on the rig, so moving it makes everything move along.

11. Once you set the name of the cycle action, click on the plus (**+**) sign next to its name to create a new action. Define its name as **Stride**.

12. In the 3D View, go to frame 1 (or the first frame of your cycle action), select the Root bone and insert a **LocRot** keyframe (*I*) for it. We need to position the Root bone forward on the exact same timing and spacing it takes from the first Extreme of the cycle to the last. But how do you know exactly how much you need to move the Root bone forward? Using the **Transform** panel on the 3D View!

13. Still in the first frame, enable the **Transform** panel on the 3D View (*N*), select the Foot.R bone (which is planted on the ground), and check its Y location value. In this case the value is 0, as you can see in the following screenshot:

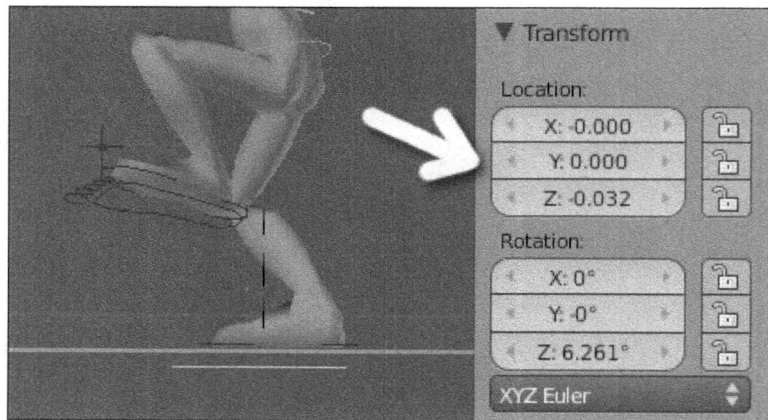

14. Now, navigate through the timeline until the last position of the cycle, on the third Extreme. Look at the value of the Y location for that bone again. In this case, it's 7.668. This is how much we need to move the Root bone forward, on its Y axis. The math for this is the last position minus the first one.

15. Go to the last frame of your cycle and move the Root bone forward to the position you've got at the previous step. You may accomplish it through the **Transform** panel, typing the value on the Y field and inserting a new keyframe (*I*) for it.

16. Now, with the `Root` bone still selected, open a Graph Editor window and look to its **Y Location** curve. We need to turn it from a soft curve to a step where the bone "jumps" from one position to the other directly. We also need to repeat this movement in an incremental way: the `Root` bone should go forward more steps in order to allow more repetitions of this cycle.

17. With its **Y Location** channel selected, go to the **Key** menu at the header and choose **Interpolation Mode | Constant**. This will make the Root bone "jump" from one position to the other directly, without inbetweens.

> Another good way of accomplishing this non-interpolated motion is through the Stepped F-Curve modifier, adjusting the **Step Size** and **Offset** according to the Timing of your cycle.

18. Once you set this stepped motion for the `Root` bone, let's make it repeat incrementally. With the Y Location channel still selected, open the **Properties** (N) panel on the Graph Editor window and look for the **Modifiers** section. Click on the **Add Modifier** button and choose the **Cycles** modifier. Leave the **Before** values unchanged. For the **After** values, set **Repeat with Offset** on the first field and the number of cycles you need on the **After Cycles** field. Your curve and modifier values should look similar to what's shown in the next screenshot:

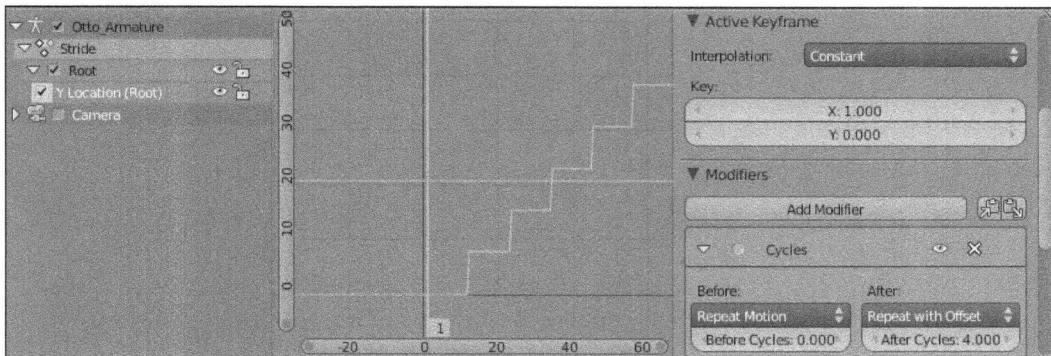

We're almost done. Now we have two actions: one with the weird jog run cycle animation and the other with the Root bone "steps", to move the cycle forward. It's time to do some NLA magic!

19. Open a NLA Editor window. On its left-hand side panel it should have your currently open active Action highlighted in red, which should be **Stride**. Click on the snowflake icon next to its name to turn into a **NLA Action Strip**.

On the **Properties** (*N*) panel to the right-hand side, set this new track name as **Stride** on the **Active Track** section. Scroll down the panel and look for the **Action Clip** section. The **End Frame** field has the number of frames of the **Action**, but it doesn't consider the cycle modifier we've set, so we need to multiply this value by the number of cycles we need.

20. In a **DopeSheet** window, open the **Cycle** action. Back to the NLA Editor window, you'll notice this action is now highlighted in red as the active action. Click on the snowflake icon to turn it into another NLA Strip and set its name as **Cycle** on the **Active Track** section. You'll see both actions layered on the NLA timeline, as seen in the next screenshot:

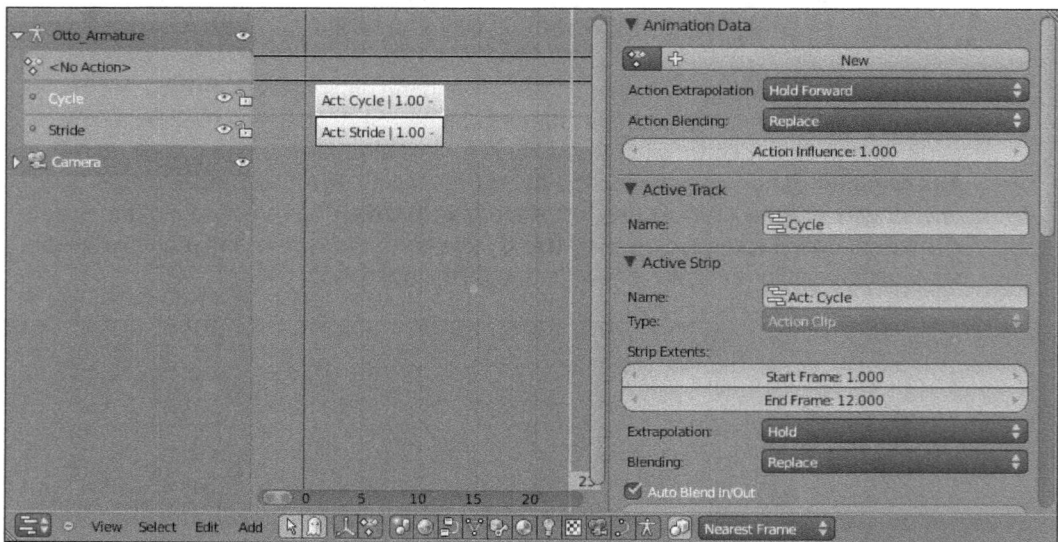

21. Scroll down the **Properties** panel and look for the **Action Clip** section for the **Cycle** action. On the **Playback Settings** values, change the **Repeat** field to the number of cycles you need.

> The number of cycles for the run cycle here is one unit higher than the number of cycles set on the **Stride** modifier. For example, if the stride moves forward four times, the cycled run must repeat five times. It happens because the stride controls the starting point of the cycle, so the fourth stride jump is actually the beginning of the fifth run cycle.

Almost done! If you hit *Alt + A* to play the animation, you'll notice that there is a weird jump between each cycle. It happens because we need to remove the last frame of the **Cycle** action from the NLA evaluation, since it overlaps with the first frame of the next cycle.

22. Back to the **Action Clip** section on the NLA window, with the **Cycle** strip still selected, just reduce the value set on the End Frame field by 1 and you're done. Now the playback (and your character) should run just as expected.

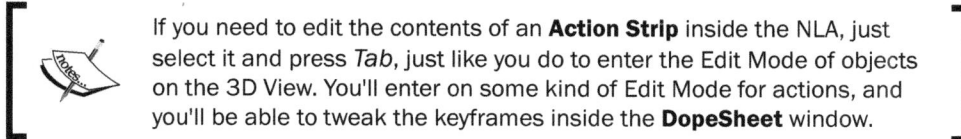

> If you need to edit the contents of an **Action Strip** inside the NLA, just select it and press *Tab*, just like you do to enter the Edit Mode of objects on the 3D View. You'll enter on some kind of Edit Mode for actions, and you'll be able to tweak the keyframes inside the **DopeSheet** window.

The file `009-RunCycle-complete.blend` has this finished recipe for your reference.

## How it works...

By carefully building a cyclic run, where the first frame equals its last, you can use the NLA Editor and the `Root` bone to repeat the cycle as you wish. The `Root` bone, which is the parent of all bones in the armature, should move forward the exact length of the cycle without any interpolation between its first and last position. The length of the entire run can be controlled through F-Curve modifiers and the NLA strips.

## See also

*Appendix*: *Extremes, Breakdowns, Inbetweens, ones and twos*

*Chapter 6*: *Non-linear animation*

*Chapter 6*: *Animating in layers*

*Chapter 7*: *Easy to Say, Hard to Do: Mastering the Basics*

# 9
# Spicing it Up: Animation Refinement

In this chapter, we will cover the following topics:

- ▶ It's time for secondary actions
- ▶ Hold, but not still: using moving holds
- ▶ Animating characters with appendages
- ▶ Like clay: refining with the AniSculpt technique

## Introduction

A strong foundation is important to make your actions express the feeling of weight and strength behind each motion, but you can enhance the fluidity by using "layers" of refinement. It's in the details of your animations that you can really make your audience forget they are watching a virtual puppet.

With a consistent base, you'll be able to deliver animated shots of reasonable quality with tight deadlines. But as you get more generous time frames, you can work on top of this good foundation and add engaging refinements to make the shot even more fluid, entertaining, and believable. In this chapter, we'll see some useful tips to make refinements to our animated shots.

# It's time for secondary actions

We may be used to seeing the term "multitasking" related to computers, where they are able to run multiple programs at the same time. Something quite similar happens with us all the time, when we're doing more than one action at once.

The animation principle of secondary actions deals with this nature: while we're performing a main action there are a number of complementary secondary actions. For instance, if our character is walking on the sidewalk in a hurry to catch a bus, some possible secondary actions may be looking at his wristwatch—meaning he's probably late—or adjusting his necktie—meaning he was so late when leaving home that he couldn't even properly wear it.

The important thing to notice here is that secondary actions should be used in your shots just as an accessory to the main action. They should reinforce the idea of your shot and add to the main idea you're trying to portray.

## How to do it...

1.  Open the file `009-Secondary-actions.blend`. It has our character Otto walking in a hurry through a rough sidewalk model, as you can see in the next screenshot:

After hitting *Alt + A*, you'll notice that he's marching down the sidewalk with a fast pace and a serious facial expression. The action itself may look a bit boring, since it's just a repeating walk cycle. Let's make it more interesting by adding a secondary action to reinforce the feeling of hurry in our character.

2.  Go to an NLA Editor window and look at the existing layers. We have one called **Stride**, which is used to make the character walk forward, and one called **Cycle** containing a repeating two-step walk. The cycle is set to repeat 14 times within the NLA editor, as you can see in the next screenshot:

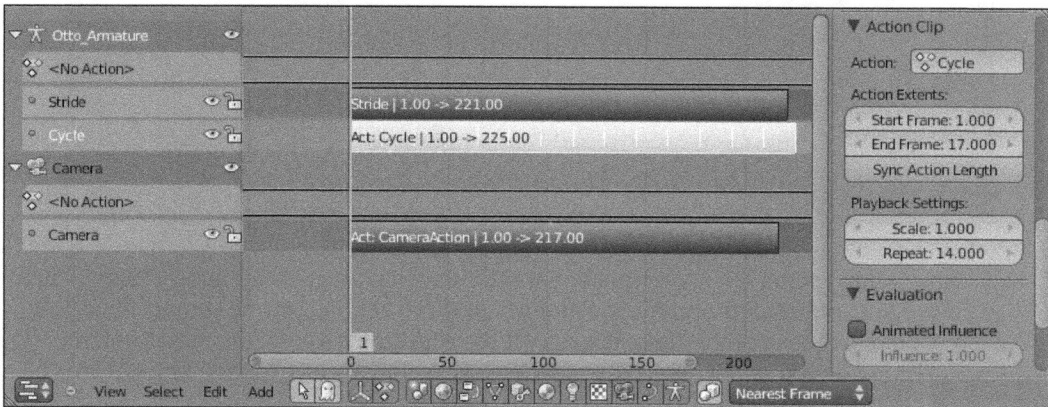

> You can select each strip in the NLA and enter its "Edit Mode" by pressing Tab and changing its keyframes on a DopeSheet window.

3.  Open a **DopeSheet** window and select the **Action Editor** mode on the header. Click on the **New** button next to it in order to create a new action and name it **Watch**. In this action we're going to pose only those bones necessary to make him look at his wristwatch.

4.  Move the timeline marker to frame 50, so our character walks a few steps before he starts looking at his watch. Select the following bones:

    ❑ FK_UpperArm.L

    ❑ FK_LowerArm.L

    ❑ Shoulder.L

    ❑ Hand.L

    ❑ Neck

    ❑ Head

5. With these bones selected, insert a new **LocRot** keyframe (*I*) for them. Your DopeSheet window should look like this:

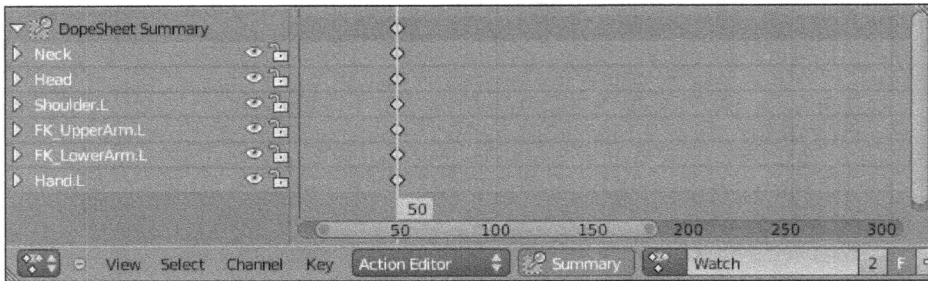

Now, when you hit *Alt + A*, something weird happens: up until frame 50 the animation looks fine, but after that the bones for which we've set a keyframe remain still. That happens because of the default way that the NLA Editor works: this new "Watch" strip is layered on top of the existing animation, replacing any information below it.

In order to change that behavior, we need to change the **Action Extrapolation** value for this strip in the NLA Editor.

6. Open an NLA Editor window and make sure the Properties (*N*) panel is opened. On the **Animation Data** section, ensure the active **Action** is "Watch" and change the **Action Extrapolation** field to **Nothing**. Leave the **Action Blending** field unchanged.

That will make our new action overwrite any animation below it, but without considering anything after its last keyframe set.

7. Go back to a **DopeSheet** window and move the timeline marker to frame 111. Select the same bones as you did in step 4 and insert a new keyframe for them. Now we have set our first and last positions for this action, and they are identical to the positions set on the actions beneath it on the NLA Editor. This will ensure our secondary action will be added seamlessly on top of the walk cycle.

8. After that, go to the 3D View window and pose our selected bones between frames 50 and 111, making our character raise his left arm, look at his wristwatch, and return to his cycled and worried walk. The next screenshot shows the DopeSheet with some poses set for this action, along with the character pose on frame 60:

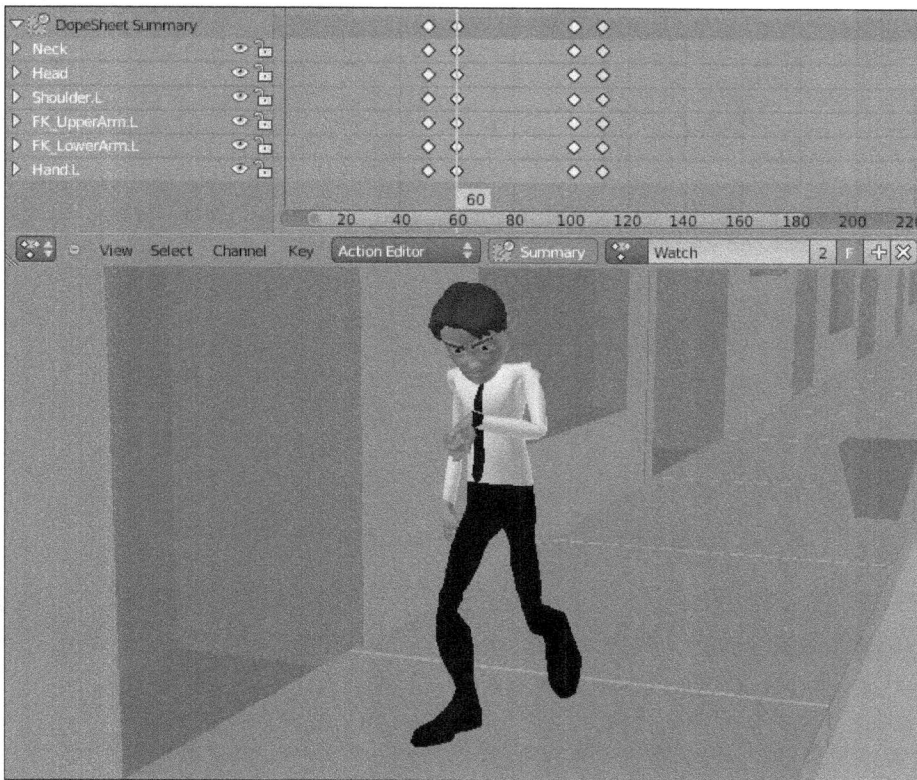

9. Now you may select the keyframes set on frame 60, representing the final position of him looking at his wristwatch, duplicate (*Shift + D*) them on the DopeSheet window and move them to frame 100.

10. Change their rotation (*R*) slightly on the 3D View and replace the keyframes (*I*). If you hit *Alt + A* again, you'll see that the walk animation transitions seamlessly to the secondary action of looking at the watch.

11. Back to the NLA Editor window, you can click on the snowflake icon to convert the **Walk** action into a NLA strip. This way you can repeat the process shown in this recipe to add more subtle secondary actions, making the scene look more natural. The file 009-Secondary-actions-complete.blend has this complete example for your reference.

## How it works...

After having a solid base animation complete, you can add secondary actions using the NLA Editor. The secondary actions are layered on top of the base animation, using its positions as a starting point to make a seamless transition. The secondary actions should be an accessory to the main action, supporting the basic idea of the scene. This approach leads to a non-destructive workflow, meaning your main action remains unchanged as you add new layers of secondary animations.

## See also

*Appendix: Understanding Extremes, Breakdowns, Inbetweens, ones and twos*

*Chapter 6: Non-linear animation*

*Chapter 6: Animating in layers*

*Chapter 7: Easy to Say, Hard to Do: Mastering the Basics*

# Hold, but not still: using moving holds

Since the Golden Age of traditional animation in the previous century, animators know that regardless of the action performed by our characters, they must feel alive to our audience. When a character reaches the end of one action, it shouldn't remain completely still. When it happens, it looks like something went wrong—is he dead? Frozen? Is the TV broken?

To avoid that, we must add a slightly modified and carefully built pose after the hold so the character keeps moving and "alive". This is specially true in CG animation, where the animation is on **Ones** (meaning that each new frame brings a new "drawing") by default. In traditional 2D animation, where the number of drawings per second of footage is normally reduced, this principle is relevant but not always so crucial.

The animation principles are often related, so we generally find and use moving holds along with the principles of Follow Through, Anticipation, Slow In, and Slow Out. Thus, we shouldn't just add a random pose after the hold just to keep our character moving. This motion should be relevant to the timing and spacing of its surrounding poses.

## How to do it...

1. Open the file `009-MovingHolds.blend`. It has our character Otto with a basic action where he turns his head from his right to his left, as if something called his attention. The next screenshot shows the last keyframe, where he looks to his left:

2. Although it does have a saved position on frame 1, our character holds its position until frame 12, when he starts the head turn. If you press *Alt + A*, you'll notice he's still like a statue before and after the turning action. Nobody (except some robots) move like that. We need to add some slightly different poses before and after the head turn in order to make the action look natural. This transformation on the poses shouldn't be random, though. Move the DopeSheet timeline marker back and forth until frame 19, where the Breakdown position is set, and check the speed and direction each of these bones go.

3. Since his body makes a quick turn to the left, it's a good idea to make this moving hold also act as a subtle anticipation. Go to frame 12 and rotate (*R*) some bones such as the `Belly`, `Head`, `FK_UpperArm.L`, `FK_UpperArm.R`, `FK_LowerArm.L`, and `FK_LowerArm.R` slightly (hold *Shift* for precision) to the opposite direction of the main action.

The next screenshot demonstrates this subtle difference by comparing the before and after using the local Y rotation axis curve of the `Belly` bone:

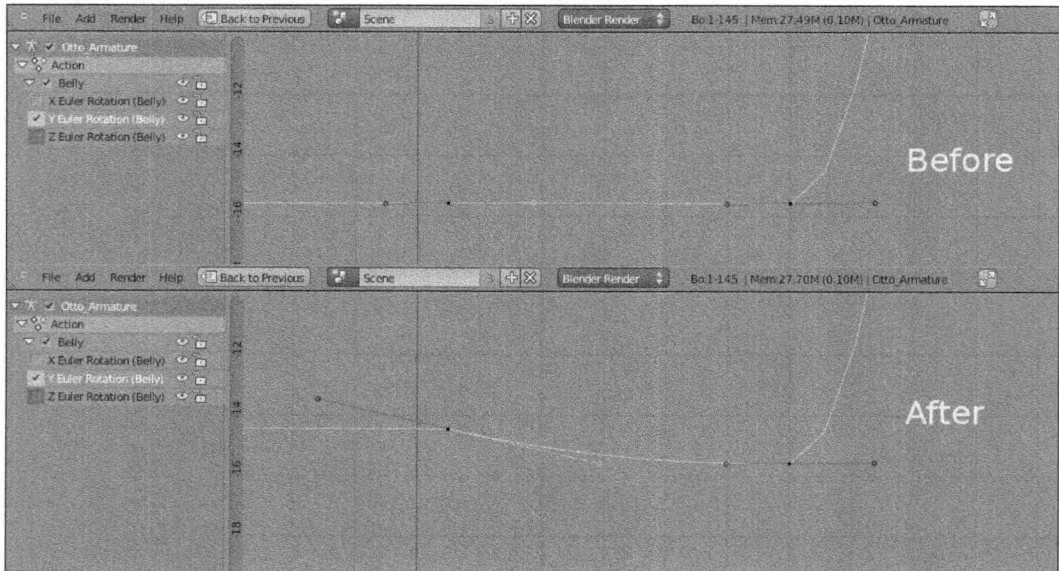

By making the moving hold go in a direction opposite to the main movement, we create a contrasting movement that acts as an anticipation to the turning action. The transformation for the hold should happen in a balanced amount and, although there are no rules for a moving hold (as they rely on the nature of each movement), here are some general issues to care about:

- ❑ If the transformation difference is subtle and the timing of the hold is too big, the action will look weightless.

- ❑ The hold should happen with a consistent speed to its surrounding actions, reinforcing the feeling of weight and avoiding linear movements.

- ❑ Remember: it's a moving **hold**, so you should avoid too much movement on it.

- ❑ You also shouldn't go the other extreme and add an unperceivable movement, or it won't have any effect.

- ❑ If the moving hold happens in the same direction as the related main action, the Extreme positions next to it will lose their strength. The action will lose contrast, and the poses won't be very defined.

Now that you have created the moving hold preceding the action, let's create another one after it.

4. Hit *Alt + A* again and notice that our character stops suddenly just after the turn. The last Extreme set for this action happens on frame 25, so go up five frames on the DopeSheet timeline.

5. On the same bones as before, make a subtle adjustment on their rotation (*R*). Make them rotate back slightly, as if the Extreme set on frame 25 was **too** extreme and needed to go back and settle. This will bring fluidity to the movement, making it come to rest in a gradual pace while emphasizing the Extreme position.

   The next screenshot shows the same Y local rotation curve for the `Belly` bone, with the Extreme position set on frame 25 followed by its moving hold:

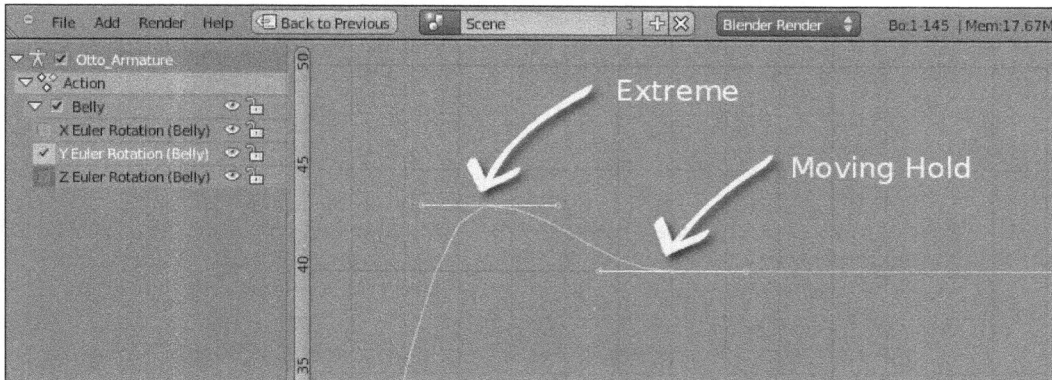

The file `009-MovingHolds-complete.blend` has this finished example for reference. Take a look at how the torso and arms bones have their moving holds at different frames, enhancing the movement with a subtle overlapping action.

## How it works...

Before and after each action, our characters normally stay in a held position. While at it, it's important to add subtle movements in order to keep them moving—or look alive—to the eyes of our audience. With this in mind, it's also crucial to add this Moving Hold while considering the preceding and succeeding actions in order to make this motion look natural.

## See also

*Appendix: Understanding Extremes, Breakdowns, Inbetweens, ones and twos*

*Chapter 6: Animating in layers*

*Chapter 7: Easy to Say, Hard to Do: Mastering the Basics*

*Chapter 9: Animating characters with appendages*

# Animating characters with appendages

We often need to animate characters with appendages such as long ears, tails, antennas, a necktie, or even mesh-based hair. Their motion follows the body part they are attached to, usually at a different pace due to their soft and bouncy nature.

When the character stops its movement, the appendages continue to follow it and keep moving for some time until they overcome inertia. This nature is described by the Follow Through principle of animation, and is often applied as a layer of detail over the main action.

The appendages are often animated after the main body parts—as the torso or head—because it's easier to visualize and test their behavior after you have finished the main action. In this recipe we'll apply the Follow Through principle to a ponytail.

## How to do it...

1. Open the file `009-Appendages.blend`. You'll see our character Otto with a beard and new hairstyle—and a ponytail—with the same action we got as a result of the previous recipe on moving holds, in which he turns his head to the left. Press *Alt + A* and you'll notice something looks weird, since the ponytail is too stiff and doesn't have the delayed and soft action we would expect. Did he use too much hair spray?

We need to add a nice follow-through action to his ponytail. This principle tells us that soft appendages must follow the main source of movement in a delayed and bouncy fashion.

> Blender offers a wide range of simulations tools, including the ability to create hair, cloth, and bouncy elements such as gelatin. These tools allow us to simulate very realistic movements, but are beyond the scope of this book. Our goal here is to understand the animation principles so we can create realistic or exaggerated movements.

To achieve this, it's good to use a FK bone setup to control the ponytail, since the head leads the movement of the hair. With a FK setup, we can control the base of the ponytail and adjust each bone of the chain until the tip. There is a simple FK setup linked to the Head bone to control the ponytail. The bones in that chain are:

- ❑ D_Tail.1
- ❑ D_Tail.2
- ❑ D_Tail.3
- ❑ D_Tail.4

All bones are set to have 16 segments, so they perform a curved deformation on the mesh. The next screenshot portrays them in a resting position:

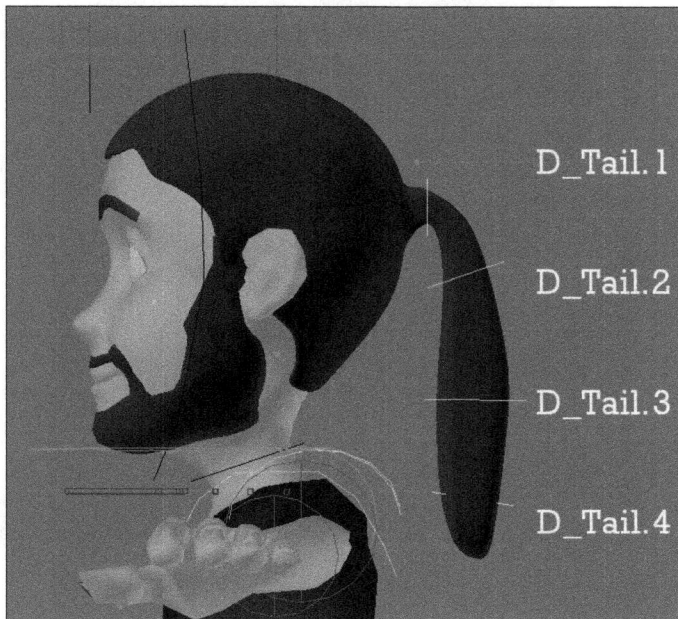

Now, for the actual animation! Since the head action is roughly a rotation on the global Z axis, we're going to mainly use the top (*Numpad 7*) and side (*Numpad 3*) views. We're going to animate the ponytail in four "steps"—one for each bone of the chain, starting from its root.

2. Select the D_Tail.1 bone. On the **DopeSheet** window, go to frame 12 (which is when the head turn begins) and set a rotation keyframe (*I*) for it.

3. Move the timeline marker to frame 19, which has our character's head in the Breakdown position for the turn. Using the top and side views, rotate the D_Tail.1 bone so that the ponytail looks like it follows the head with a small delay.

If you move the timeline marker back and forth, you'll notice that the character's head goes from looking to its right-hand side (frame 12) to looking to its front (frame 19). A delayed rotation to the D_Tail.1 bone means that it shouldn't be pointing in the same direction as the head on frame 19, but to a point a few frames in the 'past'; make it point a bit to the right, as is highlighted with a curve in the following screenshot:

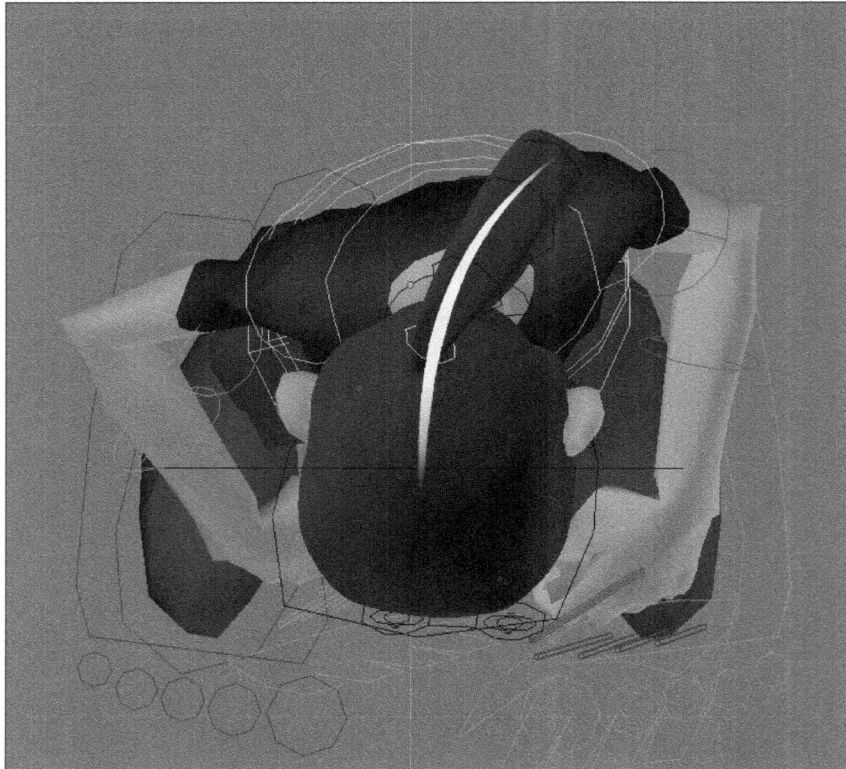

4. Go to frame 25, which is when our character's head begins to stop its movement. Rotate the `D_Tail.1` bone so that the overall shape of the ponytail describes a curve pointing to the character's back. The root of the ponytail is now closer to the head movement, but the remaining bones of the chain are still 'in the past'. That means the farther on the chain a bone is, the greater is its delay to the source of the movement.

On frame 28 the character's head is almost still, but the ponytail movement should continue. Rotate the `D_Tail.1` bone so that the ponytail now points to the opposite side of frame 25. That will bring the feeling of "bounciness" to the ponytail. The head stopped its rotation on frame 25, but the ponytail reaches its peak movement on frame 28. The next screenshot shows a comparison between frames 25 and 28:

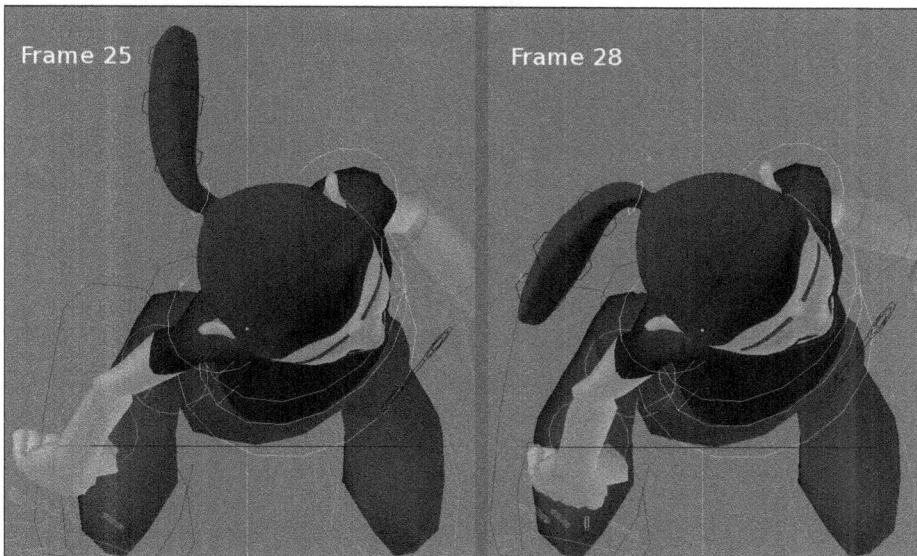

5. Now, to complete the base movement of the ponytail, add four more rotation keyframes to it—each will make the hair point to its opposite direction, gradually reducing the spacing and timing until it stops, around frame 41.

6. After you're happy with the follow-through action, timing, and spacing, applied to the root of the ponytail, move on to the next bone on the chain, `D_Tail.2`. Go back to frame 12, where the head turn begins, and save a keyframe for this bone on its current rotation.

7. Now it's time for the second "step": it's just a matter of repeating the process you did for the ponytail's root bone, but now you should use the `D_Tail.1` bone as a reference for movement instead of the `Head` bone. The `D_Tail.2` bone will now be delayed in comparison to the `D_Tail.1` bone. This will lead to a "S" shaped ponytail, as you apply the follow-through to the remaining bones of the chain in steps 3 and 4.

The following screenshot shows some frames of the ponytail movement after completing the animation for each of its bones:

The file `009-Appendages-complete.blend` has this complete example for your reference.

## How it works...

The follow-through animation principle tells us that soft body parts or objects continue their movement in a delayed fashion after the main source of the motion stops. To achieve this effect, it's optimal to use a Forward Kinematics chain and animate it from its root to its tip, always using the parent object's motion as reference.

This technique is useful to animate soft elements such as hair, clothing, or fat when the use of built-in Blender simulations tools is out of the question.

## See also

*Appendix: Understanding Extremes, Breakdowns, Inbetweens, ones and twos*

*Chapter 6: Animating in layers*

*Chapter 6: Tracking animation arcs*

*Chapter 7: Easy to Say, Hard to Do: Mastering the Basics*

*Chapter 9: Hold, but not still: using moving holds*

# Like clay: refining with the AniSculpt technique

Among Blender's very interesting features is the ability to "sculpt" meshes in the 3D view, deforming their shapes without having to worry about individual vertices, edges, or faces. While—at first—this is something useful only for character modelers, it's been used as a new paradigm for animation refinement in Blender.

The use of sculpting tools in Blender to enhance the character's shapes in movement, saving separate Shape Keys for each enhancement during the timeline, is called **AniSculpt**. This technique was first demonstrated by the well known character animator and teacher Daniel Martinez Lara, also known as *Pepeland*.

This technique is incredibly useful because it liberates the character riggers from the impossible pursuit of the "perfect character rig", suitable for every single action imaginable. Every character rig brings imperfections and gives some unwanted deformations that animators dread. Fixing every imperfection is a somewhat tedious, slow, and painful task, since the model has to "look good" from every possible position and angle.

With AniSculpt, the animator can sculpt the shapes of the characters after the animation is finished, as a layer of refinement to fix imperfections and make the overall shapes nicer on the screen. It represents a new step in the animation workflow, but can save a lot of time in the rigging stage. The rigs no longer need to give "perfect" deformations, only "acceptable" ones to be adjusted in the sculpting phase.

It doesn't mean, of course, that the rig shouldn't be good. The better the rig, the fewer the corrections that need to be made. It's a matter of leaving the right amount of work for each stage, without overloading either the rigger nor the animator.

At the time of writing this book, Blender doesn't allow the use of AniScupt on linked group meshes. You have to append the objects before the AniSculpt stage. A workaround for it is animating with a linked group and, when the animation is finished and ready to render, appending the needed objects and applying the action to it before sculpting.

## How to do it...

1.  Open the file `009-Anisculpt.blend`. It has our character Otto with a run cycle action applied to it. All deformations on its mesh are made by the rig, and we need to adjust it in order to make the shapes look better.

    Take a look at the NLA Editor window. It has two layers of actions set for the run cycle, as you can see in the following screenshot:

2.  Since the sculpting phase is the final "layer" of refinement, we can create an actual layer on the NLA Editor window to accommodate these changes. Select the `Otto_Body` object on the 3D View, go to a **DopeSheet** window, select the **ShapeKey Editor** mode on its header, and press the **New** button to add a new action. Name it **AniSculpt**.

3.  Back on the NLA Editor window, you'll see a new line for the `Otto_Body` object. Click on the triangle next to its name to unveil the line underneath named **Key** (reserved for Shape Key actions).

4.  Click on the triangle next to **Key** to see the layer containing our **AniSculpt** action. This is where our refinement layer will be placed, as you can see in the next screenshot:

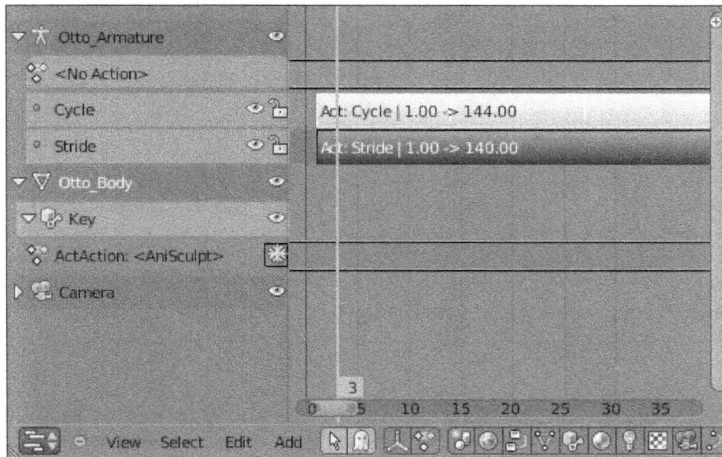

5.  Go to the 3D View window and make sure our character's mesh is selected. Open a Properties window, in the **Object Data** tab, and locate the **Shape Keys** section. Select the **Basis** shape and click on the plus (**+**) sign on the right-hand side to create a new shape based on it. Name this new shape as AniSculpt.01 and click on the pin button in order to enable the sculpting on this shape. The following screenshot shows our new shape selected and the enabled pin button highlighted:

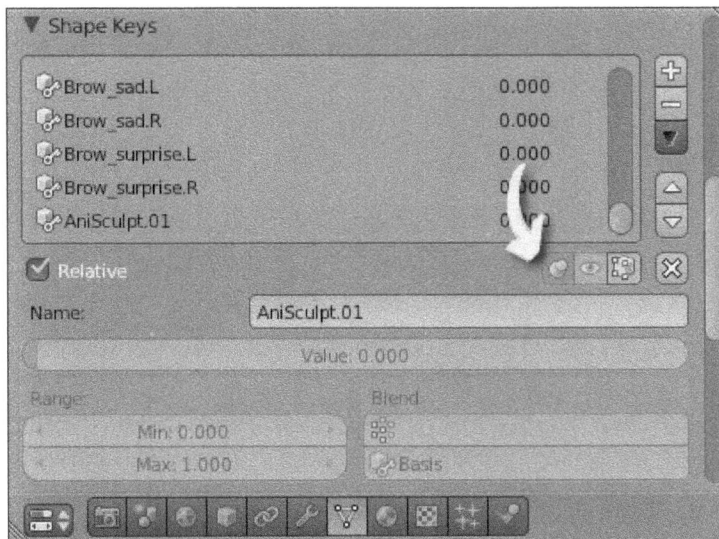

    This shape is where our first sculpted correction will be stored. There may be dozens of sculpted shapes for your scene, and that number can be as high as one sculpted shape per frame, although normally one sculpted shape works for more than one frame. For each new shape you need to repeat step 5.

6. Go back to the **DopeSheet** window with our **AniSculpt** action selected. Move the timeline marker and look closely at our character's mesh to find places that need correction (you can even hide the Armature layer, since we won't touch it anymore).

7. Now, the fun part! When you find a frame that needs corrections, make sure your mesh is selected and the Shape Key you've created in step 5 is pinned. Enter in Sculpt Mode on the 3D View window header and start sculpting your corrections. You'll get finer control if you're using a pen tablet, since Blender can use the pressure information to the sculpt brush values.

8. Sculpting the mesh is easy: the mouse cursor becomes a sculpting brush and lets you change the shape interactively with tools such as Grab, Smooth, or Inflate on the Toolshelf (*T*). Try creating nice arched shapes that follow an imaginary line of action.

> Try to avoid going too crazy with the sculpting; just make the corrections to the overall shape of our character on that position. Altering the mesh too much can give you a hard time when trying to blend all different shapes seamlessly on the timeline, but that's up to your artistic choice.

The next screenshot shows our original mesh (left) and our sculpted shape (right) with the added refinements. Notice how some skin folds were softened and the overall shape of the limbs and torso were curved to enhance the line of action. Also in the sculpted version the toes were correctly positioned on the ground and the elbows had their joints softened.

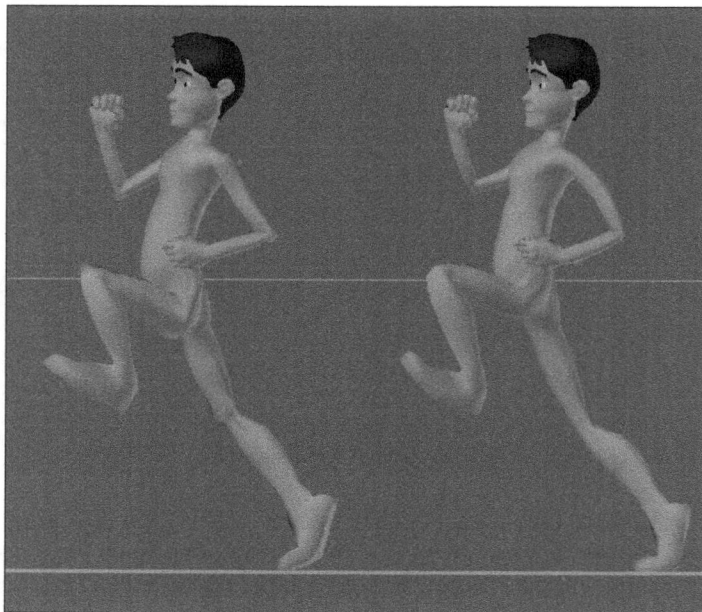

9. Move the timeline marker on the DopeSheet. You'll notice that, besides looking good on the frame you have worked on, the shape can look weird when our character reaches different positions. This is why we need to set keyframes for it.

10. Go back to the **Shape Keys** section in the Properties window, under the **Object Data** tab, and disable the pin button you've set to create the sculpted shape. On the DopeSheet window, make sure you're in the **ShapeKey Editor** mode and with the **AniSculpt** action selected. Locate and click over the **AniSculpt.01** shape on the left-hand side panel. Go to the frame where you made your sculpted corrections and insert a keyframe for it; it's just a matter of moving the slider value for that channel to 1, and a keyframe will be placed on the current frame, as you can see in the next screenshot:

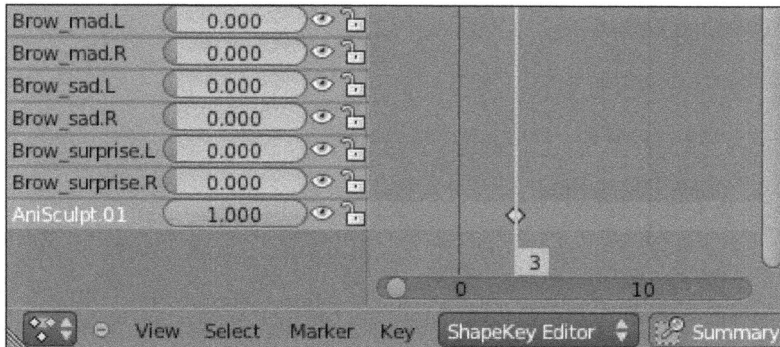

11. Now, for preceding and succeeding frames, you just have to move the timeline and adjust the `AniSculpt.01` channel slider to set a keyframe with lower values on those frames. A new keyframe will be automatically added as you change the channel slider. Change it to `0` when you feel the sculpted shape no is no longer needed.

Now it's just a matter of repeating the process from steps 5 to 12 in order to create as many sculpted corrections as you need. This can be a bit time consuming, but it is a lot easier and quicker than trying to build the all-purpose perfect character rig.

> The AniSculpt script published by the animator Pepeland on his website (`http://www.pepeland.com`) automates a good amount of the steps covered in this recipe, but it is currently (at the time of writing) not compatible with the Blender version 2.57, but now you know what is needed to accomplish the same results.

12. After you're happy with all the necessary corrections, go to the NLA Editor window and click on the snowflake icon next to the **AniSculpt** channel. This will make this layer of refinement independent and non-destructive to your already built animation.

The file `009-AniSculpt-complete.blend` has this complete example for your reference.

## How it works...

The AniSculpt technique, developed by the animator Daniel Martinez Lara, allows an easy way to make refinements to your animations. It uses Blender's built-in sculpting tools to let the animator make adjustments to the characters in an intuitive way.

## See also

*Appendix: Understanding Extremes, Breakdowns, Inbetweens, ones and twos*

*Chapter 1: Using corrective Shape Keys*

*Chapter 6: Animating in layers*

*Chapter 6: Tracking animation arcs*

*Chapter 7: Easy to Say, Hard to Do: Mastering the Basics*

*Chapter 8: Run, Forrest! (in cycles)*

# 10
# Drama King: Acting in Animation

In this chapter, we will cover the following topics:

- ▶ In the blink of an eye
- ▶ Walking with style
- ▶ Talking heads (and bodies)

## Introduction

All animation principles and techniques portrayed in this book will help you create appealing and fluid movements for your characters. But movements alone are useless: they need a reason to exist; they ought to have meaning. From subtleties such as blinking eyes, to full body motion and lip sync, everything must have a purpose.

The animator must know the character and understand the motivations behind each action. You need to ask yourself some questions before you start drawing or moving controls on screen. There is a useful and widely used acting technique known as **W.O.F.A.I.M.** that helps us answer the main questions. It stands for:

- ▶ **Wants**: Ask yourself what your character wants and, and more importantly, why does it want it?
- ▶ **Objectives**: When your character wants something, it's probably with an objective in mind. This can be an immediate one, such as throwing a baseball, or a long term objective (our character may be throwing that baseball in training for the final game).
- ▶ **Feelings**: How is your character feeling? Is he nervous? Shy? Afraid? Angry? Frustrated? Know the emotional state of your character.

▶ **As-if**: Is your character impersonating someone else? Think of a child character trying to fake his voice and talk like his father over the telephone.

▶ **Intentions**: A bit like the objectives, people perform actions with an intention behind them. If the objective is throwing a baseball, the intention may be to make the batter miss it.

▶ **Moment before**: What happened to our character just before this scene? This is important to know how and where to start.

Ask yourself these questions before each shot. This quick technique very efficiently allows you to plan and create convincing animation clips, and you should use it in every recipe of this chapter.

Note that covering all aspects of acting for animation is definitely beyond the scope of this book. Along with books, specific training in acting for animation or regular acting classes, you can try searching for tips and lessons on the Internet (once again, YouTube could be your best friend).

Something you probably already do is watch movies and TV shows. While doing that, pay attention to how your favorite characters are portrayed by their actors. Try to understand how some words written in the script are brought to life with great finesse by the actors. It's a good idea to look for movie excerpts you think have a similar mood to what you're trying to portray.

# In the blink of an eye

Although a very simple body mechanism to animate, the blinking of our eyes is a very important method of communicating. We can look at the action of our blinking eyes in the following ways:

▶ Organically, it's a way to keep our eyes moist. This is the technical aspect we needn't care about. Our audience really doesn't care if our characters' eyes are wet or not.

▶ As an "editing" device: as we look around, our blinking eyes "cut" between scenes. When you turn your head quickly from left to right for example, your eyes normally blink in the middle of this action. This blinking helps your eyes accommodate the change of focus when looking at different things. If we think of it as a movie inside our head, it would be something like: "Looking at my left side". Cut (blink). "Looking at my right side". This is relevant to our animation process, but not nearly as important as...

▶ Showing our emotional state: this should be our main concern when moving controls to make our characters blink. The frequency of blinking eyes is directly affected by our emotional state. For instance, if you are scared, you'll probably keep your eyes open for as long as possible to pay attention to what's threatening you. Shy or insecure characters tend to blink more often and at a faster pace than relaxed characters. Relaxed and sleepy characters have slow and long blinks.

Here we're going to see how eye blinks can change the overall feel of the actions. We will also talk about the eyeball movements.

## How to do it...

1. Open the file `010-Blinking.blend`. It has a Blender scene with our character Otto looking at a fixed point, as you can see in the following screenshot:

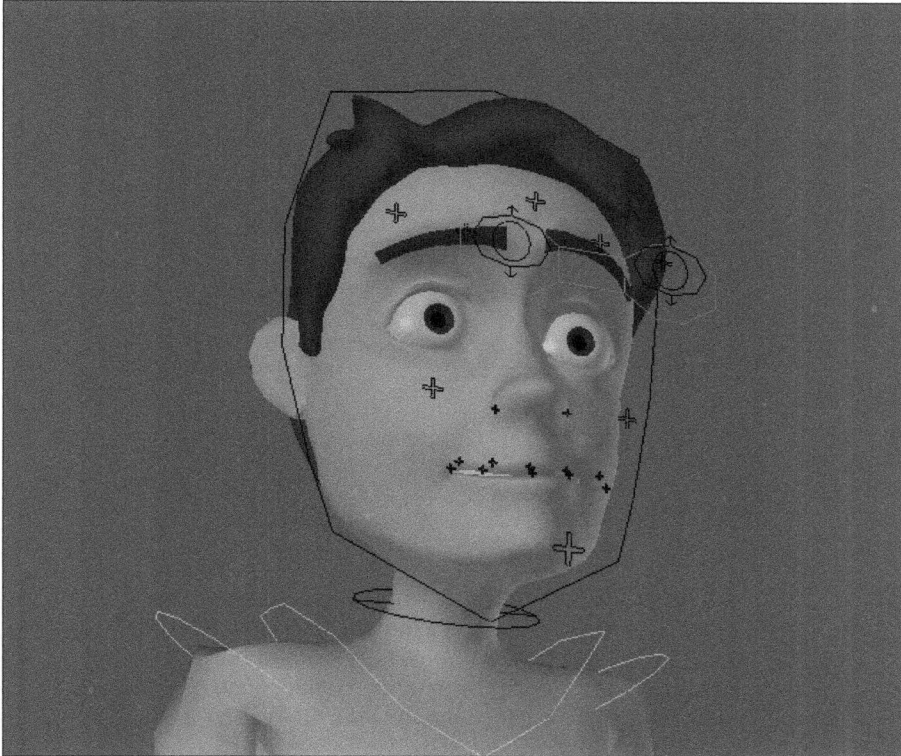

2. Hit *Alt + A* to watch this preset action. Our character's eyes are wide open while looking somewhere, then something catches his attention and he turns his head to the left. But something is not right...

   ❑ His eyes don't move a bit! He looks like a zombie! Let's first move his eyes and then make him blink.

   ❑ If you pay close attention to someone's eyes, you'll notice some very small and fast movements in the eyeballs while the person is looking at something, even if it's a fixed object. These fast movements are called **saccades**, and while recreating physically accurate eye movements is beyond our scope, it's important to add some of them to our characters.

3. A quick way to simulate these quick movements it to remove the interpolation between keyframes for the eye tracker bone. On a **DopeSheet** window, press *A* with the cursor over the timeline until all keyframes are deselected (white). Select the keyframes on the **LookAt** channel, press *Shift + T*, and select the **Constant** interpolation mode, as you can see in the next screenshot:

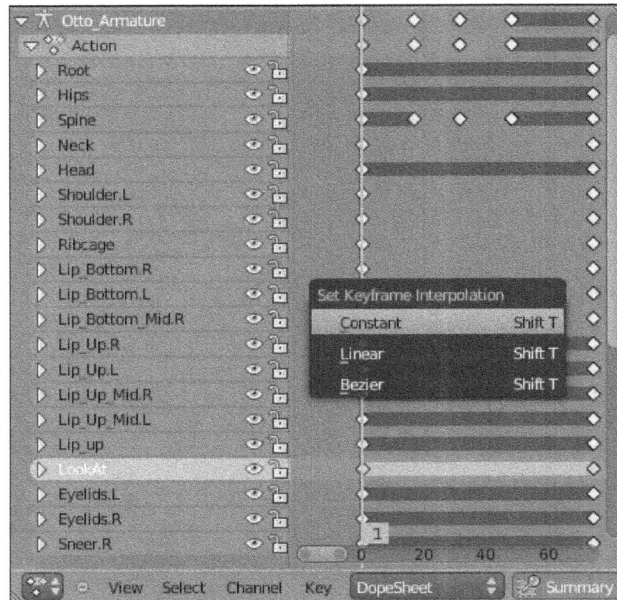

> In Blender 2.5 you can set different interpolation modes at a keyframe level, so you can alternate between modes over the timeline. This makes your current keyframe selection relevant when applying the new interpolation mode. In previous versions, the interpolation modes were applied to the entire curve channel.

4. Now you should go to frame 10, move (*G*) the LookAt bone slightly, and insert a new **Location** keyframe for it (*I*). Repeat this process a few more times between frames 1 and 72, in which the head turn action begins. Just be sure to do the following:

   ❑ Don't add too many keyframes, or the eye movements will be too distracting. Three or four (at most!) different positions should be enough.

   ❑ Make the saccades movements subtle. Try using *Shift* while moving the **LookAt** controller in order to add subtle changes to the bone's location, so our character keeps looking at the same region. Big changes are just for when our character starts looking at some other point in space, and these should have a different interpolation mode, such as Bézier.

❏   Make the timing between each movement uneven. Even timing between each change will make the movements look unnatural.

After adding the subtle and quick eye movements, you'll notice that the action appears more natural. Our character looks firmly at some point, and he's with his eyes wide open.

If we added blinking between frames 1 and 72, we would break the feeling of importance about what our character is looking at. Keeping his eyes open without blinking tells the audience that our character is concentrating on something.

In frame 72, something happened and made our character shift his focus. He turns his head to the left. The next screenshot shows him looking at his left side in frame 86:

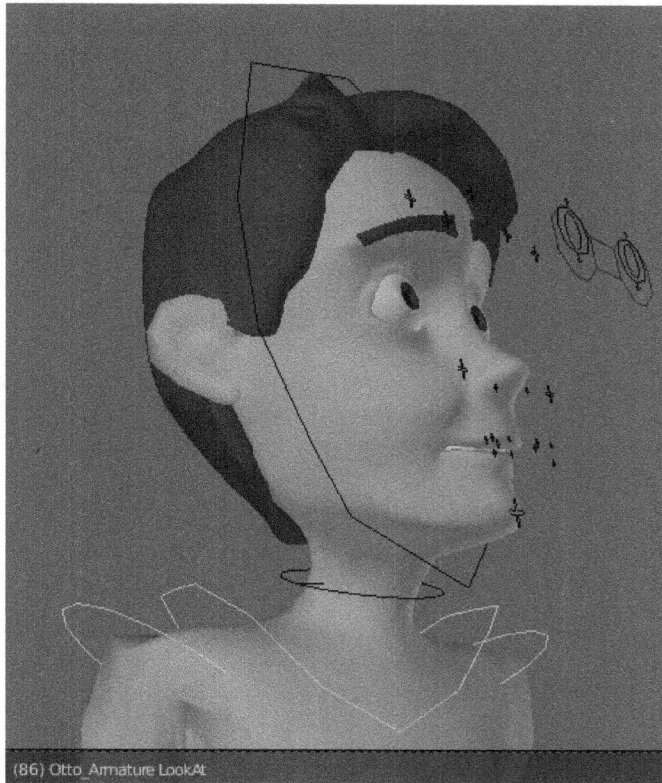

(86) Otto_Armature LookAt

5.  Anticipating this head turn, it's a good idea to lead this movement with the eyes. Go to frame 75, select the `LookAt` bone and move it so his eyes point to the new center of attention. Since this movement is not a saccade, we want a smooth movement here. Select the saved positions in frames 72 and 75, press *Shift + T* with the mouse over the DopeSheet timeline, and choose the **Bézier** interpolation mode, as shown in the next screenshot:

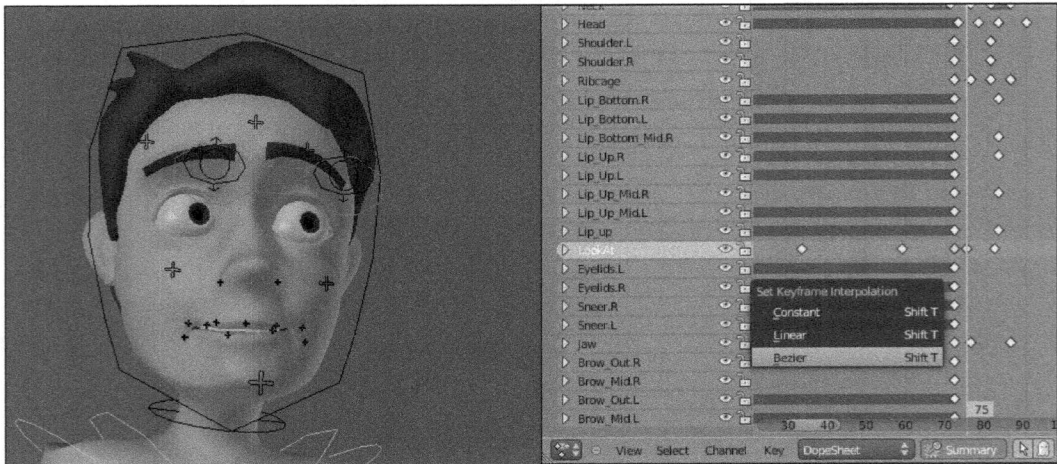

6.  It's also interesting to raise his left eyebrow a little in frame 75 to enhance this anticipation.

    In the middle of this head turn there should be a "cut" between our character's mental "scenes". He went from looking at something important to looking at something even more important to his left-hand side. To make a mental transition between these "scenes", his eyes should blink during the head turn.

7.  In frame 75, select both the `Eyelids.L` and `Eyelids.R` bones and insert a new **Scaling** keyframe (*I*) for them. This is the starting point of this blink.

> A popular approach for blinking eyes in CG is the "Pixar blink". This is an informal way to refer to an action where the eyes blink on different frames to break the symmetry. You don't have to always use this approach, but it helps in some cases, such as this example.

8.  Go to frame 77 and scale down the `Eyelids.L` bone until the left eye is closed. Go up to frame 78 and do the same to the `Eyelids.R` bone. At frames 81 and 82, fully open the left and right eyes respectively. This asymmetrical blinking happens in a subtle but efficient way to reinforce the head turn, since the left eye blinks first.

Note that "regular" blinks normally happen with a faster closing (2 frames) and a slower opening of the eyelids (3 or 4 frames long). Try variations of this pattern to achieve faster and slower blinks. For slower actions, you can even experiment with the eyes fully closed for more than 1 frame.

The file `010-Blinking-complete.blend` has our finished example for your reference.

## How it works...

Animating eyes and eyelids requires lots of attention to detail and an understanding of the emotional state of your character. The use of constant interpolation to emulate the saccadic movement of the eyes helps enhancing the realism.

The animator must plan and understand when and how often the character should blink based on its physical actions and emotional state. As a general pattern, blinking can be divided in a faster closing of eyelids and slower opening.

## There's more...

Try changing the emotional state of our character only by adding blinks. Make him blink a few times before turning his head, and make sure his eyes are not so wide open.

## See also

*Appendix*: *Understanding Extremes, Breakdowns, Inbetweens, ones and twos*

*Chapter 6*: *Animating in layers*

*Chapter 7*: *Easy to Say, Hard to Do: Mastering the Basics*

# Walking with style

In *Chapter 8, Shake That Body: The Mechanics of Body Movement* we saw both the technical aspects and body mechanics needed to create a run cycle. Now it's time to bring a little emotion into it.

A "personality" walk is nothing more than taking the emotional state of your character into account when creating the cycle. Refer to the W.O.F.A.I.M. technique at this chapter's introduction to ask and answer a few important questions before you begin.

In this recipe, we're going to create a "happy" walk. Let's imagine our character walking home just after receiving some good news. Maybe he's just got a promotion at work. He wants to celebrate, but he has to hold himself a bit because his boss is still looking at him. His walk must show this "controlled celebration".

Technically speaking, this chapter is quite similar to other recipes talking about cyclic runs and walks. The main difference is the subjectivity behind the creation of poses and the timing adjustment.

## How to do it...

1. Open the file `010-WalkStyle.blend` and you'll see our character Otto with some clothing and in its rest position, as seen in the following screenshot:

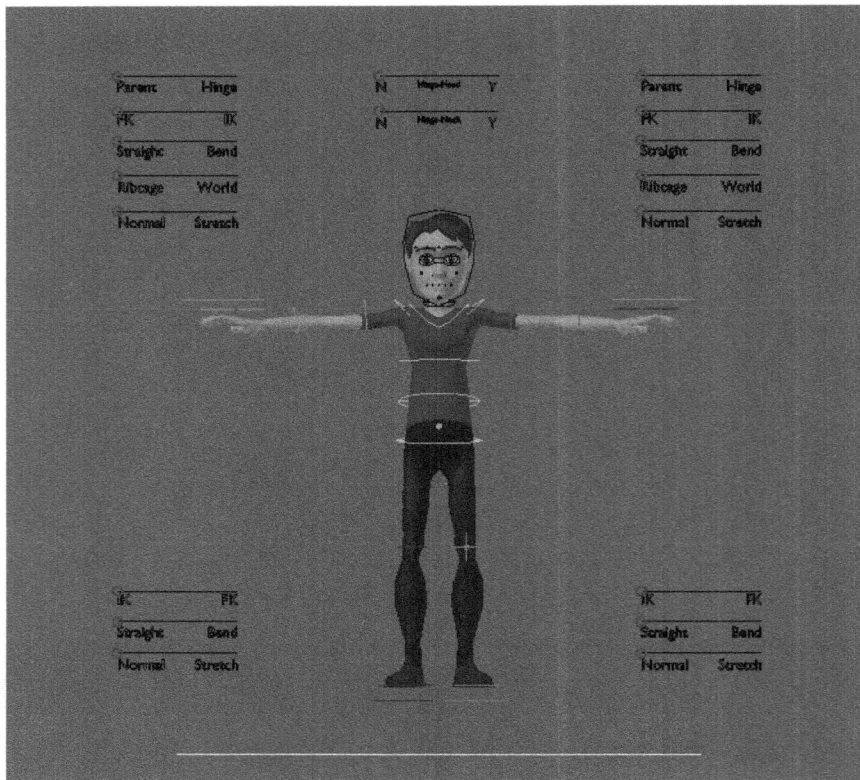

2. Go to the side view (*Numpad 3*) and let's pose our character in its first key position. Since this is not a "regular" walk, it's important to use the animation principle of exaggeration.

   We're going to use the first key position as the moment where our character makes contact with the ground using his left foot. Since acting nuances are a matter of personal choice, feel free to make this contact position as you wish. The following screenshot shows an example of this first pose in both front and side views. Notice how the position of the limbs and torso are exaggerated in comparison to a regular walk.

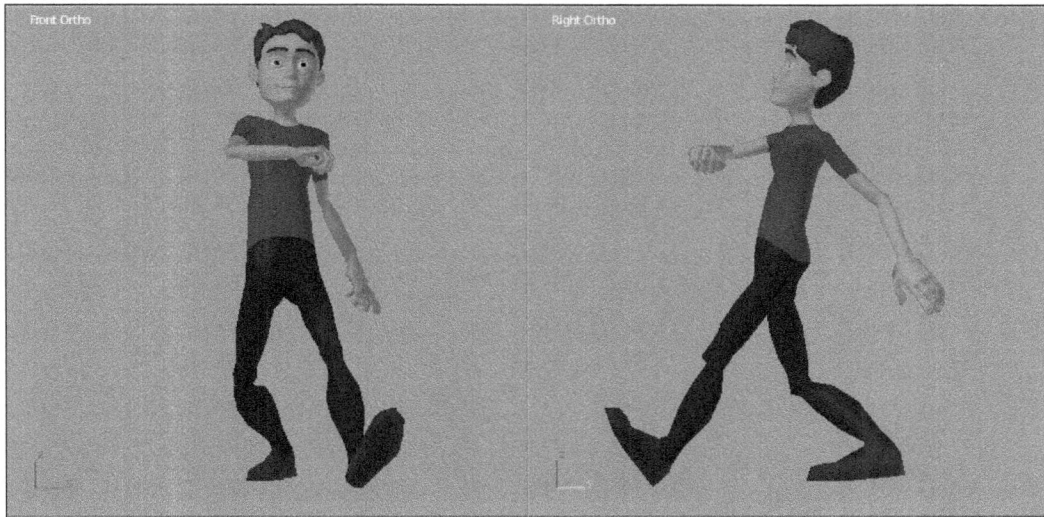

3. When you're happy with the first pose, select all related bones and insert a keyframe for them (*I*) in frame 1. Go up a few frames (we're not thinking of timing yet, so we can set a fixed 10 frames for each pose) and insert the Breakdown position, where his left leg is straight up, supporting his body. The next screenshot shows an example of it:

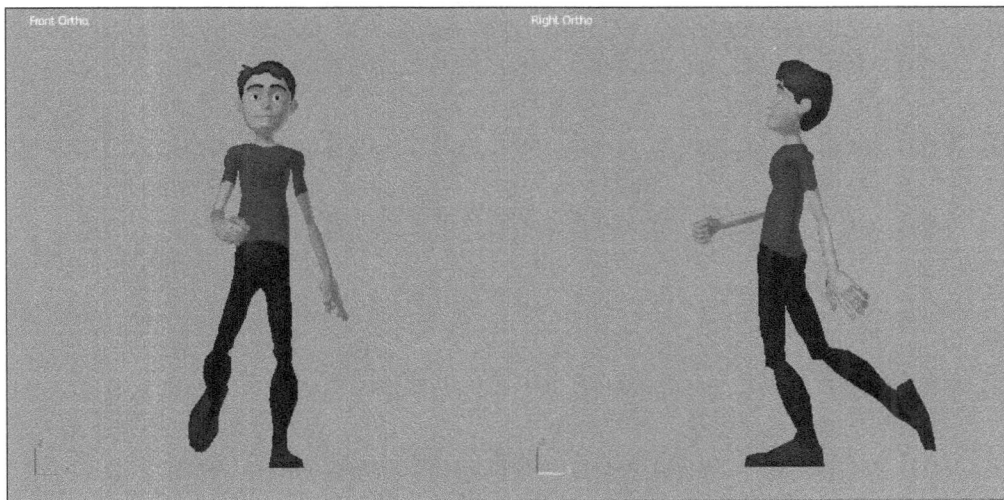

After creating the Breakdown, let's create the next key pose. This is the next contact position, where the right foot touches the ground.

4. Go back to frame 1, and select all body controls except the `Foot.R` bone (see why in the next Information box) in the 3D View. Press *Ctrl + C* to copy their transformation.

5. Go 10 frames after the Breakdown pose and press *Ctrl + Shift + V* with your mouse cursor over the 3D View. This will paste the flipped pose of our first contact position to serve as the starting point for our second key position. Notice that things will look weird, since flipping the first key pose will make our character go back in space to the position of the first step, as shown in the next screenshot:

> The naming conventions applied to the rig, using the `.L` suffix for bones on the left-hand side of our character and the `.R` suffix for the right-hand side bones, are used by Blender to calculate the flipped pose.

6. Now it's just a matter of selecting the `Hips` and the `Foot.R` bones and moving them (*G*) forward, and our pose will look normal again. Select all body controls and insert a new keyframe for them here.

> When copying the first key pose to make a flipped version, we didn't select the `Foot.R` bone. When pasting a flipped pose, the `Foot.R` transformation would be applied to the `Foot.L` bone, but the `Foot.L` bone was already planted on the ground in the Breakdown pose. We need to keep the `Foot.L` bone in its place to avoid any "slipping" during the walk.

7. Repeat this process to add a new Breakdown position based on the one you have already created and a final key position, which should be a copy of the first keyframe set (but, of course, two steps ahead). The next screenshot shows an overlay of these positions:

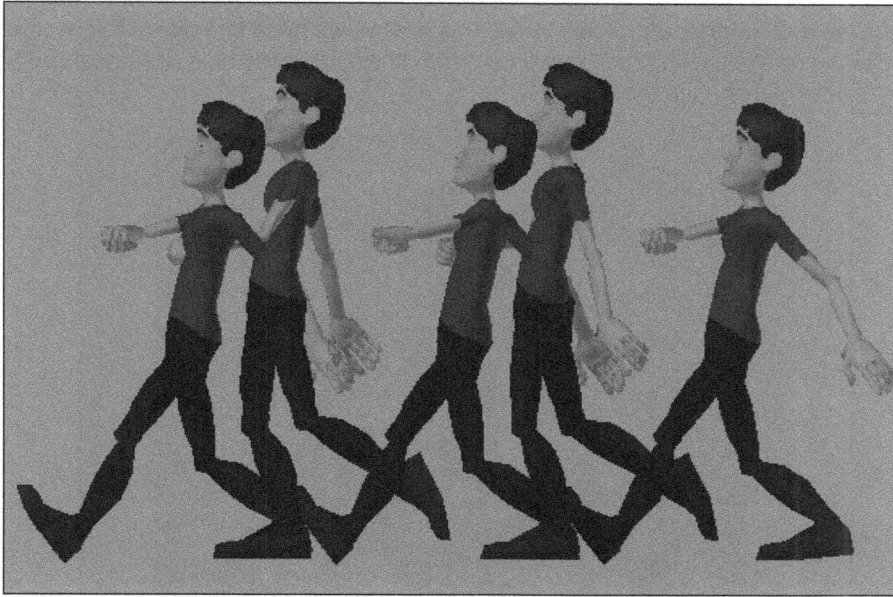

Once you have your Extreme and Breakdown poses set, it's time to work on the remaining poses. Now you can play with the timing and intermediate poses to bring even more "style" to this walk cycle. You can speed up the Breakdowns, emphasizing the contact key positions. The intermediate poses can be exaggerated, adding funny movements (such as little jumps) instead of just following the "natural" curve of motion.

It's always good, for organization's sake, to define the colors of each keyframe set on the DopeSheet. Select all keyframes set in frame 1, for example, press *R* and choose **Extreme**. This will give a reddish hue to those saved positions. Repeat that with Breakdown and Keyframe, or leave the default color for additional positions in order to make it what you need on the DopeSheet timeline easier to find.

Another way of bringing "happiness" to this walk is to refer to a widely used kind of cycle in the 1930's: the double-bounce walk. This is achieved by adding a second "down" position to a regular walk.

Normally our body goes down in a walk just after the contact of the foot with the ground, going up to the Breakdown position. In a double-bounce walk, we keep this down position and add another just after the "up" position of the Breakdown. This was often in sync with the upbeat music of the cartoon.

8.   Go a few frames after your Breakdown position and add two more positions: one down and another up, in this order. This is what we need to achieve the second "bounce". The next screenshot shows the difference between our regular (above) and double-bounce (below) walk:

9. Once you're done with your happy walk cycle, you can make it really cycle using the NLA Editor, in the process described in *Chapter 8, Shake That Body: The Mechanics of Body Movement*.

The finished example for your reference is in the file `010-WalkStyle-complete.blend`.

## How it works...

By carefully adjusting the timing and creating exaggerated poses, you can turn a regular (and boring!) walk into something appealing. The careful construction of the 'in between' poses, without making them simply follow the imaginary path described by the Extremes and Breakdowns, can make your motion very interesting. Knowledge of animation's tried and tested historic techniques also helps, so you can be inspired by the old animation masters' legacies, such as the use of the double-bounce method in this recipe.

## See also

*Appendix*: *Understanding Extremes, Breakdowns, Inbetweens, ones and twos*

*Chapter 6*: *Animating in layers*

*Chapter 7*: *Easy to Say, Hard to Do: Mastering the Basics*

*Chapter 8*: *Run, Forrest! (in cycles)*

# Talking heads (and bodies)

Lip syncing is normally a hot topic for animation students. The good news is that it's quite an easy task, if you follow some basic guidelines:

- ▶ Animate what you hear, not what you read on the transcript.
- ▶ Focus on the basic mouth shapes first; add details and polishing later.
- ▶ Asymmetry is a good thing.
- ▶ Talking isn't just about the mouth: the whole face and body has to be taken into consideration.

As with most things in animation, lip syncing gets easier once you have an organized workflow. Looking for a good reference is also important to get inspiration: notice how every person says the same word a bit differently than the others.

## How to do it...

1. Open the file `010-Talk.blend`. It has our character Otto with all his facial controllers, looking at someone behind our camera, as seen in the following screenshot:

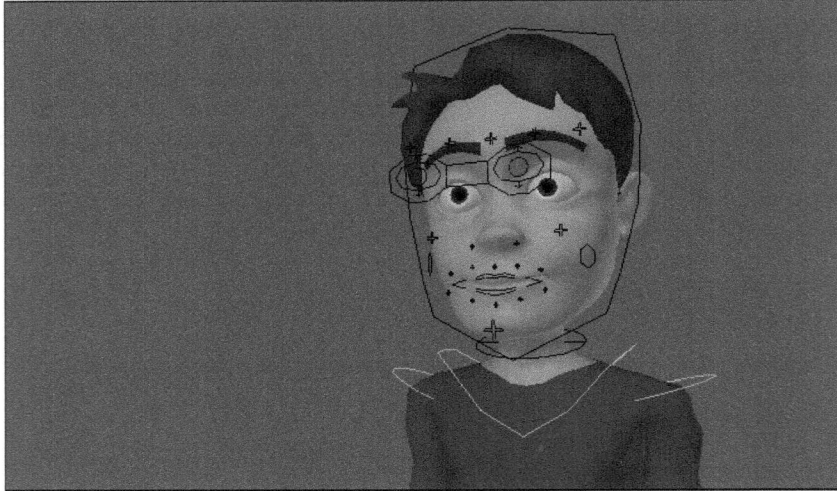

We have an audio file recorded for our scene in the file `010-Talk.wav`, in which we have a man's voice saying "So... what do you want to do?"

2. We first need to import it to our scene and set up this audio as background. For that we must use the Blender **Video Sequence Editor** (**VSE**). Open a new VSE window, press *Shift + A*, and choose **Sound** in the menu, as seen in the following screenshot:

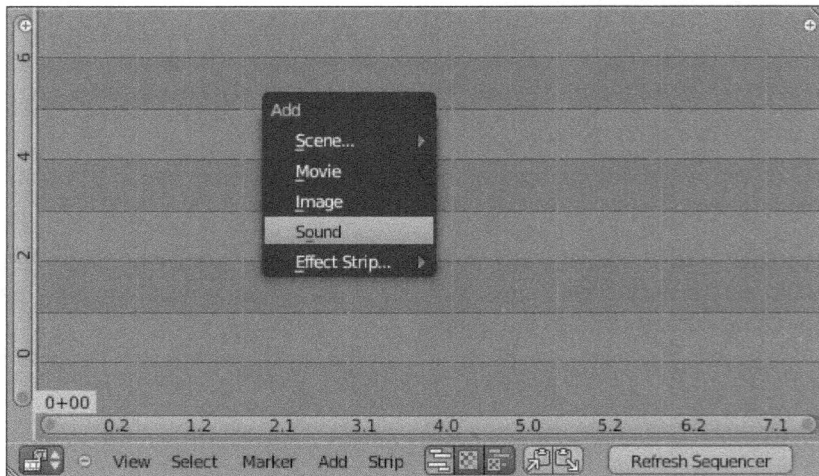

3. Blender will open a file browser window, in which you should select and load the file `010-Talk.wav`. Make sure that you set the **Start Frame** slider to 1 on the left-hand side of the window, so our sound strip starts on the first frame of our scene. You should also enable the **Cache** option to load this audio file into system memory.

> The **Cache** option is important because it enables us to actually see the audio waveform. This is useful for visually spotting the louder parts on the audio strip. You can enable caching for audio strips anytime at the properties panel (*N*) on the VSE.

4. Once your audio strip is loaded into the VSE, press *Alt + A* to listen to the file. Maximize the window (*Ctrl + Up Arrow*) to see a better visualization of the waveform. You will notice that the louder parts (or accents) of the audio are represented with larger waveforms, as seen in the next screenshot:

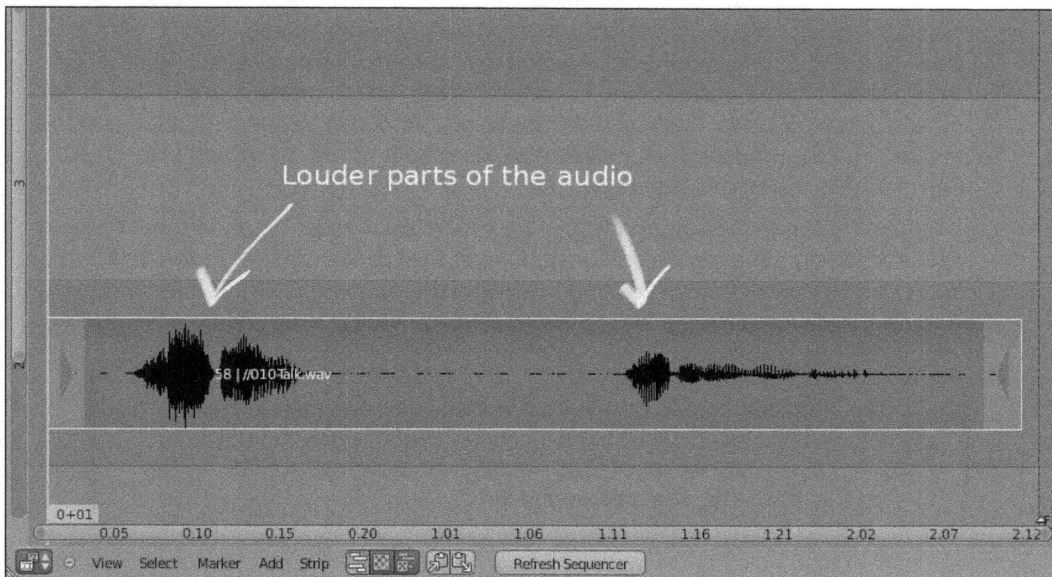

5. On a Timeline window, make sure the **Audio Scrubbing**, **AV-sync**, and **Frame Dropping** options are enabled on the **Playback** menu, so you can move through the timeline and listen to portions of the audio strip. The next screenshot shows these options:

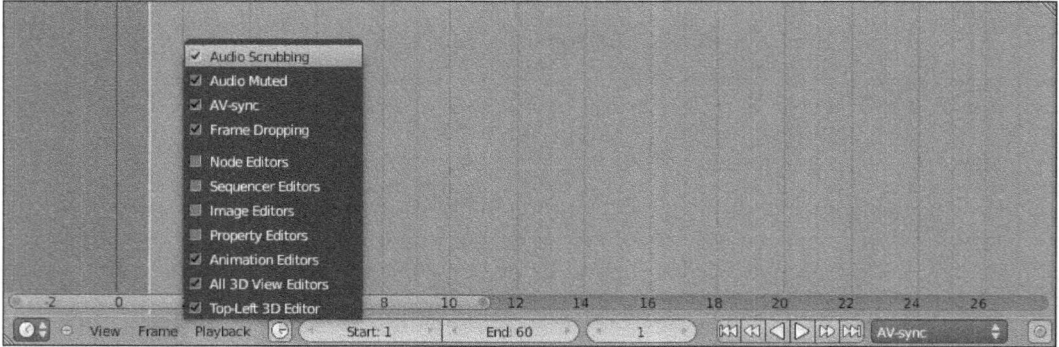

Back to the VSE window, and we're going to add some markers to indicate the syllables and frame positions we need to animate. These markers are visible in all timeline-type windows, such as the DopeSheet, the Video Sequence Editor, and the actual Timeline window. This makes it easier to spot where we should insert the keyframes to match the audio strip.

6. Position the frame indicator on frame 11, which is where we listen to the "O" sound. Press *M* to add a marker on this position, and then press *Ctrl + M* to rename it to So. You can move markers by selecting them with the right mouse button and pressing *G*. Repeat this process for the other sounds that you think are stronger.

> Remember that not every syllable should be animated. You should identify the stronger sounds, because they are the ones you should focus on. In our example, the stronger sounds are set in bold: "**So**, wh**a**t **you wa**nna **do**?"

The following screenshot shows our markers set and named properly on the VSE:

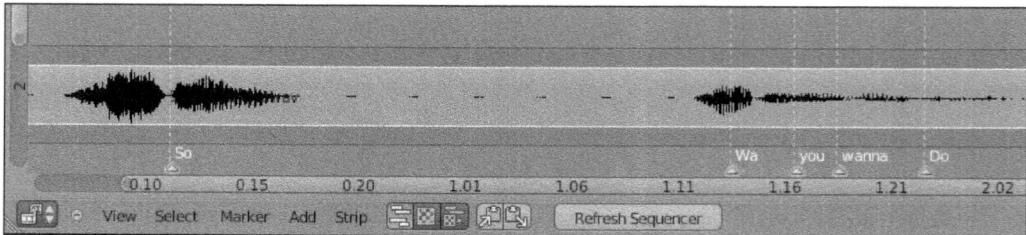

7. We now have our scene set up for animation work. Open a **DopeSheet** window and a 3D View window to start animating.

   The layered animation approach we use for our characters' bodies is also relevant for animating mouth shapes. We're going to animate the basic shapes first and then add layers of details until we finish the shot.

8. The first "layer" is created only by animating the movements of opening and closing the mouth. Move the marker through the timeline, move only the Jaw bone and insert keyframes to make our character open and close his mouth to match the sounds of the audio strip. Remember that we're only focusing on the jaw here; the lips will be taken care of in the next layer. The next screenshot shows our character with his mouth a bit open to match the sound of the word "so...".

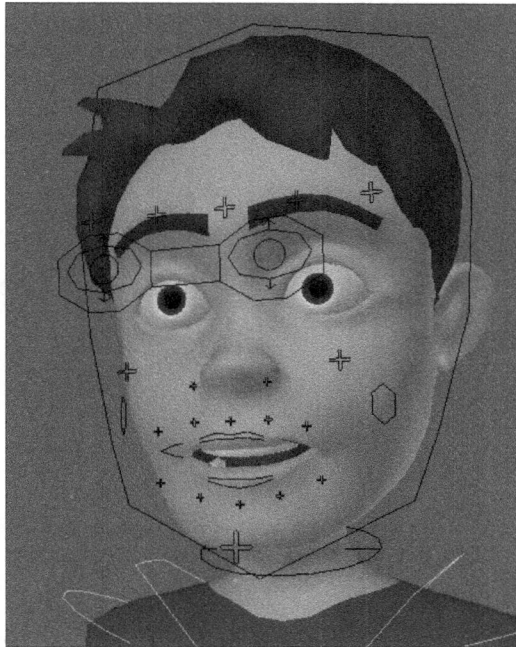

   On the next layer, we'll match the narrowing or widening of the mouth shape. The vowel sounds "O" and "U", for instance, require narrow mouth shapes while "A", "E" and "I" need wider shapes.

9. Once again, go through the timeline, move and insert keyframes for the mouth controller bones to match these sounds. Notice that some near sounds (and mouth shapes) overlap each other, such as the words "you" and "wanna"; the end of the first sound is the beginning of the second. That's why you should animate the sounds you hear, not the text in the transcript.

10. After you're happy with the second layer of mouth shapes, start adding details to make the forms more interesting. It's nice to have some asymmetrical contours: not only the mouth controllers, but the jaw and head may be changed to add some interesting shapes. The next screenshot shows the mouth closed after the word "so..."; notice that the controllers were set so the jaw is rotated a bit to his left, and the mouth shape is not symmetrical:

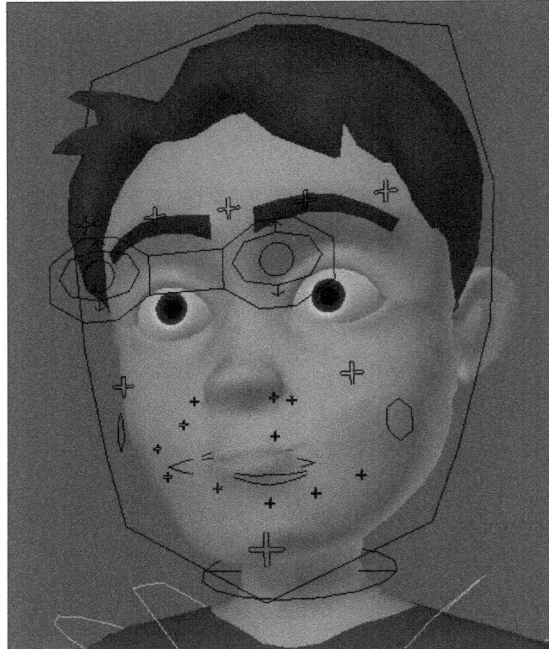

11. Repeat until you're happy with the results. Remember that nobody talks only with their mouth; head, eye, eyebrow, and body movements must enhance what's being said.

That holds true for any scene that you're animating. If your audio has someone screaming in anger at someone, for example, the whole body should follow the sound accents. In your planning phase, it's useful to act the scene in front of a mirror or camera, sketch thumbnails of your pose ideas regarding those sounds and then transpose them to your character rig.

A useful tip when making these acting choices is to avoid being too obvious or literal; if your character says the word "big", you don't have to make his pose say the same. Try to make your character's body match the emotional state, not the word's meaning.

The file `010-Talk-complete.blend` has this finished recipe for your reference.

## How it works...

By loading an audio file and setting up markers for the sound accents, you can have visual feedback to help create the mouth shapes for lip syncing. Building the mouth shapes in a layered fashion—just like you do with the body motion—is a good way to be more productive when animating your character while speaking.

You should always build asymmetry into the facial movements in order to achieve natural and fluid results. Remember that nobody speaks only with their mouth; the full body must be taken into account. When animating the body on top of a sound file, try to match the emotional state of your character. Avoid being too obvious and literal in your acting choices.

## See also

*Appendix*: *Understanding Extremes, Breakdowns, Inbetweens, ones and twos*

*Chapter 6*: *Non-linear animation*

*Chapter 6*: *Animating in layers*

*Chapter 7*: *Easy to Say, Hard to Do: Mastering the Basics*

# Planning Your Animation

In this chapter, we will cover the following topics:

- ▶ Creating thumbnails with Grease Pencil
- ▶ Naming conventions
- ▶ Extremes, Breakdowns, Inbetweens, ones and twos

## Introduction

When we think of animation, all we want is to get our hands dirty as soon as possible and bring our characters to life. But if we do that, we'll soon face problems that could easily have been solved with some careful planning.

To model facial shape keys, for example, a good planning phase will offer a list of necessary facial expressions, so you won't face any surprises such as missing shapes at the animation stage. You will also have a clearer picture of what rigging features you'll have to build for your character; this way you won't spend too much time creating things that won't be used.

## Creating thumbnails with Grease Pencil

Creating a finished animation in 3D isn't usually a quick task. We have to model, create materials, textures, rig controls, light setups, animate, and render. It may take a very long time until you see something moving on your screen.

That's why it's useful to quickly sketch our poses to see if what we have in mind will work on screen. Those sketches are great to test the poses and timing in a matter of minutes, and lots of animators draw them on paper or 2D animation programs to use as reference.

Fortunately for us, Blender has a great feature called **Grease Pencil**, which allows us to sketch directly over the interface. It's very useful not only for creating thumbnails, but also for the director to annotate the corrections directly over the scene as reference for the animators.

> The name Grease Pencil is based on the wax writing tool used by some directors to draw over the physical CRT monitors to annotate over the work of the animators of early CG productions. Since it can be easily removed, that was a quick way to make corrections and annotations over early digital work.

Drawing with Grease Pencil over the 3D View is as easy as holding *D* and sketching with the left mouse button. If you have a drawing tablet, Blender interprets the pressure applied to the drawing. You can erase the lines by holding *D* and pressing the right mouse button. The next screenshot shows a quick sketch with Grease Pencil's default settings:

In the previous screenshot, you can also see the Grease Pencil section on the Properties panel (*N*). There you can add new layers, change the color and thickness of the drawing, and enable **Onion Skinning**. This last feature indicates you can animate with Grease Pencil!

When you draw something in a frame, it's just a matter of sketching. A new keyframe drawing is created automatically at the new frame, and you can see a translucent version of the previous and next drawings with the **Onion Skinning** feature, as you can see in the next screenshot:

After you create a few keyframes with Grease Pencil, you can adjust the timing on the **DopeSheet** window by selecting the **Grease Pencil** mode on the window header. In this mode, everything works exactly like regular keyframes for objects in the 3D view; you can select and move them around. Every drawing is held on the screen until the next keyframe.

The Grease Pencil drawings are not visible to the internal renderer, but you can transform those sketches in images using the **OpenGL** render feature, by clicking on the clapperboard icon in the 3D View window header.

Since we're drawing on the 3D View, we can set how the drawing will be positioned on the 3D space by using the options in the panel section; the drawings can be aligned to your current view, to the cursor position, to the surface of existing objects, or to the surface of existing Grease Pencil drawings.

The lines you create can even be converted to **Blender Paths** or **Bézier** curves, so you can edit them and even make a vector based animation! One advantage of that is converting your drawings into something visible by Blender renderer, so you can even use Blender for producing 2D-ish animations.

# Naming conventions

Naming conventions seems like a boring subject huh? Well... it's not the most exciting part of the animation process, but it helps keeping all other activities more pleasurable and streamlined.

Blender 2.5 has a nifty feature of searching for the name of virtually anything you built in your 3D scene, but that doesn't mean we don't need to be organized. A very useful feature in Blender and most 3D apps is the ability to view your scene in a hierarchical tree-like structure, the **Outliner** window, as you can see in the following screenshot:

The Outliner shows all objects in our scene organized alphabetically and these are displayed according to their Parent-Child relationship. This is very useful, but you can make things easier to manage by adopting some organized naming conventions.

Our character Otto, for example, has his name as a prefix to all related objects. Meshes, Armatures, Lattices, Materials, and Textures—all start with `Otto_`. This is useful to separate them from any other object on the scene.

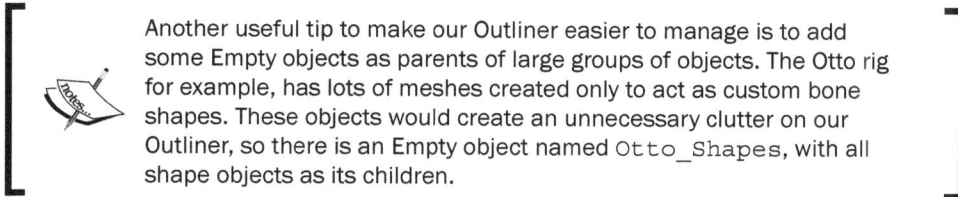

> Another useful tip to make our Outliner easier to manage is to add some Empty objects as parents of large groups of objects. The Otto rig for example, has lots of meshes created only to act as custom bone shapes. These objects would create an unnecessary clutter on our Outliner, so there is an Empty object named `Otto_Shapes`, with all shape objects as its children.

We can have two characters on the scene. Both of them may have a "skin" material applied to them, but they are not necessarily the same. Which one is Otto's skin and which is from the other character? And what about that "Shoe" object? It's easier to indicate the object's owner in the prefix, especially in larger productions.

When rigging, it's important to name bones according to their functions. Having prefixes such as `D_` for deformation bones or `M_` for mechanism, `T_` for target, and so on, is useful for understanding the role of each bone, especially in complex rigs.

For the bones actually made visible to the animator, it's best to name them by their functions or areas of control, such as "Head", "Hand.L", and so on.

# Extremes, Breakdowns, Inbetweens, ones and twos

So you want to create great animations but are still confused by some terms? Let's try to make them clear for you.

Every time you press *I* on the Blender 3D View for an object or bone, you're creating or replacing a keyframe. In digital animation, a **keyframe** is a saved property for an object at one frame of the timeline. This can be the location, rotation, scale, color, and basically any property value that you can change and save.

One thing that causes confusion is the fact that a vast terminology developed during years of 2D animation is still used in 3D, and there is an overlap of old and new terms. For the software, every property saved in the timeline is a keyframe. For an animator, each keyframe can be something else.

The digital keyframes can be:

- ▶ Key drawings: This is the most important drawing of the scene. It's the storytelling snapshot (or frame), which can alone be used to tell the story behind the scene. Normally key drawings were made by the director, so that animators could work based on it. The Key drawing is often also an Extreme, but not all Extremes are Keys.

- ▶ Extremes: These are the drawings that reproduce the maximum points of movement by a character or object. These points usually happen when a change in the direction of motion occurs.

- ▶ Breakdown: This is the intermediate drawing to portray the motion between two Extreme drawings. It's very useful to describe curved natural motions (or arcs), so the movement between two Extreme poses don't happen in a straight line.

Since we need 24 frames to make one second of animation for movies, more drawings are needed in order to fill the gaps between the Extremes and Breakdowns. This is where we have the **Inbetween** drawings. In traditional animation these are drawn by assistant animators, while in 3D the computer is responsible for the interpolation between keyframes. So, when we define the Interpolation Mode in Blender, we're actually telling the computer how to draw the Inbetween positions.

The big difference is that the computer is a "dumb inbetweener", without any sense of aesthetics. While it does help by automatically creating the Inbetweens, it requires the animator to create more keyframes and adjust the animation curves in order to guide the computer on how to create proper Inbetween drawings.

Since the computer is very quick to create these Inbetween drawings, we often have 3D animation "on ones". Animation "on ones" means that every frame of a movie clip has a different drawing. This is very expensive to do in traditional 2D animation, so normally one drawing is held on the screen for *at least* two frames.

When we have 12 drawings for a second of animation, we say that this was made "on twos". It means that every drawing is held on the screen for two frames. It's very common to see animations on 3s and 4s, and even a mix between them. From an administrative point of view, it's quicker and cheaper to produce animations with fewer drawings.

Although the default mode in 3D is to make animation on ones, you can change that depending on the style that you want to achieve. 3D animations that try to emulate analog visuals are often rendered with fewer drawings per second to enhance that analog feel.

In Blender, we can achieve that by using a modifier over the animation curve on the F-Curve editor. Select the desired channel, click over the **Add Modifier** button at the Properties panel (*N*) and choose **Stepped**. The **Step Size** value is the mode you want to achieve: 2 for an animation on twos, and so on. This modifier has to be applied over all channels of animation on which you want to enact this effect.

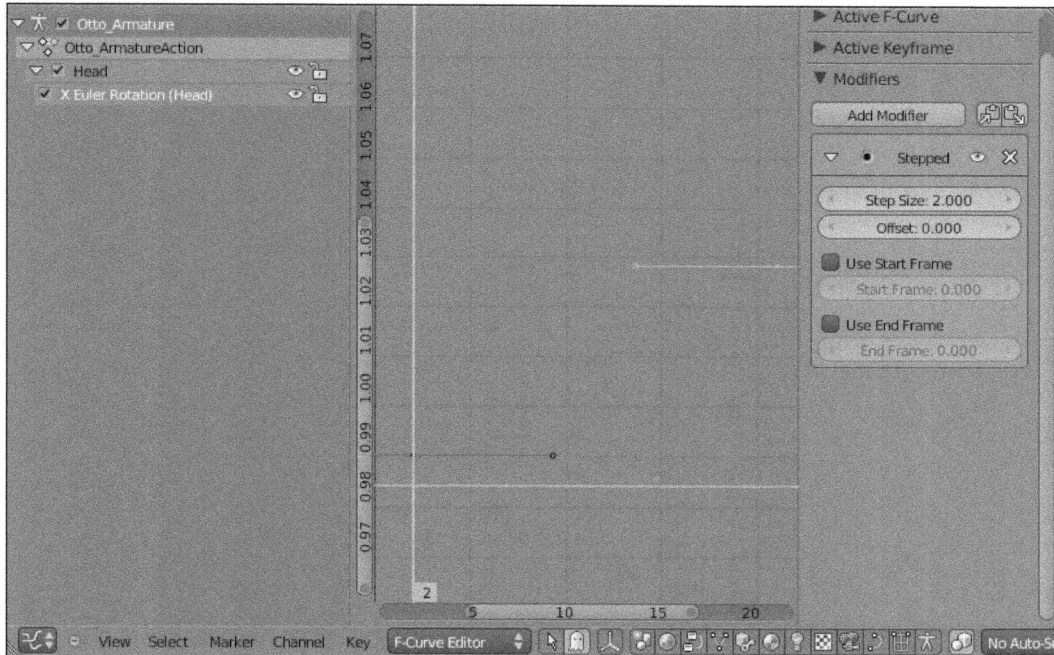

# Index

## T

T_BottomEyelid.L  76
Tennis_Ball obejct  207
Tennis_Racket obejct  207
tennis serve exercise, body mechanics  206-
    212
T_Eye.L  70
three-pivot foot
  IK legs, creating with  119-126
thumbnails
  creating, with Grease Pencil  273-276
timing
  about  182, 186
  adjusting, in animation  182-185
  tracking, in animation  182-185
tongue
  004-Tongue.blend file  110
  004-Tongue-complete.blend file  111
  controlling  109
  D_Head vertex group  111
  D_Jaw bone  110
  D_TongueBase  110
  D_TongueBase bone  110, 111
  Invert option  111
  Otto_Body mesh  111
  Otto_Tongue  110
  Otto_Tongue object  110
  Stretch To constraint  111
  TongueTip bone  110, 111
  With Automatic Weights, selecting  110
TongueTip bone  110, 111
Toolshelf panel  223
Topology Mirror option  44
traditional animators  160
Transform Channel  108
Transform channels  86
Transform Panel (N)  54, 73, 76
T_UpEyelid.L  74

## U

user interface bones  40
User Preferences window  43

## V

var-1 value  87
Vertex Groups section  100
video
  using, for background reference  167-171
Video Sequence Editor (VSE)  266
Visual LocRot keyframe  155
VLC  168

## W

wax writing tool  274
weight lifting exercise, body mechanics  213-
    219
weight painting
  about  40
  settings, for brush  45
Wireframe box  22
With Automatic Weight option  17
With Automatic Weights, selecting  110
W.O.F.A.I.M. technique  253, 254

## X

X-Axis Mirror mode  85
X-Axis Mirror property  85
X-Ray property  18, 117

## Z

Z Location channel curve  150

[PACKT] open source
PUBLISHING
community experience distilled

# Thank you for buying
# Blender 2.5 Character Animation Cookbook

## About Packt Publishing

Packt, pronounced 'packed', published its first book "*Mastering phpMyAdmin for Effective MySQL Management*" in April 2004 and subsequently continued to specialize in publishing highly focused books on specific technologies and solutions.

Our books and publications share the experiences of your fellow IT professionals in adapting and customizing today's systems, applications, and frameworks. Our solution based books give you the knowledge and power to customize the software and technologies you're using to get the job done. Packt books are more specific and less general than the IT books you have seen in the past. Our unique business model allows us to bring you more focused information, giving you more of what you need to know, and less of what you don't.

Packt is a modern, yet unique publishing company, which focuses on producing quality, cutting-edge books for communities of developers, administrators, and newbies alike. For more information, please visit our website: www.packtpub.com.

## About Packt Open Source

In 2010, Packt launched two new brands, Packt Open Source and Packt Enterprise, in order to continue its focus on specialization. This book is part of the Packt Open Source brand, home to books published on software built around Open Source licences, and offering information to anybody from advanced developers to budding web designers. The Open Source brand also runs Packt's Open Source Royalty Scheme, by which Packt gives a royalty to each Open Source project about whose software a book is sold.

## Writing for Packt

We welcome all inquiries from people who are interested in authoring. Book proposals should be sent to author@packtpub.com. If your book idea is still at an early stage and you would like to discuss it first before writing a formal book proposal, contact us; one of our commissioning editors will get in touch with you.

We're not just looking for published authors; if you have strong technical skills but no writing experience, our experienced editors can help you develop a writing career, or simply get some additional reward for your expertise.

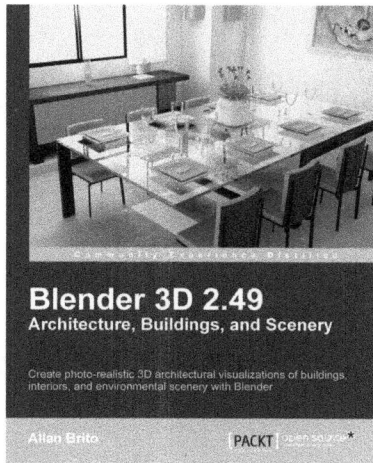

## Blender 3D 2.49 Architecture, Buildings, and Scenery

ISBN: 978-1-84951-048-6     Paperback: 376 pages

Create photo-realistic 3D architectural visualizations of buildings, interiors, and environmental scenery with Blender

1. Study modeling, materials, textures, and light basics in Blender

2. Learn special tricks and techniques to create walls, floors, roofs, and other specific architectural elements

3. Create realistic virtual tours of buildings and scenes

4. Develop a library of textures, materials, and objects that you can use over and over again

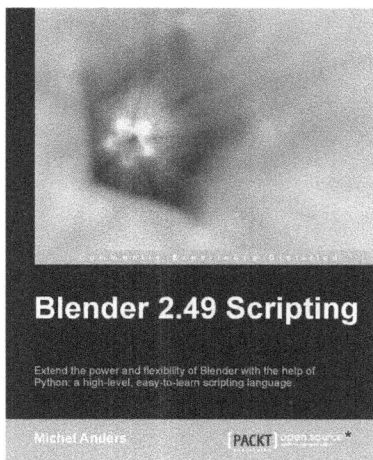

## Blender 2.49 Scripting

ISBN: 978-1-849510-40-0     Paperback: 292 pages

Extend the power and flexibility of Blender with the help of the high-level, easy-to-learn scripting language, Python

1. Gain control of all aspects of Blender using the powerful Python language

2. Create complex meshes programmatically and apply materials and textures

3. Automate the rendering process and extend Blender's image manipulation capabilities

Please check **www.PacktPub.com** for information on our titles

www.ingramcontent.com/pod-product-compliance
Lightning Source LLC
Chambersburg PA
CBHW080936220326
41598CB00034B/5804